SAKE METER VALUES

+7 and up	(probably) very dry
+4 to +6	dry
+1 to +3	slightly dry
+1 to −1	slightly sweet
−2 to −5	sweet
−6 and below	(probably) very sweet

日本酒度
Nihonshudo

CONVERSION CHART

Traditional Japanese Measure	Metric	U.S. Standard	Comments
————	100 ml	3.4 oz	
8 *shaku* 八勺 /*hasshaku*	140 ml	4.7 oz	small decanter
1 *gō* 一合/*ichi gō*	180 ml	6 oz	regular decanter
————	300 ml	10 oz	common bottle size
2 *gō* 二合/*ni gō*	360 ml	12 oz	large decanter
————	600 ml	20 oz	
4 *gō* 四合/*yon gō*	720 ml	24 oz	common bottle size
5 *gō* 五合/*go gō*	900 ml	30 oz	typical bottle size
1 *shō* 一升/*isshō*	1,800 ml	1.9 qts/60 oz	typical sake bottle

NOTE: One Imperial/British fluid ounce equals 25 milliliters, thus 100 ml = 4 oz, 1 *gō* = 180 ml = 7 oz, and so on.

The Insider's Guide to
SAKÉ

The Insider's Guide to SAKÉ

Philip Harper

KODANSHA INTERNATIONAL
Tokyo • New York • London

AUTHOR'S NOTE

In English texts, the Japanese word "sake" is often italicized or given an accent (saké) in order to distinguish it from the English word "sake," as in "For Pete's sake." Feeling that the cumulative effect in a book of this nature would be distracting, I have followed the standard pattern of romanization, and taking a course found more often of late, chosen to drop the accent and italics. For Japanese names, I have used the Western approach, given name before surname.

Jacket material and sake labels are reproduced courtesy of individual brewers. Additional jacket photography and interior shots by Mizuho Kuwata.

Published by Kodansha International Ltd., 17-14 Otowa 1-chome, Bunkyo-ku, Tokyo 112-8652, and Kodansha America, Inc.

Distributed in the United States by Kodansha America, Inc., 575 Lexington Avenue, New York N.Y. 10022, and in the United Kingdom and continental Europe by Kodansha Europe Ltd., 95 Aldwych, London WC2B 4JF.

ISBN 4-7700-2076-7

www.thejapanpage.com

With thanks to Fujiki,
who has a lot to answer for;
and to Yasuko, for living nobly with
the consequences.

Contents

Introduction

I am a sake brewer, an unusual trade in Japan, and still more so for a foreign resident. In fact, as far as I know, I am the only non-Japanese member of this tradition-laden, rather secretive profession. Brewing has been my life for long enough now for it to seem as natural as eating breakfast, but, once in a blue moon, a memory or a stray scent reminds me of other worlds, and I experience a sudden and vertiginous sense of what a strange path it is I am treading. It seems only proper to explain at the outset how I came to brew sake for a living.

In 1988, I came to Japan for the first time, armed with three or four words of Japanese, a fresh degree in English and German Literature and a liberating paucity of any ideas about careers. I arrived on the popular ticket of English teaching, and was fortunate enough to work in public high schools in Osaka, western Japan's largest city. Almost all Japanese people go through high school, so it is a key stage in the system, as much about socialization as about education as such. It showed me the warts-and-all face of the society, not the touched-up version I later saw in private language schools, where the environment is colored by the desire to accommodate the Westerners around. My place of work also meant that my first taste of sake was destined to be at *enkai*—the festive gatherings of colleagues, which may take on the character of a banquet or a night at the pub, according to the occasion and the members.

Liking a drink as much as the next person, I was keen to try the sake of rumor: some kind of wine made from rice. It seems to be unthinkable to hold an *enkai* without cold beer and hot sake, so I had ample opportunity to consider the matter. Sake is served in china decanters, and drunk from tiny porcelain cups. They require constant refilling, and pouring for each other is one of the pleasanter conventions of such gatherings. It also permits a graceful escape from boring conversation; you simply grab a decanter and go round the room pouring drinks. This wins you enormous kudos for your knowledge of polite Japanese custom, allows you to talk to anyone you want to for a while, and frees you from the tedious partner whose lecture on internationalization would have been your fate for the entire evening at a Western-style dinner party.

So my first encounters with sake were, fittingly, bound up with its social usefulness. In a land where so much real business takes place off the record, sake is the oil that keeps the wheels of society turning smoothly. Though I could not, as yet, talk to my colleagues (or at least only to those few with some English and the courage to use it), I could, and did, drink with them. I soon discovered that, for all the refinement of the utensils used for drinking sake, it delivered a hangover about as delicate as a pneumatic drill. After a few cautionary experiences, I resolved to limit my fluid intake on such occasions to beer, which exacted a less painful price for its use as a social lubricant.

At this stage, I mentioned my reservations about the stuff to Fujiki, a Japanese chap with whom I had struck up a friendship on the foundation of a shared taste in music. He immediately dragged me off to drink "real sake." We were served *chilled* sake, and it was hard to believe it was the same thing. Some of it tasted quite clearly of rice, unlike the steaming potions of the *enkai*. Still more startling, though, were those whose aroma was sublimely and unmistakably fruity. How on earth do you make a drink with the fragrance of fruit from rice? My curiosity was piqued and my palate seduced; I was hooked. My enthusiasm was undimmed by the Olympian scale of the bill at the end of the evening, and was reinforced when I awoke the next morning with a clear head and a fur-free tongue.

I set out to learn more, and consumed my salary by the glassful. My fascination grew as the number of brands I tried rose into the dozens— every one distinct. I could not yet read Japanese and spoke very little into the bargain, so I progressed as an illiterate, ordering remembered names, greeting familiar labels like old friends. The linguistically challenged struggle I went through is the reason I decided to write this book. In time, I heard about the odd (and decidedly complicated) brewing process that miraculously conjures such fruity delights from humble grains of rice. My friend and I joined a sake-tasting club, and I visited a few of the beautiful buildings, or *kura*, that produced some of my favorites. Breweries are amongst the finest and oldest examples of architecture in many Japanese towns. Though some modern breweries are housed in nondescript ferro-concrete factories, and other traditional *kura* are now nothing more than lovely museums attached to larger firms, many concerns, both great and small, still brew in these wonderful, hoary, massive-beamed structures. On these visits I also met some of the modest craftsmen who brew Japan's national drink, and began to appreciate the demands traditional brewing makes on its practitioners.

The club's activities were not all spectating and drinking. With the farmer's amused cooperation, for example, we hand-planted a rice-paddy, and handed our harvest over to a local brewery to turn into sake. Our rice was not, to say the least, of the highest quality, but the brewer somehow contrived to turn it into a toothsome sake, at once both fruity and full of rice flavor—the last bottle now a fond memory.

Time passed, and after two years of English teaching, I was ready for something new. After considerable investment in both time and bar tabs, it occurred to me that sake-related work of some kind would be interesting. I satisfied visa regulations by teaching at a private English school, and worked in the evenings in the same bar in which I had previously spent so much of my salary.

At about the same time Fujiki, the friend who had instigated the whole thing, gave up his nice, safe job and joined a small, highly traditional brewery in neighboring Nara Prefecture, the producer of an extremely distinctive sake that had held a high place in my esteem since the first days of discovery. When I could find time off, I went to see what the life of a brewer was like. My schedule, teaching until 9 P.M., then working in the bar until the small hours, seemed like hard work sometimes, but it was a picnic compared to the grueling life Fujiki was living: long, long hours and heavy physical labor, day in, day out—and never a day off. Traditional brewing happens only in the coldest months, and brewers have, for centuries, left their families and the snowbound fields of their home regions to work the winter brewing season. They live in the brewery for the duration, and Fujiki was obliged to fall into line, returning to his own home only for baths. At the New Year, I stayed for a week, rising hours before dawn, and working through till half past five. (For the brewers, working at the punishing pace set by the microorganisms, which drive fermentation, it was business as usual. The only concession to the most important holiday of the year was a long lunch hour!) In the highly traditional world of the *tōji* (master brewer) and his team, even Fujiki was an exotic presence, so they must have been alarmed to find such a bizarre guest as myself in their midst. However, as far as I could tell (their dialect defeated me almost completely), they accepted me with great courtesy, and were pleased by my obvious interest in and regard for their work— and its delicious results, in particular!

The working visits I made to the brewery left a profound impression. Everything about it was so pungent, from the extraordinary feudalistic structure of the labor force, to the occasionally medieval details of the brewing process: even the fragrance of the brewery air was unforgettable.

Meanwhile, I was learning more while working at the bar—about myself, as well as about sake. It was a common enough arrangement for Japan; a long counter, with room for fifteen customers at a push. At that time, it was still quite rare for a drinking place to stock anything more than one "house sake." In contrast, my employer listed more than a hundred on the menu, and there were always about fifty more lurking in the fridge. People came from miles away to sample the rarities available. Most of the customers, sharing my interest in what they were drinking, were interesting conversation partners. Inevitably, though, there were the odd sake snobs. In little bars like this, the customer takes the owner (or barman) for granted as a captive audience. I discovered that it is never the really knowledgeable people who insist on lecturing the assembled company. Whenever some would-be connoisseur inflicted his (always *his*) particular mix of misconceptions and garbled plagiarisms on me, I found it tremendously hard to maintain the air of polite interest my station required. By this time I knew enough to know when someone was talking rubbish, and I had a perilous, unprofessional urge to puncture the self-importance of this stamp of snob. I was also in a situation to do so in particularly devastating fashion, since these people also generally assumed that blue eyes correspond to a complete ignorance of matters related to sake (and, indeed, all things Japanese), and seized the opportunity to flaunt their wisdom with a corresponding lack of modesty and inhibition. Finding it increasingly irksome to bite my tongue, I decided to try my hand at brewing, for which an imperishable smile is not a necessity.

Many people have subsequently remarked to me that they can understand sake becoming a hobby, but not such a drastic choice of career. I lived in Germany and enjoyed the country's wine and beer copiously, but it never occurred to me to think of making the stuff. I suppose the difference lies in attitudes. Germans are proud of their wine and positively idolatrous about their beer. Both industries are thriving and highly regarded. In contrast, I found that most Japanese people were dreadfully unaware of this jewel of their culture. When talking to people involved in the industry, I found a distressing consensus. Everyone agreed that sake had never been better: veteran craftsmen were using traditional skills and new technologies, and the resulting masterpieces were more widely available than ever before. This rosy picture was then qualified by the sad prospect of things to come, for the industry is suffering a critical shortage of manpower. Young people in the rural areas, the traditional source of labor for brewing, are turning to alternative careers, and the current generation of brewing craftsmen will be the last, as many retire with no successors to whom they can pass on their secrets. The average age of the men in the brewing unions is over sixty, and breweries go out of business every year for want of staff. A sense of crisis influenced my decision. Not that I had any illusions that a single literature graduate with no brewing experience whatsoever could turn the tide, but if the industry had plenty of young apprentices, it is safe to say that I would spend my New Year's holidays drinking warm sake in front of the TV, not working a twelve-to-fourteen hour day in a chilly brewery.

The company president said later that he never—at first—thought I was serious. A television reporter asked the master brewer what his first reaction was when he heard that he would have a foreigner on his team. He is an alarmingly honest man: without missing a beat, he said: "How awful!" Despite this reaction, he and his team of five were very kind to me from the start, and their misgivings seem to have been allayed once we had worked together for a while.

Though I had visited several times during the previous season, the rigors of that first winter were beyond anything I had imagined. The new environment, the long days and the punishing physical work load, the enormous amount of information to be absorbed, and the mentally and physically testing nature of hand-brewing—all combined to reduce me to a rambling zombie.

Still quite early in the season, I pulled off the trick of falling asleep while cycling back to work for the 9 P.M. session, rolling right into a river. I awoke in the bitter-cold water, soggily aware that my shoes were floating downstream, and that I was going to be late for work. Somehow, I hauled my bike up the river bank, and set off groggily for the brewery. When I arrived, everyone was just climbing the stairs to start the last communal task of the day. As I approached, they all froze. Fujiki enlightened me: "You're covered in blood, you are."

I went off to wash my face, and discovered a haggard extra from a splatter movie looking at me from the mirror. I had evidently cracked my head on a rock when I sleep-cycled into the river. I went back the next day to look for my shoes and hat, but never found them. I couldn't even find a place where it seemed possible to cycle into the river at all, a mystery which remains unsolved.

The season began in November. In January, I got married; my wedding day and the day after were the only two days off work that winter. In February, I compounded insult with injury in the form of a broken hand suffered in a car accident. Until the cast came off, I spent my days struggling up vertical ladders and handling thirty-kilogram bags of rice, literally single-handed. I survived; and finally, in mid-March, the last batch of rice was steamed—the moment that signals the end of midnight labor, the chance for recuperation, and perhaps the long-forgotten luxury of a day off in the near future. That first season, this happy event fell on my birthday, a coincidence that has yet to be repeated.

Since the 1991–92 season, I have brewed every winter. Conditions have never been quite as hard—and I have never fallen asleep on my bicycle again—but each season is a grueling test of stamina. In compensation, each year sees a fine new vintage unique to my brewery. Which, of course, is the point of hand-brewed sake.

This, in short, is how I came to be a sake brewer. As far as I know, I am still the only non-Japanese member of the industry, and it is a pleasure to use my peculiar vantage point to put in a good word for my adopted profession. Over the years, I have inevitably learned a great deal (though not nearly enough!) about the technical side of brewing, some of the edited highlights of which you will find in the following pages. On the other hand, I first encountered sake from the viewpoint of a consumer, and a certain unprofessional drinker's enthusiasm has never left me: it is that enthusiasm (along with the support of my colleagues and my wife) which sustains me through the season's inevitable moments of bone-crushing exhaustion. I hope to share both this amateur's enthusiasm, and such professional insights as may be of interest, in the coming pages.

I begin with a discussion of the varieties of sake, and a brief look at the basic features of brewing methodology. After considering the various ways sake is served and drunk, I have included a section showing how to recognize the various grades. Next, the reader will come to the heart of the book, the sampler. This is a selection of over a hundred brands of sake made by 83 breweries. I made my selections almost entirely from a few of the higher-quality grades (see Chapter 2, Categories of Sake). Although these currently account for only about a quarter of all sake made in Japan, they are also gaining ground, reflecting growing consumer interest at a time when sake's overall market share is declining.

Also included are lists of retailers, and restaurants and bars carrying a wide or interesting selection. At the rear of the book, the reader can find a glossary of terms in both English and Japanese.

The emphasis in this book is on the domestic situation. Those fortunate enough to live or visit in Japan have the enviable opportunity to experience sake at its diverse and delicious best. My first concern has been to help such people make the most of this opportunity. While overseas readers will, sadly, not be able to get hold of many of the individual products in this guide, I hope the brief notes on particular firms may be of use. I have also provided some information specifically for them.

I

SAKE FOR STARTERS

1

A Brief History of Sake

Sake, the dictionary says colorlessly, is a fermented liquor made from rice. It is also Japan's national drink. There is so much more to say, though: it comes in thousands of varieties, has a fascinating history stretching all the way back to the semi-mythical *shinwa jidai* ("Age of Legend"), is made by unique processes refined in the vacuum of a Japan isolated from the world for over two hundred years, is great for cooking, and is by far the most pleasant approach to learning the preposterously complicated Japanese writing system. All this, and delicious, too! First, a quick sweep of its history.

Like almost every people in the world (except, I am told, the Eskimos and a tribe or two in Papua New Guinea) the Japanese discovered the giggly juice very early. Alcohol was certainly already being drunk in prehistoric Japan. Japanese legend recounts that people learned about alcohol by observing monkeys, who stuffed fruits into hollows in trees and drank the results, made into "monkey sake" by natural fermentation. Sadly, experts (tiresome people) insist that the stories of *saru-zake* (*saru* means "monkey") are apocryphal. Indeed, all kinds of raw materials can be used to make alcoholic drinks, and reports of simple concoctions produced in parts of Southeast Asia and remote islands of the Japanese archipelago cite such appetizing ingredients as millet and acorns, though rice seems to have been by far the most common. Chew up such dainties and spit them into a vat, and enzymes in the saliva will make you alcohol of a kind. This type of *ur*-sake is known in Japanese as *kuchikami-zake* ("mouth-chewing sake") and was made for festivals in some areas of Japan well into this century.

The oldest physical evidence for the production of alcohol is pottery containers excavated in Nagano Prefecture. Some are believed to have been drinking cups. A larger one, found with wild grape seeds inside, is thought to have been used for making wine in the mid-Jomon period (ca. 10,000 B.C.–ca. 300 B.C.).

However, the history of a drink fermented from rice is necessarily relatively recent, since rice cultivation is said to have been introduced from the continent only about 2,500 years ago. A Chinese text of A.D. 300 refers to the Japanese as drinking, dancing, and singing. By this stage, they were almost certainly carousing with drink made from rice. The *Kojiki* ("Record of Ancient Matters," compiled in A.D. 712) refers to sake and

A

Alcohol

Sake has the highest percentage of alcohol by volume of any fermented beverage. In its natural undiluted state, it may contain a potent 20%, compared to 3 to 5% for beer, or 9 to 12% for wine. Fortified wines (port, sherry, and so on) may be stronger, but this is achieved by the addition of (distilled) grape alcohol. The essential brewer's miracle of water into wine is at its most potent in the case of sake.

early brewing methods on several occasions. The excellent story of an eight-headed monster defeated by the use of "eight-fold sake" is one such. Reference is also made to the arrival in Japan of a skilled brewer, one Susukori. The emperor, on sampling his productions, is quoted as saying, "I have become intoxicated with the august liquor distilled by Susukori. I have become intoxicated with the soothing liquor, with the smiling liquor." This would seem to have been in the fourth or fifth century.

As in many other fields, the Japanese no doubt learned much from their continental neighbors, the Chinese and the Koreans, though the many unique features of Japanese brewing leave a question mark on the extent of their borrowings. On a more truly historical note, a brewing department was established within the Imperial Palace (on a site near my home in modern-day Nara Prefecture) in A.D. 689. (Pottery utensils of the time are preserved in museums today.) In the classic formulation of Kin'ichirō Sakaguchi (1897–1994), microbiologist and author of several renowned books on sake, the history of sake production moves through the following phases:

1. sake made by the people (*minzoku no sake*),
2. sake made by the court (in the Nara and Heian periods, 710–1192; *chōtei no sake*),
3. sake made by specialist breweries (the middle ages; *sakaya no sake*),
4. sake made in production centers and in scattered regional breweries (*honba no sake* and *inaka no sake*—the Edo period, 1603–1868).

The distinction between these last two is very clear in British chemist R. W. Atkinson's 1888 account of the procedures in Nada and Itami (major brewing centers then as now), and the relatively unsophisticated methods of a Tokyo brewery of the time.

Other authorities also point to the many technical advances made in brewing in temples in the middle ages as representing an important stage. Records (such as the famous *Tamon'in Diary*, an amazing account of daily temple life over the period from 1478 to 1618) show that many of the typical features of brewing as we know it today were already established. Examples are the polishing of all rice used in brewing, and the addition of ingredients to the main fermentation mash in separate stages.

The modern structure of the industry took form in many essentials by the Edo period. It is not known exactly when the highly effective (and chemically extremely complex) *kimoto* method of making the yeast starter was developed, but it is described in numerous documents from the seventeenth century onwards, and remained the standard until the twentieth century. The *kan-zukuri* (winter only) style of brewing was firmly established by this period, and is still followed by most breweries today. The ancestors of contemporary schools of *tōji* (master brewers), too, were already refining their particular skills by the Edo period.

Though the modern period has undoubtedly seen great changes— the industry has benefited from scientific research and automation—it is still in many ways a very traditional (and even superstitious) industry. It offers many examples of the ultra-modern and the exceedingly old-fashioned rubbing shoulders. The fruits of research in biotechnology are perhaps the industry's biggest talking point today. Computer-supervised brewing has been a reality for years, and the largest firms and central research bodies are constantly developing new techniques. Yet many breweries still brew by methods that would be basically familiar to the craftsmen of a century ago. In many cases the buildings would be the same as well!

Currently, the biggest spur to change is a dire shortage of labor—breweries are struggling to survive as traditional sources of manpower dry up. The next decade or two will undoubtedly see major changes as a result.

Outsider's View

The first reference to sake from the pen of a European is a comment from the Jesuit Francis Xavier, dating from 1552. He records that the only alcoholic beverage available was made from rice, and further observes that the fact that the raw material was also the staple food resulted in scarcity and high prices. According to the *Oxford English Dictionary*, the first reference in English to sake is in a text from 1687. Of the Japanese people, it says, "Their ordinary drink is a kind of Beer (which they call Saque) made of Rice." The third edition of the *Encyclopedia Britannica* (1797) says that "Sakki, or rice beer, is as clear as wine and of an agreeable taste." Such early reports notwithstanding, sake has remained a rather mysterious quantity to the West. After Japan reluctantly re-opened its doors in the mid-nineteenth century, the first heroic translators of Japanese literature were still puzzled as to whether sake should be rendered as a wine or a beer. The confusion about spelling persists even today, the *OED* listing "sake" and "saki." Since the "ke" in Japanese calls for a short "e" sound (as in "get"), the second spelling clearly owes its existence to mispronunciation. (It is also how my mother pronounces it. In the face of endorsements from such authorities as the *OED* and my mum, it seems unlikely that my protests will have much effect at this late stage.)

The first thorough, scholarly study of sake and its chemistry was written by the previously mentioned Atkinson, who was a visiting professor at the newly established Tokyo Daigaku (Tokyo University). His book, *The Chemistry of Sake-Brewing* (1881), based on his own experiments and observations of brewing procedure in Tokyo, Itami, and Nada (this last the primary area of production even today), is acknowledged to be the foundation of scientific study in this field, and gives a fascinating insight into the techniques of the day. Yet despite this early and thorough report, misconceptions remain common more than a century later. Though accurate, up-to-date technical information has been available in English textbooks for some time, even recent editions of the *Encyclopedia Britannica* offer a muddled combination of misconception and error in its entry on sake. (The description of contemporary sake brewing seems to be a garbled version of the type of brewing observed by Atkinson more than a hundred years ago.) The *Britannica* is, unfortunately, not the only source of misinformation in English. The extent of the difficulties of comprehension offered by the complexities of sake brewing can be judged by the frequency with which it is inaccurately reported, even, it must be said, by Japanese sources. For non-Japanese writers, the innate difficulty of the subject is inevitably compounded by the particularly obstructive barrier of the Japanese language, and by an extensive technical jargon. All such problems notwithstanding, there are signs of an increasing interest in sake beyond its native shores. On the Japanese side, thought is currently being given to the possibility of a more international market for sake, and a number of new plants have even been set up overseas in recent years. The flow of information should improve accordingly. Sake is set to enter a new international era.

Sake in Japanese Life

Sake has a special place in Japanese life. It is served, for instance, at wedding ceremonies, where the couple seal their vows by sipping *san-san-kudo* (nine times: the lucky number three thrice repeated). In World War II, it was sake which sent kamikaze pilots off to their macabre glory. It is offered to the Shinto *kami* (gods) at shrines, and is even today a part of the ceremonies performed by the priest when work begins on the building

Bottled sake first appeared in Japan in the 1860s, though it took some time for bottles to replace wooden casks. The standard size is the big 1.8-liter bottle, an amount stipulated one *shō* by traditional Japanese reckoning. This type of bottle, still by far the most common, is known as an *isshō-bin* ("1-*shō* bottle"). Other common sizes are the *yongō-bin* (4 *gō*, 720-milliliter bottle), 900- and 300-milliliter types. The old Japanese measures are still in wide colloquial use, although all official statistics are given in the metric system. One *gō* is 180 milliliters; *tokkuri* (sake serving carafes) are most commonly either *ichigō* or *nigō* (180 or 360 milliliters).

of a new house. Ceremoniously breaking open a cask of sake is a common way to celebrate everything from a wedding to an election victory.

Though sake is still indispensable in many of these traditional roles, recent decades have seen its once-unchallenged position in Japanese life under threat. The word *sake* means "alcoholic drink" in a general sense,

CHRONOLOGY OF SAKE DEVELOPMENT IN JAPAN

Jomon period (ca. 10,000 B.C.–ca. B.C. 300)	• 300 B.C. • Techniques of rice cultivation imported from the continent
Yayoi period (ca. 300 B.C.–ca. A.D. 300)	• A.D. 1
Kofun period (ca. 300–710)	
Nara period (710–794)	• 689 Establishment of brewing department in Imperial Palace
Heian period (794–1192)	• 905 Records of brewing ritual/technique in *Engi Shiki* (905–27)
Kamakura period (1192–1333)	• 1264 Sale of sake forbidden; more than 30,000 casks destroyed in Kamakura
Muromachi period (1333–1573)	• 1569 Technique of pasteurization recorded in *Tamon'in Diary* (*Tamon'in Nikki*)
Momoyama period (1573–1603)	• 1578 *Morohaku* (sake made from 100% white rice) mentioned in *Tamon'in Diary*
Edo period (1603–1868)	• 1696 Technique of adding distilled alcohol to fermenting sake in use
	• 1700–1870 *Kan-zukuri* brewing becomes the norm at this time
	• 1784 Waterwheels used to drive rice-polishing machines

Meiji period (1868–1912)	• 1840 Discovery of *Miyamizu* brewing water
	• 1878 First sale of sake in glass bottles
	• 1881 Atkinson publishes first scientific treatise on the chemistry of sake brewing
	• 1903 Horizontal type of rice-polishing machine introduced
	• 1906 First sale of pure sake yeast by Japanese brewer's association
Taishō period (1912–1926)	• 1910 *Yamahai* and high-speed techniques for yeast starter developed at this time
	• 1923 Wooden vats replaced by enamel tanks around this time
Shōwa period (1926–1989)	• 1926 Almost 10,000 breweries in existence
	• 1933 Vertical type of rice-polishing machine introduced
	• 1944 Technique of alcohol addition becomes standard
	• 1956 Rice-cooling machines introduced around this time
	• 1961 First plant for year-round brewing established
	• 1969 Use of preservatives prohibited
	• 1971 Around 3,500 brewers in existence
	• 1970–1990 Production levels peak and begin to decline
Heisei period (1989 to present)	• 1992 Abolition of system of dividing sake into Special, First, and Second Class tax brackets
	• 1997 Number of brewers falls to 1,742

as well as referring specifically to what the Japanese, to differentiate, also call *nihonshu* (literally, "Japanese sake"). Once, the national drink enjoyed such a universal role as to make the two meanings synonymous. (Wine and beer were almost unknown until the end of the nineteenth century, and even beer remained a luxury item until after World War II.) The peak of sake production came in the 1960s. Since then, its share of the market has been eroded by competition, from the bland *mizuwari* (a shot of whisky mercilessly drowned in water) to the sound but monotonous products of the beer colossi. Now the word *sake*, in its broader meaning, encompasses not only *nihonshu*, but the full range of alcoholic beverages, including wine, beer, whisky, and cocktails. After a long period of digging in against the competition, sake has, in the last few years, moved into an era of change, with a welcome upswing in quality the happy result. A renaissance is under way as ever more people wake up and see sake for the national treasure it truly is. It is possible that the current harmonic convergence of technical advancement and traditional expertise represents the zenith of a long history. The bottom line is that there has never been a better time to drink sake. For the interested non-native, however, it can be hard to know where to begin. Even with some knowledge of Japanese, the terminology particular to sake is a daunting barrier, baffling even to many Japanese people. Information in English is scarce. Though random exploration has its own appeal, it can be a disappointing and expensive enterprise. Every nugget of information will make your activities more interesting, cost-effective, and fun.

So to business. Let us begin our sampling of sake's delights by considering the many forms in which it is to be enjoyed.

C

Comics are read by everyone in Japan, and there are *manga* about everything: sake is no exception. *Manga* artist Hitoshi Takase has written many strips (and books) for the sake fanatic. Many sake lovers have also read the series *Natsuko no Sake* (Natsuko's Sake), by Akira Oze. This is based on the true story of the revival of a lost variety of sake rice, and is packed with closely observed details of life in a small brewery. It makes entertaining and educational reading for anyone interested in sake. It was also made into a television drama, about which the less said, the better.

2

Categories of Sake

T he world of sake is above all one of profuse variety. Though, sadly, a number of breweries go out of business every year, there are still almost two thousand. Each firm offers a range of products, so the sake lover is spoiled for choice—to the tune of thousands of brand names. Varying criteria are used to divide this huge range into pieces of a more manageable scale. Some connoisseurs rave about the wonders of their favorite brand, or the virtues of particular rice or yeast varieties. Others are passionate about the characteristics associated with regional brewing styles, or the methodologies of different schools of brewers. All these factors and more are the subject of debate and devotion. To join the fray, it is first necessary to know the various categories of sake.

Sake is categorized in three basic ways: by the raw materials used (and their grade), by the method of brewing, and by how it is processed *after* brewing. In the next section, I introduce some basic categories, which are graded primarily in terms of raw materials. (On page 33, I explain some further, somewhat unusual varieties.) All those introduced up to this point are defined by what happens *during* the brewing process. The next section, from page 34 to page 38, explains certain subdivisions defined according to the treatment of the finished sake. In other words, the varieties in the first group, until page 33, are defined by what happens until their birth, so to speak. Those discussed from page 34 onwards are defined in terms of their "upbringing."

Grades of Sake Defined by Raw Materials

Sake is made from rice that has been "polished." Brown rice is milled, and the smaller white rice grains that remain are used in brewing. Brewers long ago discovered that the further rice is polished, the finer the flavor of the resulting sake. As a result, one of the most important criteria for categorizing sake is the grade of white rice used. This is given as a percentage of the grain remaining, a figure called the "rice polishing ratio"—*seimai buai* in Japanese. The lower the number the more the rice has been polished.

$$\text{rice polishing ratio} = \frac{\text{weight of white rice}}{\text{weight of brown rice}} \times 100$$

The first three categories introduced below belong to a premium group known as Special Designation Sakes. Details vary for each of them, but the basic requirement for inclusion in this group is the use of white rice polished to 70% or further. Most of the sakes introduced in the Sampler in this book belong to these categories, beloved of connoisseurs.

D

Doburoku

This is home-brewed sake, and is sadly illegal, as is all home brewing in Japan. It's a far cry from the clear sake made commercially—generally cloudy if not actually lumpy!

A portion of the rice used in brewing is made into rice *kōji* (a variety of mold used in "malting" rice). Beer and sake brewers face the same problem of producing fermentable sugars from a grain. Rice *kōji* is sometimes called "malted rice," since it is seen as a parallel to the barley malt used in making beer. (Though, as the reader will see, it is very different from anything known to Western brewing. Details of this highly distinctive feature of sake brewing can be found in Chapter 3, Making Sake.)

Junmaishu (純米酒)
"Pure Rice Sake"

The two basic ingredients of all sake, then, are white rice and rice *kōji*. Some sake is made *only* from these two ingredients, and this type is called *junmaishu*.

To qualify for this ranking, the sake in question must be made from rice polished to 70% or less. In terms of taste, *junmai* sakes tend to be full-bodied with a rather stronger flavor than other varieties, though exceptions abound. Their relatively high acidity also distinguishes them from other sakes. *Junmai* brews are sometimes strongly reminiscent of the rice of which they are made. This type of sake is becoming more popular, but still holds only a small share of the market.

Militant *junmai* lovers (an increasingly numerous breed) insist that pure rice sake is the only genuine article, unsullied by any but natural ingredients. This extreme view is still the minority position of a very small percentage of connoisseurs; the lighter (some say smoother) flavors of alcohol-added varieties (see below) still outsell *junmai* brews massively. A subdivision called **tokubetsu (special) junmaishu** also exists. The maker is entitled to use this tag if the rice used is polished to 60% or less—or if a "special production method" has been used. This is obviously open to interpretation by the maker, who may use the term without specifying in what fashion the product in question is "special."

Honjōzō (本醸造)
Sake with a Limited Addition of Brewer's Alcohol

This type of sake must also be made from rice polished to 70% or less. It is distinguished from pure rice sake by a limited addition of brewer's alcohol—introduced to the fermenting mash before pressing. Brewer's alcohol is ethanol, usually commercially produced, though a few brewers distill their own. The quantity of the addition is subject to an upper limit of 116 liters of pure alcohol to 1,000 kilograms of white rice. This means that about a quarter of the alcohol in the sake you buy has been added. In terms of flavor, *honjōzō* sake tends to be lighter than pure rice varieties, since flavor components are effectively diluted.

Rigid-minded *junmai* purists often refuse to admit any merit other than economy to the technique of alcohol addition. If the only motivation were economic, however, the addition could equally be made to the sake *after* pressing. The reason that this is not the case is that brewers aim to retain the fragrant (but volatile) components which otherwise remain to a large extent in the lees. Most brewers have had the depressing experience of pressing a superbly fragrant batch, only to find themselves left with a tank of almost odorless sake and a heap of sweet-smelling rice-cake, destined to end up as animal feed or in a pickle factory. Because the substances that are the source of the aroma are highly soluble in alcohol, the small addition brings out the nose in a way not possible with a *junmai* sake. (As I write, I suppress the urge to dive for cover; this is probably the favorite skirmishing-ground for sake militants. What kind of a bouquet should a sake have? How prominent should it be?) The *junmai* camp point out that almost all sake made until World War II was pure rice sake, but it is worth considering that the technique of adding alcohol before pressing was known as long ago as the seventeenth century. I enjoy both, myself.

You may come across the subdivision **tokubetsu (special) honjōzō**, with the same additional requirements as for *tokubetsu jun-maishu*.

Ginjōshu (吟醸酒)
"Special Brew" Sake

The "gin" (pronounced as in "gingham," not as in my mother's favorite tipple) comes from the phrase *ginmi suru*, which means to select carefully, or to be particular or scrupulous about something. "*Jō*" is a reading of the character 醸, *kamosu*, which means "ferment." In other words, *ginjō* is "specially brewed" sake, made by painstaking special methods from the highest grade of rice. Where the rice used in making *junmai* and *honjōzō* varieties must be polished to 70% or less of its original size, the minimum requirement for *ginjō* sake is a costly 60%. If the rice used was polished to 50% or further, it qualifies for the label **daiginjō** (大吟醸), or "great *ginjō*." (In contrast, the term **chu-ginjō** ["middle

E

Enzymes and ebriety

Everyone knows the word "sobriety," but its sibling is rarely remembered: "ebriety"—a word that simply means drunkenness and carries no sloppy sentimentality or judgement! When alcohol is broken down in the body (and in the liver in particular), the first product is acetaldehyde, a volatile compound which causes strong reactions if it accumulates in the bloodstream. This is then further converted by an enzyme (aldehydedehydrogenase by name). The liver of a normal Westerner metabolizes acetaldehyde so quickly that none gets into the blood at all. However, it is said only a small percentage of Westerners have a deficiency in this enzyme, which means that they are much more drastically affected by alcohol than people with a normal allowance. In contrast, about half of the Japanese are said to suffer from the same deficiency, which is why they tend to move from sobriety to ebriety so quickly.

ginjō," 中吟醸] is sometimes used for sake made from rice polished to between 60 and 50%.) It is further stipulated that the brewer use *ginjō-zukuri*, the peculiar techniques associated with the style. (Terminology becomes circular: "*Ginjō* sake is to be made by the methods used to make *ginjō* sake.") An array of particular, labor-intensive techniques are used in brewing these luxury sakes in the small lots that their demanding methodology requires. They are prized for their refinement and superb, fruity aroma, so distinctive that it, too, is self-defining: *ginjō-ka*; the aroma of a *ginjō*! There are both alcohol-added *ginjō*s (with brewer's alcohol added within the same limits as for *honjōzō* sakes) and pure rice varieties, which are called ***junmai ginjō***, or ***junmai daiginjō***.

For the lover of rarities, the world of *ginjōshu* is one of many treasures. Heavy drinkers may quail at the price, and *junmai* (pure rice) zealots may insist on the more down-to-earth delights of their favorites, but everyone, when push comes to shove, admits the right of *ginjō* sake to the crown of the sake kingdom. At once the epitome of traditional wisdom and the fruit of modern technologies, *ginjōshu* is the paragon of Japanese brewing.

Sanzōshu and *Futsūshu* (三増酒, 普通酒)
Lower Grades of Sake

Sakes made from rice polished by less than 30% do not qualify for the Special Designations. Neither do those that have greater additions of brewer's alcohol than the strictly limited amount permitted in the making of a *honjōzō* (or an alcohol-added *ginjō*). While the market share of the Special Designation styles has grown enormously in recent years, their extraordinary rate of growth is partly a reflection of the tiny share they originally had. The bulk of all sake consumed belongs to one of the lower grades introduced below. Most sake connoisseurs would rather have a cup of tea, but can millions of Japanese drinkers be wrong?

The most common kind is called *sanzōshu*, "triple sake." Brewer's alcohol is added in bulk, and certain other additives are also permitted. Where the addition of alcohol to *honjōzō* sake represents a fractional increase in yield, enough is added to *sanzō* brews to triple the amount of sake produced per batch, thus the name. It is a tremendously economical method of production, developed in the 1940s in Manchuria, then a colony of Japan. In the war years (and for some time thereafter), Japan suffered cruel food shortages. The situation was still more dire for those stationed in Manchuria. There was certainly little rice to be spared for brewing, so research was begun to find ways of making more from less.

SALES OF SAKE BY TYPE

YEAR	GINJŌ SAKE	JUNMAISHU	HONJŌZŌ
1985–86 (61 BY)	6,980	19,787	72,114
1986–87 (62 BY)	9,465 (136%)	26,972 (136)	87,862 (122)
1987–88 (63 BY)	11,123 (118)	35,370 (131)	107,258 (122)
1988–89 (1 BY)	19,877 (179)	34,121 (96)	140,282 (131)
1989–90 (2 BY)	26,564 (134)	36,079 (106)	158,717 (113)
1990–91 (3 BY)	32,095 (121)	43,318 (120)	176,563 (111)
1991–92 (4 BY)	38,682 (121)	46,596 (108)	182,807 (104)
1992–93 (5 BY)	47,363 (122)	51,196 (110)	212,478 (116)
1993–94 (6 BY)	51,279 (108)	54,733 (107)	219,221 (103)
1994–95 (7 BY)	51,583 (99)	53,453 (98)	204,948 (94)

NOTE: Sales figures in brackets show sales as a percentage of the previous year's record. Sales periods run from July, when the brewing season begins, to June of the following year. "BY" is an acronym for English "Brewer's Year," given in the year of the Emperor's reign. Thus, 63 BY signifies the final year of the reign of

The solution was to boost the yield by adding raw ethanol (with sugars and organic acids to balance the flavor). In the most extreme form, a sake-like drink was produced using no rice whatsoever! However, the method that became standard (to the point of almost universal use within a year or two of introduction) was known as *sanbai-zōjōshu*, "sake brewed and increased three times." This lengthy phrase from brewing law is commonly shortened to *sanzōshu*.

Although the market has diversified in recent years, it is still true to say that if you simply order "sake" in a bar or restaurant, the chances are good that a *sanzōshu* will arrive. For years, though, sake has been losing its share of the overall liquor market. Until recently, very few people had an inkling of any other variety of sake than *sanzōshu*, so it would seem that its dominance brought certain problems for the industry. Admittedly, the national drink had to face an unprecedented level of competition from

SPECIAL DESIGNATION SAKE TOTAL	LOWER GRADE SAKE	TOTAL	*NAMA* SAKE
98,881		1,377,513	
		(103)	
124,299		1,424,869	
(126)		(103)	
153,751		1,403,438	
(124)		(98)	
194,280		1,417,293	
(126)		(101)	
221,360		1,388,858	
(114)		(98)	
251,976	1,169,921	1,421,896	48,477
(114)		(102)	
268,685	1,142,003	1,410,088	52,950
(106)	(96)	(99)	(109)
311,037	1,099,418	1,410,455	59,589
(116)	(96)	(100)	(113)
325,233	1,072,937	1,398,170	62,949
(105)	(98)	(99)	(106)
308,985	1,010,450	1,319,435	66,336
(95)	(94)	(94)	(105)

the Emperor Shōwa (Hirohito) and 1 BY indicates the first year of the current Emperor's reign. The overall drop in figures for 1995 is due to the Great Hanshin Earthquake in Kobe in January 1995—the peak of the brewing season.

newly popular arrivals—notably beer. Nonetheless, sake (in the sense that sake equaled *sanzōshu*), was undergoing an image crisis. Triple sake had been a tremendous blessing in the hard years of bitter want, but it was an anomaly in cornucopian modern Japan. In a country where surpluses had to be contained by subsidizing farmers not to grow rice, the industry was still churning out cheap sake suited to a harsh world of scarcity. Another factor was probably concern over the additives used, as health-consciousness increasingly affected consumer trends. It is a fact that many people who dislike sake know only this variety; it is also undeniable that some kinds deliver apocalyptic hangovers. For all these reasons, triple sake has seen a long period of decline. If there were no *sanzōshu*, though, the resultant drought would be colossal. Despite the growing popularity of the Special Designation Sakes, they account for only about a quarter of the total market.

The tripling method was developed to make sake cheaply, and the resultant tendency to consider cost more than quality has left it with a considerable image problem. However, times have changed, and many sake lovers with painful memories, and correspondingly robust preconceptions, might be surprised by some of the *sanzō* products now available. Triple sake may yet ride again with a combination of raised standards, low cost, and drinkability.

Another variety is *futsūshu* (普通酒). *Futsū* literally means "ordinary" or "standard" sake, but the term "standard sake" is rather misleading. This type is in fact no more common than *sanzōshu*. (The rather confusing terms come from tax law, which distinguishes between the *zōjōhō*, the method for producing triple sake, and *futsū jōzōhō*, literally "standard brewing method," which is the legal definition of the procedure for making *futsūshu*.) In the making of this kind of sake, a greater addition of brewer's alcohol is permitted than for *honjōzō* types, but the quantity of additives is not permitted to the same extent as it is in triple sake. Organic acids may be used, but sugars are not permitted.

CONDITIONS FOR GRADING OF SAKE VARIETIES

| Grade | Rice-polishing ratio (minimum level) | Permitted Additions | | Sugars | Organic acids |
| | | Brewer's alcohol | | | |
		limited addition	major addition*		
"Triple sake" (*sanzōshu*)	No limit	X	✓✓	✓	✓
"Standard sake" (*futsūshu*)	No limit	X	✓	X	✓
Honjōzō	70%	✓	X	X	X
Junmaishu	70%	X	X	X	X
Ginjō					
Chū (middle)	60%	✓	X	X	X
Dai (great)	50%	✓	X	X	X
Junmai ginjō					
Chū (middle)	60%	X	X	X	X
Dai (great)	50%	X	X	X	X

*Though the scale of the addition for "standard sake" (*futsūshu*) is considerably larger than that for *honjōzō* varieties, it is in turn dwarfed by the bulk additions permissible in making triple sake.

Kimoto and *Yamahai* (生酛, 山廃)
The Old School

An important stage in the making of sake is the production of the yeast starter mash. In Japanese, this is called *shubo* or *moto*. (Details of production can be found in the following chapter.) There are two schools, the modern "high-speed" method, and the classical *kimoto* ("live" or "raw" *moto*) style. This latter, in turn, has two forms, the original *kimoto* method and a revised (and slightly less laborious) form, *yamahai*, which was developed at the turn of the century. (Though the expressions *yamahai* and *kimoto* strictly refer to the method of production of the yeast starter, the terms are also used to refer to the finished sake itself.) Sake for which the yeast starter was made by one of these methods tends to be deeply flavored—though this rule, too, has its exceptions. In the current climate of approval for all things light (and—horrors—lite), they are a distinctive presence. Because of the burden they place on the brewer (requiring twice as long as the modern high-speed method), and because of the nationwide trend towards lighter flavors, they are unlikely to become truly popular styles, but enough connoisseurs enjoy their punch and character that their niche seems assured.

Kijōshu (貴醸酒)
"Precious-brewed Sake"

This peculiar style of sake has parallels with the port of the wine world. Around half of the water used in brewing is replaced with sake. The resulting sake is very sweet, and is, like port, usually matured for several years before sale. Makes an excellent pre-prandial or dessert wine.

Nigori-zake (にごり酒)
"Cloudy Sake"

The "English" slogan "The Refined Japanese Sake" can be found on many sake bottles. It is an attempt to render the Japanese term **seishu** (清酒)—literally "clear sake." *Seishu* is defined as sake that has been passed through a mesh of some kind—actually a legal requirement for all products sold as sake. Thus, *seishu* is simply the generic term for all legally marketed sake today.

An odd subdivision is that variety called *nigori*. *Nigori* means "cloudy." This kind is only passed through a very coarse mesh (though some makers apparently put lees *back* into the clear sake after pressing in the normal way). Whereas most sake is almost completely clear after pressing, the wide mesh used in the case of *nigori-zake* allows a certain quantity of rice solids through, and the resulting sake is milky white (when the bottle is shaken to disturb the sediment).

To be sold legally as *seishu*, a sake must be passed through a mesh. This includes both *nigori* sake and *ori-zake* (page 38), both defined by their turbidity. Since they have in fact passed through a mesh filter, the paradoxical consequence is that *nigori* sake, being by definition *seishu*, is "cloudy clear sake." Is this the world's only drinkable oxymoron?

Categories Defined According to Treatment of the Finished Sake

The various categories listed above are defined mainly in terms of the ingredients used (and their grade). The sakes that follow are defined by certain features of their handling *after* brewing has finished.

Genshu (原酒)
Undiluted Sake

Eighty percent of sake is water, but water is never listed as an ingredient. It is, naturally, used during brewing, but is usually also added once again before sale. In its raw state, sake may contain more than 20% alcohol by volume. This can be a bit fierce for the wimpy modern consumer, so it is generally diluted to about fifteen-and-a-bit percent. Occasionally, though, it is sold in its natural state. Such sake is called *genshu* (*gen* means "origin" or "base").

It's fun to drink on the rocks: starting off strong, it dilutes, little by little, as the ice melts. What is exactly the right strength? After a few minutes, the sake reaches a moment of perfect balance between temperature and strength; a few moments later, and it is suddenly watery and thin—necessitating reinforcement from the bottle, and returning the whole process to stage one. This game is fun, but it is easy to get through a lot more of the potent stuff than you expect.

Nama-zake (生酒)
Unpasteurized "Live" Sake

Sake is made by the skillful handling of microorganisms: yeast and the amazing *kōji* mold in particular (discussed in detail in Chapter 3, Making Sake). However, the same microorganisms can cause problems during storage. For this reason most sake is heat-treated (pasteurized) twice to kill all these microscopic beasties off, once before storage and once before shipping. This makes handling both safer and simpler, since it renders the sake more stable and less prone to spoil. In recent years, refrigerated storage and transport have made sake in its original "live" state (formerly virtually unknown outside the trade) easily available to the consumer. This type of sake is known as *nama* ("live" or "raw," 生) in Japanese. In

F

Filtration

Most sake undergoes carbon filtration before it is shipped. This lightens the flavor and inhibits the changes in color and flavor associated with maturation. When the sake has colored during storage (a common phenomenon), filtering can return it to its original clarity. In its natural state sake has a slight greenish-yellow cast, but some sake on the market is completely colorless, a sign that it has been heavily filtered.

This technology is a two-edged sword, particularly for brewers of premium *ginjō* sake. While filtration may remove unwanted heavy tastes and color, there is a real danger that the delicate flavors and precious *ginjō-ka* aroma may also be eliminated—the brewer's equivalent of throwing the baby out with the bathwater.

terms of flavor, its most easily distinguished characteristic is an aroma known as *kōji-bana*. Rather than attempt to describe this unmistakable smell in terms of something else, I shall leave it to the reader to discover at first-hand (or first-nose). *Nama* sake is generally rather robust, with a "thickness of flavor," (*atsumi*) as is said in Japanese. It used to be conventional to say that young sake was rough-tasting: today, that certain untamed flavor is exactly what appeals to *nama* fans. It has a freshness and pizazz all its own, but also changes very quickly, thanks to the still-active microorganisms; this is both its delight and its danger. It requires extra care in storage, and should always be refrigerated. Once open, it should be finished off as quickly as possible. In other words, the storage and transport of *nama* sake require all the care necessary in looking after any good sake, except more so.

A variation on the theme is **nama chozō shu** ("live storage sake"). In this case, the sake is left unpasteurized throughout the storage period, and only heated at the bottling stage, immediately before shipping.

This leads to a slightly more robust sake than the completely untouched **bon-nama** while retaining a certain amount of the characteristic *nama* zing. Alternatively, you may come across **nama-zume** ("live bottled sake"), in which case it is pasteurized only once, before storage, and not when bottled.

Because of its freshness, and also because it is almost invariably served cold, *nama-zake* sells best in the fearsome heat and humidity of the Japanese summer. Japanese culture (including poetry, food, and letter-writing) displays a connoisseur's appreciation of the passing seasons and their particular aspects. Sake is wonderfully suited to these seasonal modulations: warm sake when the swallows leave; cold, refreshing *nama* to alleviate the midsummer heat.

In market terms, *nama* inevitably has a relatively small share because of the difficulties of transport and storage, but it is gaining ground slowly. The debate about the relative virtues of *nama-zake* and sake that has undergone the standard double pasteurization process (*hi-ire*, 火入れ) is one of the most heated of all. I know extremely knowledgeable people in both camps.

Koshu and *Shinshu* (古酒, 新酒)
Something Old, Something New

In the good old days, more or less all sake was made and consumed in a very Japanese, seasonal, one-year cycle. Once the first sake of the season was pressed, all the previous year's production (or what remained thereof) was referred to as *koshu* ("old sake"). The new sake, with admirable simplicity, was called *shinshu* ("new sake"). This usage is still current. However, big makers now brew year round, which inevitably necessitates

G

Gold flakes

Sake containing gold flakes is a common gift, the rationale being that they lend a sense of luxury to the product. (Gold is inert, and so has no effect on the taste of the sake.) Japan has a very complex culture of gift-giving, though, in which the appropriate price often decides the suitability of a gift. In this sense, sake with gold flakes is a cousin to individually wrapped apples (not made of gold, despite the price).

different storage and sale patterns, and hence, terminology. The traditional terms are still common, but use the brewers' year (from July to the end of the following June) as the measure. Those involved in traditional winter brewing still use the term mainly to distinguish between this year's sake, just pressed, and that of the previous season, in storage.

The word "*shinshu*" remains safe enough, but "*koshu*" is also colloquially used to signify highly-aged brews. You may also come across the expressions **ō-goshu** (大古酒—"great, old sake"), **ko-ko-shu** (古古酒—old, old, sake) and **hizōshu** (秘蔵酒—"treasured sake," literally "sake stored in secret"). There seems to be a certain amount of flexibility (read: confusion) about the use of these terms. It's not really worth worrying about. Just remember that *koshu* is old sake, and you'll know as much as the rest of us.

Much more interesting than all these definitions is what actually happens when sake matures. After a few years (or longer in cases where storage takes place in refrigerated conditions and the speed of maturation is correspondingly glacial), color deepens, a strong and distinctive bouquet develops, and a range of powerful flavors emerge. Sometimes there is a resemblance to sherry: smoky, caramel flavors develop. The pace and character of change is also drastically affected by the method of storage; sake stored in tanks (still the most common method) ages much more quickly than that matured in bottles. It is becoming common to distinguish between the two styles, calling the lighter kinds "*jukuseishu*" (熟成酒—"matured sake"), and the darker, more pungent (generally tank-matured) variety simply *koshu*.

The effect of well-aged sake is radically different from the familiar freshness of young sake. Those who dislike the pungent *koshu* tastes and aromas hate aged sake with a vengeance; the converted wallow in the depth and complexity of flavor. Until recently, the characteristic odor of *koshu* was generally referred to disparagingly as *hine-ka* ("old smell"), and was automatically counted as a defect, but more people are coming to see *koshu* as a genre of its own, deserving of a different set of standards. It is still a relatively minor niche of the sake world, but interest is picking up. It is one area where whisky-loving, sherry-swilling Westerners may be quicker off the mark than the Japanese, who lack a tradition of pungent, matured beverages.

Ori-zake (おり酒)
Sake with Lees

After normal pressing, sake *looks* completely clear. It is returned to a tank before final storage. There, after several days have passed, a fine sediment (*ori*) collects at the bottom of the tank. Usually, the clear sake is drawn off, leaving the lees behind, a process called *ori-biki*. Occasionally, though, this process is omitted, and the sake is bottled, lees and all. This is called *ori-zake*.

Both *ori-zake* and *nigori-zake* have a taste reminiscent of the fermenting mix, which people tend to either love or hate. The solids they contain are loaded with the microorganisms that drive fermentation before pressing. These are the same bunch that make unpasteurized *nama-zake* prone to spoil, and they are here in force. This means that these types really don't keep well, and are best kept refrigerated (of course) and drunk as quickly as possible (naturally).

Taru-zake (樽酒)
Keg Sake

Taru-zake has undergone an aging period in Japanese cedar barrels. Such sake has a distinctive aroma, directly attributable to the wood of the keg. The finest wood for this purpose is held to be from Yoshino in Nara Prefecture. At weddings, festivals, election victories, and other moments of celebration, sake is often served from the keg (frequently in *masu*, square boxes made of Japanese cedar). This is not *taru-zake* in the sense given above, since it is not *aged* in wood, but filled shortly before use. Even so, the aroma of the wood imparts a distinct—occasionally even overpowering—smell and flavor.

Such are the main varieties of sake. While one or two more minor categories exist, they are relatively unimportant. Should you come across them, you will find them listed and explained in the glossary. At the risk of stating the obvious, it is worth pointing out that these categories are not all mutually exclusive. For example, a sake may be *ginjō*, <u>and</u> *genshu*, <u>and</u> *nama* into the bargain.

Having introduced the various types of sake, let's consider how they come about.

3

Making Sake:
An Inside Look at the
Brewing Process

Sake making is complex, old-fashioned, automated, labor-intensive, idiosyncratic, traditional, and high-tech. It is not easy to give a "typical" example, because there are such wide variations. The common phrase is *sake zukuri banryū*, which means "ten thousand schools of sake making"! I shall do the conventional thing, and begin at the beginning, sticking, for the moment, to the practical processes involved in contemporary brewing.

Rice Polishing (*Seimai*, 精米)

As has already been mentioned, the rice used in sake brewing is polished white rice, from which the outer layer has been milled away. The outer portion of the rice contains minerals, fats, and proteins that affect fermentation adversely and contribute to off-flavors in the finished sake. (Eating rice is also polished, but only to 91%.) Rice used in brewing is generally polished to 80% or less of its original size—and to less than 40% for some top grades. The powdery unused portion is generally used in making *tsukemono* (Japanese pickles) or as animal feed, although the fine, high-grade powder from the rice used for *ginjō* sake is used in making Japanese cakes and sweets. As the expression *kome-nuka bijin* ("rice-powder beauty") suggests, it is also held to be good for the complexion, and is used in some cosmetic products.

Rice polishing was the first of all the processes of sake brewing to be mechanized, when Edo-period (1603–1868) brewers began using mills driven by waterwheels. A later advance in the 1930s introduced a "vertical" type of machine in which the millstones turn on a perpendicular axle, as opposed to the earlier horizontal arrangement. Still more recently came computer-monitored equipment. The vertical design enabled brewers to polish their rice effectively to higher grades than ever before; computerization meant that the process could be completed without some poor devil having to oversee it day and night.

Handmade sake

More than a few labels carry the legend 手造り (*te-zukuri*) which means handmade. There is no legal definition of this term but the idea is that many of the various brewing processes are (literally) in the hands of the craftsmen brewers. In such cases, many crucial decisions are made by brewers solely on the strength of their five senses, and the sixth sense which comes with long years of experience. In contrast, there are many companies whose sake is entirely machine made. Obviously, such operations continue on a quite different scale, and there is no necessity for midnight labor. From raw ingredients to bottled sake, all is untouched by human hands. As technologies have developed, the quality of machine-made sake has improved enormously, and, today, many truly fine sakes come out of completely automated plants. That being said, many companies whose operations are otherwise totally automated brew one or two tanks of sake by hand for the prestigious industry contest held each spring. Many romantics (and a goodly number of quite unsentimental critics) insist on the more idiosyncratic character of handmade brews, but it would be a very dry world if it were not for the enormous production capacity of automated plants.

During polishing, friction heats the rice considerably. This means that there is very little moisture in freshly polished rice. If it is washed too soon, the parched grains crack when they come into contact with the water. Therefore, it is usual to let the rice stand before use, during which time the moisture content of the grain recovers. (This waiting period is called *karashi* in Japanese.)

In short, the brewer polishes the rice to eliminate substances concentrated in the outer portion of the grain that cause unpleasant flavors and adversely affect the fermentation pattern. The further the rice is polished, the cleaner and lighter tasting the resulting sake will be.

Rice Washing (*Senmai*, 洗米)

After the rice has been polished, *nuka* (rice powder) still clings to the surface of the grain. This is removed by washing. Machine washing, in one of a variety of forms, is now most common. The simplest method is to transport the white rice from the place of storage by pumping it through a pipe with water, washing it in the process. However, for top quality *ginjō* sakes, gentle, laborious hand washing is still the rule, rather than a rare exception. White rice, polished to less than 50% of its original size (as for *daiginjō*), is very delicate, and brewers take every care to prevent the precious grains from cracking.

Steeping (*Shinseki*, 浸漬)

After washing, the rice must be soaked. The purpose of this is to allow the rice grains to absorb the desired amount of water. This stage is crucial to establishing the consistency of the rice, which is to be steamed the next day. The texture of the steamed rice in turn determines the quality of *kōji* that is produced, and affects the pattern of fermentation in the main mash. To backtrack for a moment, it is also true to say that the success of this process depends on how skillfully the rice has been polished. This domino effect, where a mistake in one step resonates through the entire production of a batch, is a major concern for brewers, who must be unfailingly vigilant at every stage throughout the season. It is also one reason that teamwork and cooperation are so crucial to successful brewing, since a mistake at any stage will affect all the subsequent processes.

For the "average" batch of rice (polished to about 75%), steeping will take several hours. Many brewers leave the rice to soak overnight. However, the more the rice has been polished the quicker it absorbs water. Thus, in the case of the highly-polished rice used in brewing *ginjō* sake, the rice may well be soaked only for a matter of minutes. In such instances, an error of minutes—even seconds—may have dire consequences for the subsequent processes and the end product.

Steaming (*Jōmai*, 蒸米) and Cooling (*Hōrei*, 放冷)

The washed rice is steamed the following morning. Steaming softens the grains and breaks down the starch molecules, facilitating the growth of the vital *kōji* mold. (It also has the bonus effect of killing off all other microorganisms, leaving an initially sterile environment in which to propagate the sake mold.) The time varies considerably, from twenty minutes to an hour according to the particular brewer and the apparatus used. According to the traditional method, the rice is steamed for forty minutes to an hour in a pot called a *koshiki*, a process that does not really lend itself to large-scale production. The "continuous rice-steaming machine" (*renzoku jōmaiki*), on the other hand, steams the rice on a conveyor belt, along which it travels for about twenty minutes. The development of this equipment in the 1950s allowed the steaming of up to twenty tonnes (twenty-two tons) of rice a day compared to one or two tonnes in the traditional way. This was a major breakthrough in mechanization and mass-production. Some breweries have never changed from the *koshiki*; in recent years, others have returned to the *koshiki* in response to the growing demand for higher grades of sake. Today both methods exist.

The resulting steamed rice (*mushi-mai*) is considerably firmer than eating rice. If the steamed rice is too hard, the mold will be unable to grow into the hard center of the grain; if the steamed rice is too soft, the mold propagates abundantly, but fail to produce the required quality of enzymes. The correct firmness is also vitally important for the progress of fermentation in the main batch, due to its effect on the delicate balance of sake brewing's extraordinary pattern of "multiple parallel fermentation."

The steamed rice is divided according to how it will be used. Some is cooled (usually by air blowers, though that for *ginjō* brewing is often cooled naturally in the cold winter air) and then goes directly into the mix. Between 20 and 30%, however, is taken to a heated culture room, where it is infected with the spores of a mold called *Aspergillus oryzae*. This is *kōji*, the magical sake mold.

Kōji Making (*Seikiku*, 製麴)

Despite all the social and cultural paraphernalia that the world of sake glories in, the undeniable bottom line is alcohol. This is produced when yeast converts sugar into alcohol (plus carbon dioxide, chemistry fans). Here, sake brewers face quite different challenges than winemakers, for example. The grapes from which wine is made contain glucose (which is actually called *budō-tō*, "grape sugar," in Japanese). Naturally occurring or cultured yeast changes this sugar to alcohol in a simple process, appropriately known as simple fermentation. In rice grains, however, there is no sugar. It is created by the action of the *kōji* mold, which converts the starch in the grain into sugars.

The propagation of *kōji* on steamed rice is considered to be the very heart of sake brewing, and is also one of its most distinctive features. (Although the use of mold cultures does occur in brewing in other parts of Asia, the methods of Japanese brewers bear little resemblance to practices elsewhere.) Explained here is the most common form of the classical method. Almost all of the figures given are subject to variation depending on the school and methodology of the individual brewer, and the stage of brewing in which the finished *kōji* is to be used.

Inshu unten (飲酒運転) means drunk driving, and is illegal, but regrettably common, in Japan.

First, the steamed rice is cooled to about 35° or 36° C (95° to 97° F) before being taken to the *kōji* culture room. (This is known as the *muro* and is kept heated at around 30° C/86° F.) This first stage is called *hikikomi*. Spores of the mold (*tane kōji*) are sprinkled like fine dust on the rice when it has cooled to about 33° C, or 91° F. (The spores are bought from specialist makers.) Once the spores have been kneaded into the steamed rice (*tokomomi*), the rice is heaped and wrapped in cloths to prevent heat and moisture loss. The growth rate of the mold is enormously sensitive to the two factors of temperature and moisture: their skillful control is the key to successful *kōji-zukuri*—*kōji* making. So the *kōji* mold begins to grow on the rice. To maintain an even temperature the rice is usually spread out and mixed about ten hours later, then wrapped up once more, a task called *kirikaeshi*. When the mold has been growing for about twenty hours, it at last becomes visible to the naked eye in the form of white flecks. By this stage, too, the temperature of the rice begins to rise, and it is divided into smaller lots and transferred to wooden boxes to facilitate more precise control. This division is called *mori*. The classical method uses tiny traylike boxes called *kōji* "lids" (*kōji-buta*). Though no longer the most common method, these are still quite widely used in the making of *kōji* to be used in the production of sake for entry in the yearly industry contests, but most brewers find them too demanding to use all the time. Slightly more common, and a touch less exhausting, are larger boxes that hold about fifteen kilograms each (ten times as much as the tiny trays). About seven or eight hours later, the temperature of the rice has risen considerably, and the batch is mixed again to reduce variations in moisture content and temperature (*naka shigoto*). By this stage, the mold covers roughly one-third of the rice grain, exhibiting its characteristic white color, and begins to give off a distinctive aroma. When the tiny trays are being used, each is individually agitated to move the rice around. Then the stacking order is reversed to compensate for the variation in moisture and temperature in different parts of the culture room. The trays at the top are hotter than those below. Trays will also be shifted from left to right and front to back. Each tray is rotated and moved. Carried about by an experienced craftsman, this is a most elegant dance to watch. While all handmade *kōji* requires checks in the middle of the night and the small hours of the morning, this method requires considerably more midnight labor than the others.

As the mold grows, it generates considerable heat, and frequent checks are necessary to prevent overheating. On the other hand, if it is over-exposed, and the temperature drops too far, the propagation will be impeded. Six or seven hours after *naka shigoto*, the temperature will have reached about 38° or 39° C (100° to 102° F). The opaque, white spots of *kōji* mold will cover most of the grain. At this point, the rice is remixed;

J

Ji-zake (地酒) means "local or regional [as opposed to national] sake"; it is one of the industry's most potent buzzwords. Until the recent past, the majority of brands were only available in their region of production, the exceptions being the nationally distributed wares of the giant makers. However, improved transportation links and a change in the expectations of consumers over the last couple of decades have seen many more "country sakes" reach urban markets throughout Japan. In a sense, they thus cease to be *ji-zake*. Though there are still a great many sakes that are almost never to be found away from home, there are few people today who would insist on restricting the definition of *ji-zake* to these local brews alone. The problems concerning the definition of the term recall the debate regarding the expression "microbrewery" in the United States. For most people who like to use it, the expression *ji-zake* simply refers, in a rather vague way, to the products of smaller, traditional-style breweries.

this final stage is called *shimai shigoto*. The temperature rises once more, and generally climbs well over 40° C (104° F). When the trays are being used, they are usually re-stacked once more, three or four hours later. When the *kōji* rice has reached the desired balance of taste, temperature, and aroma (which translate to enzyme content and balance in chemical terms), it is removed from the culture room and allowed to cool, thereby stopping the growth of the mold. (This is called *dekōji*, and usually takes place about twelve hours after the final *shimai shigoto* mixing. The "standard" time to produce one batch of *kōji* seems to be between forty and forty-five hours.) The finished *kōji* is sweet to taste, because of the all-important sugars that have been produced, and smells rather like roasted chestnuts. During the last hours in the *muro* room, moisture content of the grain decreases considerably through evaporation, so the *kōji* is quite hard to the touch. The finished *kōji* rice is usually left for a day before use.

There are many variations in the methodology of *kōji* making, according to the style of sake to be brewed, the grade of rice in use, the stage of brewing the finished *kōji* is to be used in, and various other factors. Machine-made *kōji* is now very common, and this too comes in many forms and degrees. The simplest machines are nothing more than arrangements of fans that blow air through to cool things off according to preset criteria, leaving much of the work to be done by hand. At the top end of the market are *kōji* robots (the cutely-monikered *Tōji-kun*, for example), or the completely automated two-story type of apparatus.

NOTE: Among the dozens of enzymes known to be produced in rice *kōji*, the key groups are amylases and proteases. Both acid and alkaline proteases are produced; the former act in the main fermentation mash to decompose proteins, forming peptides and amino acids that affect the flavor of the finished sake. However, the most crucial enzymes that are formed are Alpha-amylase and the diastatic enzyme—a saccharifying enzyme called amyloglucosidase. The former breaks down long starch molecules into shorter chains. These intermediate products are unfermentable sugars, or oligosaccharides. Next, the saccharifying enzyme reduces these in turn to glucose molecules, which the yeast can use in the actual alcoholic fermentation.

Starter Mash (*Shubo*, 酒母)

This stage is also colloquially known by the name *moto*, written with a character (●) unused except in this context. You will look for it in vain in most dictionaries, and word processors are no help either, as I know only too well. It incorporates an element signifying "source" or "origin," which gives a good idea of its importance. (The characters for *shubo* signify "sake mother.") The use of this yeast starter (or seed) mash is another peculiar feature of sake brewing. It is in essence a technique to produce a superbly pure, dense culture of sake yeasts, excluding wild yeasts and rogue bacteria.

Finished *kōji* rice, water, and yeast are mixed together in a small

SAKE MAKING—THE BREWING STAGES

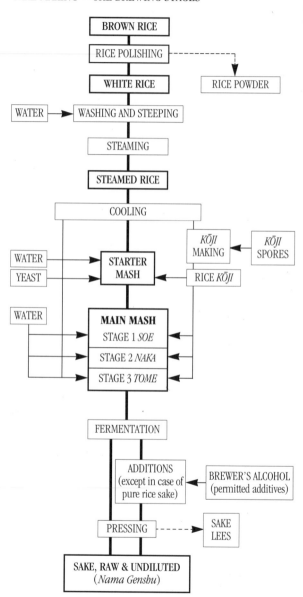

tank. To this, lactic acid is added, raising the acidity of the mix, and thereby inhibiting the growth of unwanted bacteria, which may have a disastrous effect on fermentation. Afterwards, fresh steamed rice completes the mix, bringing the overall temperature up to the required range of about 18° to 20° C (65° to 68° F). The yeast is nurtured, multiplying over a period of ten to fifteen days. With careful attention to temperature, the mix is tended to produce the yeast-heavy starter desired. During this period, a glorious, fruity smell arises, a tangy amalgam of apple, melon, and banana elements. The aroma of a healthy *moto* is probably the most enticing I have ever encountered.

The technique described above is called *sokujō* (quick-fermentation method), and is the standard today. One other method is *kō-on tōka,* a variation on the basic *sokujō* theme. *Kō-on tōka* means "high tempera-

K

Kura and *kura-bito*

Kura (蔵) is the Japanese word for a (sake) brewery. Even Japanese people often confuse it with the more common *kura* (倉), which simply means a warehouse, never having taken on the extra, specific meaning gained by the former character. Things are often clarified by referring to a 酒蔵 (*sakagura*). Sake brewers are referred to as *kura-bito* (蔵人), or "brewery people." (The job description on my business card is *kura-bito*.) The chief brewer is called a *tōji* (杜氏).

ture saccharification." In this method, the ingredients are added at a high temperature of about 55° C (131° F), and saccharification (the conversion of starch in the steamed rice grains to sugars) proceeds at top speed. What takes several days by the standard *sokujō* procedure is accomplished in a matter of hours. After those first few hours, the procedure is the same as for the normal *sokujō*. Overall, the starter mash can be made in about half the time, a considerable saving. (It is also possible to make sake without the aid of a *shubo*, by a method called *kōbo jikomi*, which calls for the direct use of concentrated yeast cultures. Though very economical, it is not held to produce sake of as high a quality as that made with a starter preparation.) At the other end of the scale are the *kimoto* and *yamahai* methods, old-fashioned, laborious, time consuming, and correspondingly rare. They share a common and highly complex chemistry, in which a natural fermentation produces the lactic acid which, in the modern method, is added to the mix from the start. *Kimoto* was the standard procedure from the seventeenth century until the early twentieth. The *yama-hai* version is chemically identical, but omits the most exhausting feature of *kimoto*, the so-called *yama-oroshi* process, in which the mash is ground down to a pasty subsistency with long, flat-headed tools over a period of hours. (The Japanese for "discontinuation of *yama-oroshi*" — *yama-oroshi haishi* — is shortened to *yamahai*.) It was developed around the turn of the century. Where the *sokujō* style tends to yield lighter-tasting results, the *kimoto* school is associated more with strongly flavored sake. However, because of the broad range, some overlap—full-flavored *sokujō*, lighter *yamahai*—does occur. Whatever the method, the aim is a mash with such a dense population of pure sake yeast that wild yeasts and bacteria have no chance to propagate. The safe environment created at this stage is most important for a strong fermentation during the next.

Main Mash (*Moromi*, 醪) and Fermentation (*Hakkō*, 発酵)

In one of sake brewing's characteristic features, the ingredients of the main mash (water, *kōji* rice, and steamed rice) are added to the starter mash in three stages over a space of four days (*san-dan jikomi*, 三段仕込). If all were added at once, the safe environment of the starter would be thinned to a point where it would be perilously prone to infection by wild yeast and bacteria. The safety of the fermentation is further protected by carrying out the three stages at successively lower temperatures (increasingly less comfortable for the wild yeasts and airborne bacteria that can spell disaster for the brewer). Modern science has explained the chemistry of these processes only in the twentieth century. What is remarkable is the extent to which Japanese brewing methods created and protected an ideal environment for the growth of sake yeast in an era in which the nature of the contaminants was unknown.

At the first stage (*soe*), the finished starter mix is moved to a slightly larger tank. *Kōji* rice, steamed rice, and water are added, roughly in such quantities as to double the volume of the mix. Naturally, the mix becomes somewhat thinner at this stage. It is then left for a full day, during which period the yeast re-propagates, approaching the density of the yeast starter and ensuring a safer environment for the second and final stages (*naka* and *tome*). This period is known by the euphonious name of *odori*, a word that combines the original sense, of the wide step in the middle of a staircase where one pauses momentarily before resuming the ascent, and that of "dance"—which is exactly what the surface of the mash appears to do on its lively second day.

On day three, the mash is moved to the final, large fermentation vessel, and the second addition of *kōji* rice, steamed rice, and water takes place, roughly doubling the volume of the mash again. The final batch of the same three ingredients is added the following day, and doubles the volume of the mash a third time (though the exact ratio may vary). The main mash, with all the ingredients added, is called *moromi*.

$$L$$

Light

Sake is phenomenally sensitive to light and temperature and requires careful storage. Direct light, natural or otherwise, is very harmful, affecting both the taste, and, quite dramatically, the color. As sake ages, its color inevitably darkens, but this process is accelerated by exposure to strong light. Sake also spoils easily if stored in a warm place, and an *even* temperature is also important. The refrigerated shelves of specialist dealers are the answer to the problem of temperature control. How the problems of light and temperature are handled is an excellent marker of the standards of both retailers and bars and restaurants.

A few hours after all the ingredients have been added, the steamed rice absorbs all the liquid. The tank appears to contain a great swollen heap of very thick porridge. After a couple of days, the moist surface begins to crack in places, and a thin foam appears there. The mash begins to bubble as gas is given off during the burgeoning fermentation. The foam gradually spreads over the surface of the mash, eventually covering it completely. The first fine, watery foam changes into a much thicker, creamier layer of bubbles. At its peak, this foam rises well over a meter above the surface of the mash.

An experienced brewer reads the progress of the fermentation by the condition of the foam. This recedes a few days after reaching its peak, and the fermentation enters its most vigorous stage. The mix is much lighter and more obviously liquid by now, and it bubbles and seethes frantically for several days. Gradually, the activity subsides. Over the last few days, the master brewer watches carefully—he does not wish to press the batch too early, but if he delays too long, the weary yeast may begin to die off in the mash, causing off-flavors in the sake. When the right moment is judged to have arrived, the sake is pressed. (If it is an alcohol-added variety, the addition is made at this point—before pressing.) The length and pattern of fermentation may vary enormously, from about two weeks to well over a month.

Of all the various patterns of fermentation, the most distinctive form is that used in the making of *ginjō* sake. Fermentation proceeds at excruciatingly low temperatures—10° C (50 ° F) and below. It is only at such uncomfortable temperatures that sake yeasts produce the esters and higher alcohols that add up to the prized bouquet. At higher temperatures, yeast ferments more vigorously, producing alcohol in a correspondingly short space of time. (Two weeks is enough, if you're really dying for a drink.) At low temperatures, fermentation necessarily moves very slowly, and *ginjō* sake routinely requires a nail-biting month or more. This is one of the reasons why *ginjō* costs more.

Pressing (*Jōsō*, 上槽)

Nowadays, almost all sake is pressed in automatic machine presses. The *moromi* is pumped into the machine, which contains a series of panels with balloonlike sacks attached. The balloons are inflated, pressing the remaining rice solids into board forms between the panels: the clear sake flows out of the bottom of the machine, from where it is pumped to a storage tank. Though now unusual, the traditional *fune* press is still used in some breweries (my own workplace included). This classical method sees the *moromi* poured into long bags (*saka-bukuro*) holding about fifteen liters each. The mouth is folded over, and the bags are stacked in the deep rectangular body of the press. For the first few hours, the sake trickles out under its own weight; later, a heavy lid is lowered and pressure slowly applied. On the following day, the bags are re-stacked, and pressed once more. Compared to the machine press, the *fune* is very time-consuming and inefficient—requiring considerable heavy labor at various stages, and three days to accomplish what the machine press does automatically overnight—but the soft, refined flavor of the sake that results is prized by connoisseurs. The caked lees (*kasu*), the remains after pressing, are used in pickle making and cooking.

Removal of Lees (*Ori-hiki*, 滓引き)

After a few days, a fine sediment of rice particles (*ori*) settles on the bottom of the tank. Modern machine presses limit this considerably, so the

One of the culinary high points of the hungry winter season (and a side benefit of working in a sake brewery) is *kasu-jiru*, a kind of deluxe miso soup, a warming and flavorsome dish made with *sake kasu*, pressed rice lees. It is carried by many supermarkets in winter: my wife warns against dry, boardlike yellow stuff; moist, pale-colored *kasu* is best. The traditional versions use salmon and umpteen varieties of vegetable, and can be found in many Japanese cookbooks. This is my wife's simplified recipe.

Yasuko's Quick Sake Lees Soup

serves 4

9 oz (300 g) pork

9 oz (300 g) carrot

½ cup Japanese leek (*naga negi*) or long onion

6 oz (200 g) sake lees (*sake kasu*)

5 cups (1.2 liters) bonito stock (*dashi*)

3 oz (100 g) snow peas (*kinusaya*)

2 Tbsps (50 g) red miso (*aka miso*)

1. Cut pork into bite-size pieces and julienne carrots. Chop leek or long onion and break sake lees into small pieces.
2. Boil bonito stock in pot, add pork and carrots. When the ingredients are almost cooked, add lees and snow peas. Simmer for a few minutes, add red miso, and stir to dissolve.
3. Turn off the heat and sprinkle with leek/onion.

traditional process—where the clear liquid is siphoned off leaving the lees behind—is sometimes omitted.

Filtration (*Roka*, ろ過)

Most breweries carry out carbon filtration of the sake twice, once before storage and once before shipping. (There are exceptions: we filter very little of our sake.) Filtration inhibits coloring and aging.

Pasteurization (*Hi-ire*, 火入れ)

Though named in English (and, I assume, French) for Louis Pasteur, the process of heating liquids to about 65° C (149° F) to sterilize them has been in use for centuries in Japan. Heating sake kills off the remaining yeast, stops enzyme action, and knocks the dreaded *hi-ochi* bacteria (the lactic acid bacteria that spoils sake so quickly) on the head. This process, too, is usually carried out twice, once before storage and again before shipping. *Nama* sake is left unpasteurized.

SAKE MAKING—POST-BREWING TREATMENT

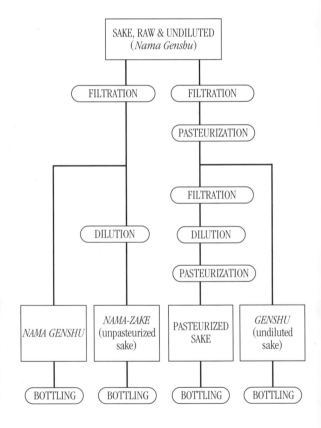

Storage (*Chozō*, 貯蔵) and Maturation (*Jukusei*, 熟成)

The traditional (and still most common) pattern is to store the new sake in tanks until sale in the autumn. Indeed, the maturation over this brief period of time is quite astounding, the edge of the new sake vanishing to be replaced by a smooth and rounded balance. (Sake at this stage is called *aki-agari* or *hiya-oroshi*, terms referring respectively to the season and the "cooling off" after the "putting in of fire," which is what *hi-ire* literally signifies).

Blending (*Chōgō*, 調合) and Dilution (*Kasui*, 加水)

Blending is an art in itself. Though not all sake is blended, most makers use the technique to ensure an even quality of product. (Those looking to emphasize character and individuality sometimes prefer to ship their sake unblended.) In its raw state, sake can be more than 20% alcohol. Most sake is diluted before being sold at around 15%, though *ginjō* sake is quite often found at 16 or 17%.

These are the essential elements of sake brewing. There are wide variations at every stage, reflecting the varying policies of individual breweries, the strengths and weaknesses of particular *tōji*, and the degree of automation, to name but a few of the many factors involved. Yet certain basic features are common to all breweries, and indeed would be largely familiar to the craftsmen of a century ago.

The story is not over at this stage: having made the sake, important work still remains; next, it has to be drunk.

M

Meimonshu-kai

The Meimonshu-kai (Prestige Sake Association) is a group of producers and retailers with a widespread national network. It has long been active in providing momentum for the recognition, distribution, and consumption of good-quality sakes. The member manufacturers label their products informatively in a standardized format. In recent years, the group has also been exporting their products.

4

Drinking Sake: Some Like It Hot

Ⅰf your image of sake is of something hot and faintly toxic, you are not alone—but not among the best informed either. My first impressions were of this sadly common kind, but I can well remember the revelationary evening when my first taste of fine sake—*chilled* sake—blew away my preconceptions in a fragrant gale of new sensations. The image of steaming plonk is depressingly prevalent, but to see no further is to miss the chance to experience the amazing variety and color of the thousands of kinds that exist. If the reader finishes this book with an impression of sake's infinite variety, I will consider my job well done.

Before going any further, let us consider why connoisseurs usually drink sake cold, when it is so often served hot.

Few would deny that the virtues of a white wine are best appreciated when it is cold, where those of a red wine are most evident at a higher temperature. In the case of quality sake, the brewers have gone to enormous trouble, fermenting long and slow at the lowest possible temperature, to create the flavor and aroma which are the joy of a fine brew. To then heat up the result of their labors—during which the painstakingly-won bouquet evaporates—is about as polite as a slap in the face, and a terrible waste. Sake-lovers, therefore, generally drink their beverage cold, the better to appreciate its beautiful flavor and aroma. There is no single "perfect temperature," although there is a point at which the flavor and balance of any particular sake are at their best. Straight out of the refrigerator is too cold for many sakes; room temperature is a little high for some, and sublime for others. One of the great pleasures of sake-drinking lies in savoring the subtle changes in flavor as the liquor warms (or cools) in the glass, searching for the magic moment when a particular brew is at its best.

Why, then, is the custom of heating sake so widespread? One of the main reasons lies in the problems of pre-modern brewing. For technological reasons, the brewers of days past were generally unable to make sake of as high a grade as is now possible. On the contrary, strange, musty flavors and earthy odors must have been a common feature. Yet, by what must have seemed like a wonderful alchemy, many of these dubious flavors could be eliminated simply by heating the brew. It went down well on cold winter days, too! Nowadays, however, all kinds of technical advances have rendered heating unnecessary (though not uncommon). To drink fine sake hot is barbarism incarnate, but warming it lightly brings out the best in many types (not to mention fortifying the chilly soul in the winter months). Experiment! Explore! But please don't overheat!

Hot sake is served in small decanters called *tokkuri*, and drunk from the delicate cups known honorifically as *o-choko*, or simply *choko*. (Oddly, the name of these exquisite sipping cups literally means "wild-boar's mouth.") Practical they are not; since they hold only a tiny mouthful, they need constant refilling. That, in fact, is their purpose. Politeness

Nada

Nada is the name of the most prolific sake-producing region of Japan, in Hyōgo Prefecture. It also had the misfortune to be in one of the worst-affected areas in the Great Hanshin Earthquake of 1995, in which a number of brewers lost their lives. Thankfully, most of the area's numerous producers were back in business before too long, but more than one brewery ceased production; a sad loss.

Other traditional sake areas are Fushimi in Kyoto, Itami in Hyōgo, Ikeda in Osaka, and Hiroshima. (Sadly, only one or two *kura* remain of the dozens that used to brew in Ikeda.) In contrast, Niigata Prefecture and other areas are booming anew. These are some of the most famous districts, but sake is made everywhere—except Kagoshima Prefecture on the southern island of Kyūshū, which has the unenviable distinction of being the only brewery-free prefecture.

requires that one's companion's cup is never empty. *O-shaku*, the congenial custom of mutual service, is wonderful for breaking the ice, and a great opportunity to leapfrog the language barrier. The small *choko*, though a great aid to communication, are rather fiddly for the serious drinker (especially later in the evening), and friends often dispense with formalities and drink from the slightly larger cups (*gui-nomi*).

Fine sake is also often served by the glass, but a more earthy receptacle is the *masu*, a square box of cryptomeria wood. It was once common to find working men drinking from these, with a pinch of salt on one corner of the box as an accompaniment. Nowadays this is a rare sight, though *masu-zake* frequently enlivens festivals even today. In the last resort, there is "trumpet-drinking" (*rappa-nomi*)—from the bottle!

Questions of Taste

Traditionally, the flavor of sake was described with just three terms: *ama*, *kara*, and *pin*. The first two are simply sweet and dry. The third, though rather hard to define, speaks for an admirable grasp of a crucial feature of the makeup of a sake. For want of a better term, *pin* is that certain something, that *je ne sais quoi*, which is not a question of sweet or dry or other flavor elements, but of a harmonious clarity of tone born of perfection of balance. *Pin* is that crisp feeling of there being nothing out of place at the finish.

Later generations, perhaps without that reliability of perception with which *pin* says all that needs to be said, found it necessary to analyze the matter more minutely. The flavor of sake came to be discussed in terms of five flavors, still a common measure of evaluation:

The Five Flavors of Sake (*Gomi*, 五味)

sweet	*amai*	甘い	(sweetness, *amami* 甘味)
dry	*karai*	辛い	(dryness, *karami* 辛味)
bitter	*nigai*	苦い	(bitterness, *nigami* 苦味)
sour/acidic	*suppai*	酸っぱい	(sourness/acidity, *sanmi* 酸味)
astringent	*shibui*	渋い	(astringency, *shibumi* 渋味)

The last term, "astringency," is rather unfamiliar to many. Imagine the astringency of strong tea (especially green tea), or the tannic feel of red wine. The word "astringent" (or, heaven forbid, "acerbic") has unpleasant associations in English; this is not necessarily the case in Japanese. A fine sake is held to require a balance of all five flavors. For any one of the *gomi* to be too strong or too faint disrupts that balance.

In time, a need was perceived for a more general framework in which particular sakes could be placed to clarify their overall flavor without

STANDARD SIZES IN THE SAKE WORLD

UNIT	METRIC EQUIVALENT	CONTEXT OF COMMON USAGE
shaku 勺	18 milliliters (0.6 fluid ounces)	Sometimes *tokkuri* pitchers come in 8-*shaku* sizes (i.e., 4/5 of a *gō*). Since most customers assume a *tokkuri* to be 1 *gō*, this is a profitable tactic for bars and restaurants.
gō 合	180 milliliters (6 fluid ounces)	Sake is often sold in *tokkuri* decanters of 1 or 2 *gō* (*ichi-gō* or *ni-gō*) in bars and restaurants, though it may as often be offered in 120- or 150-milliliter glassfuls. The common 720-milliliter bottles are often referred to as "four-*gō* bottles," or *yon-gō bin*. People who like boasting about their drinking prowess usually do it by the *gō* (or, very occasionally, the *shō*!).
shō 升	1.8 liters (1.9 quarts)	Big standard-size bottle (*isshō-bin*). Equals 10 *gō*.
to 斗	18 liters (19 quarts or 4.75 gallons)	Large bottles (*to-bin*) used to store sake intended for annual trade contests. Occasionally re-bottled and sold as a deluxe product, in which case it is denoted *to-bin gakoi* (斗びん囲い). Equals 10 *shō*.
koku 石	180 liters (47.5 gallons)	Used when describing the production capacity of a brewery. The range is vast, from tiny breweries making only two or three hundred *koku*, all the way up to giant makers, producing tens of thousands of *koku*. The brewery I work for, Ume no Yado, makes 1,000 *koku* every winter. Equals 10 *to*.

NOTE: Strictly speaking, all these figures are officially calculated in liters and milliliters, but their colloquial use is widespread.

lengthy explanations. The Central Brewers' Union divides sake into four basic flavor types, on four axes of sweet, sour, bitter, and *umai*. This last is another translator's nightmare. It generally ends up as "delicious," in which broad sense it is certainly used. It does, however have a more specific sense, in which it signifies a richness, a satisfying roundness of flavor. It is a common criticism to say of a sake that it lacks *umami*: *umami ga nai*. What this means is that the flavor lacks fullness; the taste is somehow two-dimensional. It is, of course, nonsense to talk of a two-dimensional taste. It is also next to impossible to fully describe flavors and smells in words, or to find satisfying English equivalents for the word *umai*. I know what Frank Zappa meant when he said that talking about music is "like fishing about architecture."

According to the position established along these axes, a sake is considered to be of "mature type," "fragrant type," "light and smooth type," or "full-bodied type." Obviously, no set of criteria can fully express the multiplicity of sensations that together create the flavor unique to any individual sake, but there is a perceived need for terms which quickly and simply give the general idea.

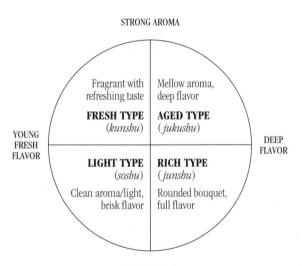

Drinking by Numbers:
What the Figures Tell You

Sake Meter Value (*Nihonshudo*, 日本酒度)

Sometimes you may find a plus or minus figure displayed on the label of a sake. This is the sake meter value (SMV), the reading on a scale of sweet and dry. A number is arrived at by using a device that measures residual sugar, like the hydrometer used in winemaking. Sweet sakes register minus, dry sakes plus; a "0" theoretically indicates a neutral flavor.

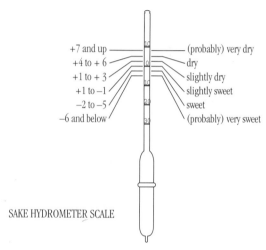

+7 and up	(probably) very dry
+4 to +6	dry
+1 to +3	slightly dry
+1 to −1	slightly sweet
−2 to −5	sweet
−6 and below	(probably) very sweet

SAKE HYDROMETER SCALE

For all I know, life may sometimes be simple, but sake certainly isn't. Generally, a theoretically slightly dry sake of +1 tastes sweetish on most palates. A −3 will likely be very sweet to most people; a reading of +6 or +7 usually indicates a very dry sake. However, the level of acidity also plays a large role. With the same SMV reading, the sake with the higher acidity will taste dryer. There are also those charming surprises when what happens on the tongue is quite different from what science would lead us to expect. The SMV is a useful rule of thumb, but the other factors should be taken into account.

Rice Polishing Ratio (*Seimai Buai*, 精米歩合)

It is simplistic but true enough to say that the lower the rice polishing ratio, the lighter (and probably cleaner) the flavor. Also, within a single category of sake you may find a wide range of quality, determined to an extent by the grade of rice used. For example, pure rice brews must be polished to 70% or less, but you can find *junmai* sake made from rice polished much further than the minimum requirement. The same holds true for *honjōzō* and *ginjō* sake, too. So this statistic can be a clue for bargain hunters.

Acidity (*Sando*, 酸度) and
Amino Acids (*Amino Sando*, アミノ酸度)

Acids and amino acids are extremely important factors in the taste. Acidity is the index of how tangy/sour a sake is. Amino acids give body, and the elusive *umami*. If these values are very low, the sake will (perhaps) taste thin and watery; if they are too high, it often feels heavy and rough-tasting. The level of these values also influences how other elements (sweet, dry, and so on) are perceived on the palate.

The yeast and, to a lesser extent, the rice variety give their own character to a sake's flavor. The yeast variety, in particular, also influences the bouquet.

🍶 ▬ ▬

All of these factors can be used as hints in building up an image of the flavor of a particular sake. However, there are plenty of products that taste surprisingly different than their vital statistics might suggest. Thank heavens for that. Some folk revel in all the number-crunching and statistics, and derive great pleasure from the insights it gives them. Others simply find all the figures intimidating and confusing. Ultimately, all that matters is the balance between your wallet and your palate, and that is as personal a matter as likes and dislikes.

With the above discussion in mind, let's take a look at how professionals judge sake.

Sake Tasting (*Kikizake*)

Formal sake tasting is done with a special tasting cup (*kiki-joko*). These are usually made of white porcelain, with a pattern of blue concentric circles (the so-called snake's eye), which makes it easier to judge the color. In cases where the color is not under consideration, smoked-glass cups are used.

Professional tasting takes place under strictly regulated conditions. Care is taken that all the samples are at the same temperature, usually about 20° C (68° F). If the sake is chilled, its aroma is less easily perceived; also, faults of balance and flavor are more evident at the higher temperature. It is also important for lighting (preferably natural) to be even, so that color can be objectively regarded. To this end, too, the tasting cups must be identical. *Choko* that have the "snake's eye" rings may appear identical, but different batches have slight variations in the depth of the blue color, which considerably affects the appearance of the color of the sample. The amount in the cup is also important; about three-quarters full is common. Here, too, consistency is crucial; large-scale tastings therefore involve a numerous and busy staff, one of whose tasks is to keep the level in the cups even. Such events take place with a variety of purposes. What they all share is the need for objectivity, hence the efforts to ensure a consistent environment, and the use in evaluation of agreed terms and standards.

Snake's eye sake cup

Etiquette is very much a question of common sense. The most antisocial (and unfortunately, most common) transgression is the introduction of strong odors into the tasting room, scented cosmetics and tobacco being the main offenders. Smokers cannot perceive the odor even their hands leave on the cup, but it causes great problems for non-smokers. To abstain in the tasting room is a minimum courtesy, but it is better not to smoke for some time before tasting begins. For the sake of the palate, it is usual to refrain from tasting shortly after eating. The following list charts the routine of professional sake-tasting sessions.

STAGES OF TASTING

1. **Color:** the color of the sake is observed. Too dark a color is considered a defect, except in a few special cases, such as highly aged sake.
2. **Aroma/bouquet:** the nose—the smell rising off the liquor—is then considered.

3. **Taste:** a little sake—about three to five milliliters, or as much as a spoonful of medicine—is taken in, and rolled over the tongue. At this stage, a little air is drawn into the mouth and through the sake. (This can be done with or without slurping sound effects. The noise is not essential, but the air is; it frees volatile aroma compounds so they can reach the nose. A lot of real "tasting" action actually happens in the nasal cavity, not on the palate.) After a few moments, the taster breathes out through the nose, concentrating on the flavors and aromas which can be perceived there. These aromas are called *fukumi-ka* in Japanese. The sample is spat into a prepared container, and the judge evaluates the aftertaste.

4. **Evaluation:** usually, the taster will assess color, aroma, and so on individually, and make an overall evaluation. There are a number of methods depending on the event and the purpose of tasting. The most common are the three- and five-point methods, in which the best sakes are given one point, and the worst (to put it brutally) receive three or five points respectively.

5

Buying Sake:
Deciphering the Label

All this talk of brewing methods and types of sake is all very well, but it's about as useful as an ice-cube in an igloo unless you have some idea how to go about finding, buying, and most importantly, drinking the subject of your studies. To that end, this section describes how to recognize the Special Designation Sakes, and gives shortcuts for spotting them in their native habitat—the bottle and the bar. Unsurprisingly, the great thing is to look at the label. This is an extremely pleasant undertaking, since sake labels are enormously varied and frequently extremely beautiful. There are charming old-fashioned labels, *ukiyo-e* labels, countless examples of exquisite (if, sadly, hard-to-read) calligraphy, labels hand-written by brewery staff, those made from *washi* (gorgeous Japanese paper), and labels depicting historical figures, famous scenes, or some of the colorful flora and fauna of Japan. If you want to study Japanese language, culture, or aesthetics, you could hardly hope to find a more engaging and varied source of material. In short, sake labels are often objects of great beauty, but tend to err on the side of form rather than function. Despite all their gorgeous, impractical variety, however, they can be deciphered fairly easily if one knows what to look for.

Labels are often crowded with mottoes, poems, and whatnot, little of which is of use, and much of which is Greek to the average Tanaka-on-the-street. However, some points provide important information. By law, the brewer is required to list the ingredients used, the percentage of alcohol by volume, and the shipping date. However, most serious sake shoppers look first for the grade—*junmai*, *ginjō*, and so on. Though this is not always as obviously displayed as one might expect, it is usually there somewhere. (Those who are stumped by Japanese characters can check with the crib list given on the endpapers.) An additional obstacle arises when this information is given in cursive script, since, in Japan, the work of a skilled calligrapher is often illegible to mere mortals.

Happily, the approximate grade can also be determined by counting the number of ingredients listed on the label. The general rule of thumb is, the fewer ingredients the higher the grade. Two or three ingredients indicate a Special Designation Sake such as a *ginjō* or *junmai*; a list of four or five ingredients is a sure sign of additives along the lines discussed in Chapter 2, and a lower grade (*sanzōshu*, *futsūshu*, and so on).

The good news here is that the ingredients section of the label is almost always clearly printed, unlike the hieroglyphics that predominate elsewhere. Look for the word "ingredients" in Japanese—原材料名 (*genzai-ryōmei*)—near the edge, often to be found at the bottom right-hand corner, though sometimes it appears vertically to one side.

For *junmaishu* (純米酒), "pure rice sake," two ingredients are listed; they are rice (*kome*, 米) and rice *kōji* (*kome kōji*, 米麹). The label reads:

> 原材料名: 米, 米麹
> Ingredients: rice, rice *kōji*

For *honjōzō* (本醸造), sake with a limited addition of brewer's alcohol (*jōzōyō arukōru*), three ingredients are listed:

> 原材料名: 米, 米麹, 醸造用アルコール
> Ingredients: rice, rice *kōji*, brewer's alcohol

Ginjōshu (吟醸酒), "special brew" sake made from the highest quality white rice, offers a snag for non-readers of Japanese. By the counting method, a *ginjō* is not to be distinguished from the other two designations. Like those books that offer to teach "instant Japanese," the labels-by-numbers method is not completely reliable. There are, however, other simple ways of spotting *ginjō* sake, apart from its generic aroma. A distinguishing feature is that it cannot be produced simply, or in bulk, so its inevitably higher price is one trademark. It is also often announced by its packaging, which tends to involve colors suggestive of precious metals and luxurious living. These products often come boxed. (The boxes themselves are as beautiful as the labels, but they also serve the important purpose of protecting the delicate liquor from light.) Some makers give the rice-polishing ratio on the label as a percentage. (*Ginjō* sake is made from rice polished to 60% or less). This type of sake is the apex of the brewer's art, and a source of pride (not to mention sleep deprivation and frayed nerves) on the part of a brewer. Few makers therefore miss the chance to display the magic word *ginjō* on the bottle. Take the plunge and learn the Chinese characters.

For *ginjō* or *daiginjō* (吟醸, 大吟醸):

原材料名： 米， 米麹， 醸造用アルコール （吟醸酒，
大吟醸酒）

Ingredients: rice, rice *kōji*, brewer's alcohol

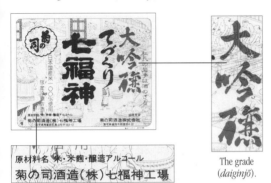

原材料名 米・米麹・醸造用アルコール
菊の司酒造（株）七福神工場

On this label, the ingredients appear at the bottom, above the brewer's name.

The grade
(*daiginjō*).

For *junmai ginjō* or *junmai daiginjō* (純米吟醸， 純米大吟醸):

原材料名： 米， 米麹
Ingredients: rice, rice *kōji*

Lower grades of sake made from rice polished by less than 30% do not qualify for the Special Designations. Neither do those that have greater additions of brewer's alcohol than the strictly limited amount permitted in the making of a *honjōzō*. The most common kind is *sanzōshu* (三増酒, "triple sake"), sake with a large addition of brewer's alcohol, which has—tellingly—four ingredients on the label. The fourth is *tōrui* (糖類)—sugars, usually glucose. The listing looks like this:

原材料名： 米， 米麹， 醸造用アルコール， 糖類
Ingredients: rice, rice *kōji*, brewer's alcohol, sugars

Sometimes triple sake has acids (*sanrui*) added—any of a number of permitted organic acids, or monosodium glutamate. This brings the number of ingredients to five. In this case, the label will read:

原材料名： 米， 米麹， 醸造用アルコール， 糖類，
酸類

Ingredients: rice, rice *kōji*, brewers' alcohol, sugars, acids

To determine a *futsūshu* (普通酒, "ordinary" or "standard" sake), a brew with a larger addition of brewer's alcohol than is permitted for *honjōzō*, a little more detection may be required. The brewer is, naturally, free to use less highly-polished rice than for *honjōzō*. While the use of organic acids for flavoring is permitted, sugars may not (as in the case of triple sake) be used. Nonetheless, organic acids are not invariably used in the making of *futsūshu*. This means that the list of ingredients may read the same as for a *honjōzō*—but without that extra designation being displayed: Just as no brewer will go to the trouble of making a *ginjō* sake without advertising the fact prominently on the label, no maker will omit the 本醸造 (*honjōzō*) tag if entitled to use it. If it doesn't *say honjōzō*, it almost certainly isn't.

As noted above, the law requires that the percentage of alcohol and the shipping date appear on the label. Both of these items are usually clearly printed in the kind of format given below.

0

Okegai

This word means "vat-buying"; its counterpart is *okeuri*, "vat-selling." Firm A buys sake in bulk from Firm B. This sake then undergoes blending and is sold under Firm A's label, a system which reached its peak in the 1970s. Although I haven't seen figures, I can't recall having come across a company that wasn't involved in this practice to some extent: it seems to have been more or less universal. Since then, however, *okegai* has suffered virulent criticism, and the practice has greatly declined, though it is far from extinct. Many big producers who bought in this way in order to meet the enormous demand for their sake later invested massively in equipment to enable year-round brewing, thereby increasing their overall production capacity and reducing the necessity of buying brew from other makers. The trend was reinforced by decreasing sales at the bottom (cheap) end of the sake market. In an ironic twist, some small concerns, their breweries dormant for lack of brewing staff, now apparently buy sake (to be sold under their own brand name) from the giant firms' factory plants—the mirror-image of the original practice, and a marker of the drastic changes the last few decades have seen in the industry.

Percentage of Alcohol (アルコール分, *Arukōru Bun*)

The figure given is a percentage. *Genshu* may have from 18 to 20%, but most sake is sold at around 15% (by volume, not weight). Recently, low-alcohol varieties with 7 to 12% have become available. The higher the percentage of alcohol, the better a sake keeps; this is often cited as a point in favor of alcohol additions.

Bottling Date (製造年月, *Seizō Nengetsu*)

Though the Japanese means "year and month of production," the date given refers to the time of shipping from the brewery. As for any food item, old stock is not a good sign. In the case of quality sake, however, there are many conscientious retailers who take great pains to provide the depth and smoothness of flavor possible with a well-kept, quality aged sake. If you are in a well-stocked specialist shop with mainly refrigerated stock, it's probably safe to assume that bottles with a long-past date on the label have been matured rather than just left on the shelf. Play safe and ask.

Other Statistics

Sometimes the label carries a whole array of technical information:

Sake meter value (SMV)	*Nihonshudo*	日本酒度	●
Rice polishing ratio	*Seimai buai*	精米歩合	●
Rice variety used	*Genryōmai shiyō hinshu*	原料米使用品種	●
Yeast variety used	*Shiyō kōbo*	使用酵母	●
Water source	*Shikomi mizu*	仕込水	
School of brewers	～ *Tōji*	～杜氏	
Master brewer's name	*Tōji*: ～	杜氏：～	
Length of fermentation	*Moromi nissū*	もろみ日数	
Ratio of lees	*Kasu buai*	粕歩合	
Acidity	*Sando*	酸度	●
Level of amino acids	*Amino sando*	アミノ酸度	●

All of these items are clues to the flavor of the sake. The three items underlined are given for every sake listed in Part II, the Sampler, and discussed in Chapter 4, Drinking Sake. It can be fun to know all these things, but it is no more necessary than it is to know the type of brush a painter used to appreciate a picture. I have marked with a *tokkuri* ● the ones I find particularly interesting to know. Trainspotters away!

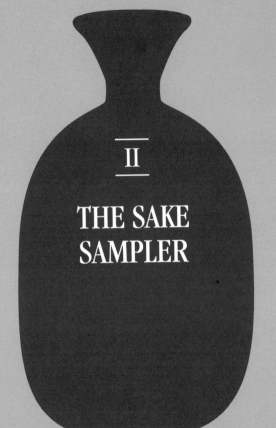

II

THE SAKE
SAMPLER

6

A Sampling from Japan's Breweries

Welcome to the sake sampler! I have endeavored to select sakes covering a wide range of styles, areas of origin, availability, and price. Choosing a mere 109 sakes from the many thousands available is necessarily problematic: to attempt it will inevitably seem an impertinence to some, since so many masterpieces must be neglected. Still, the reader will find more than enough here to occupy his or her palate.

Professional tasting requires objectivity above all else, and uses a restricted number of terms in fixed and specific senses. In this guide, while trying to be fair, I have allowed myself a certain subjective leeway and a rather wider vocabulary. Again, I am no doubt asking for trouble.

From my own experiences as a Japanese illiterate trying to find out more, I know that initial progress comes by remembering the *appearance* of brands—labels, bottle shapes, and, ultimately, the initially baffling *kanji* (or Chinese ideographs). With this in mind, I have included as many photographs as possible. Non-inclusion of a sake or brand does not reflect on the quality of any given product; this is simply a taster. All the sakes introduced here represent only a fraction of all the sakes I have tried. All the sakes I have ever tasted represent only a drop in the ocean of all the sake world has to offer. Please browse, drink, and be merry!

How to Read the Entries

Name of brewery: name of product
• Grade

Rank of product: *ginjō*, *junmai*, et cetera (see pages 25–38). The figure in brackets is the rice polishing ratio (page 59). Where two figures are given, one is for the rice used in making *kōji*, the other for the remaining white rice.

• **SMV**

Sake meter value. A rough measure of sweet and dry (see page 59).

• **Acidity**

The level of acids. A useful clue to the likely flavor profile of the sake, particularly if considered in tandem with the amino acid content (see page 60).

• **Amino acids**

See page 60.

• **Alcohol**

Percentage of alcohol by volume.

• **Price**

In most cases, for a 1.8-liter bottle. Where two or more prices are listed, the size of additional bottles is given in parentheses. The prices are before tax.

• **Body**

Under the vital statistics can be found brief tasting notes. Following these, some entries include a few words about the brewery in question—its history, brewing style and so on. Brewery information is indicated with a ⌂ .

• **Brewery**

Each listing closes with the name, address, and telephone number of the brewery. (Some breweries take orders by phone.) Note that the name of the firm may be quite different from the product name.

1. Aki-shika: Ikkan-zukuri

秋鹿：一貫造り

- Grade: *junmai daiginjō* (40%)
- SMV: +3
- Acidity: 1.7
- Amino acids: 0.9
- Alcohol: 16–17%
- ¥9,714

This is the sort of *ji-zake* thing that aficionados enjoy: this sake is made from rice grown by company staff. Very full flavor, and strong acid tang. The effect is pleasant, but surprisingly dense for sake made from *Yamada Nishiki* rice polished this much; a lighter, more delicate sake would be typical.

Anyone who has been to Osaka might find it hard to imagine pastoral scenes of rice fields, but the Nosé area of the prefecture has a long history

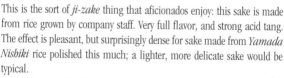

of producing sake rice, no less. It is here that the staff of Aki-shika ("Autumn Deer") grow the *Yamada Nishiki* for the distinctive sakes that delight their fans. With strong flavors and high levels of acidity, their products leave no one on the fence.

秋鹿酒造有限会社　Aki-shika Shuzō Yūgen-gaisha

大阪府豊能郡能勢町倉垣1007　〒563–0113

☎ 0727–37–0013

2. Ama no Zake: Rei

天野酒：醴

- Grade: *junmaishu* (60%)
- SMV: +1.0
- Acidity: 1.45
- Amino acids: 1.4
- Alcohol: 15–16%
- ¥2,330

Sharp, grainy aroma with a peppery touch of spice, and chocolaty notes, well-matched with a quintessentially ricey flavor. Sweet and dry, astringent and tangy, in solid, complex combination; a grassy, chocolate aftertaste lingers softly on the tongue. Warmed, the sake retains voluminous softness, and a rather sharp finish emerges. Cools to a magic moment (about 30° C/85° F) of melting sweetness with a mellow acid tang.

3. Ama no Zake: Sōbōshu

天野酒：僧房酒

- Grade: No added alcohol; does not qualify for *junmaishu* label because rice is polished only to 87%
- SMV: –87
- Acidity: 4.0
- Amino acids: 7.2
- Alcohol: 15.8%
- ¥4,885 (750 ml)

The product of a highly peculiar brewing method modeled on records of the processes used to brew the favorite tipple of medieval warlord Hideyoshi Toyotomi in Kongōji Temple on Mount Amano (called, you guessed it, Ama no Zake). Uses rice polished to a mere 87%, *kōji* made over four days (double the usual period), and an extremely dense mash. The result is a thick, silkily oily sake with an almost muddy dark brown color, revealing a reddish, tawny hue in strong light. A cocoa-and-chocolate aroma with a sour, damp-hay tang leads the way to the profound sweet-and-sour complexity of the flavor. As a bonus, the gourd-shaped bottle makes an absolutely fabulous glug-glug sound when the sake is poured. An excellent after-dinner drink, even for non-warlords.

☗ Ama no Zake makes highly distinctive sakes which show mature flavors more prominently than most (though they tell me the sake itself is not kept for particularly long before sale).

西條合資会社　Saijō Gōshi-gaisha
大阪府河内長野市長野町12–18　〒586–0014
☎ 0721–55–1101

4. Aramasa: Fū ga Kō

新政：風が香

- Grade: *ginjōshu* (45%)
- SMV: +5
- Acidity: 1.3
- Amino acids: 1.2
- Alcohol: 15.5%
- ¥1,940 (720 ml)

An unusual hexagonal bottle in blue glass is a bit precious, but the contents have force and depth of flavor. Spicy vanilla aroma has nutty hints paralleled in taste. Dry, nutty flavor followed by firm, persistent, woody astringency.

5. Aramasa: Akita-ryū Junmaishu

新政：秋田流純米酒

- Grade: *junmaishu* (60%)
- SMV: +2.0
- Acidity: 1.4
- Amino acids: 1.5
- Alcohol: 15.3%
- ¥1,893

Aroma gives a brusque, dry impression, but astringency (so pronounced as to be almost abrasive) and sharp dryness still make an eye-opening combination. Other flavors are not absent, but these two are exceptionally dominant.

"Akita-ryū" refers to the Akita region's school of brewing. The brewers of mainland Japan's second most northerly prefecture have their own distinctive style, shaped partly by the highly regarded, locally developed yeast. This recently became the latest to be nationally distributed (as Association Yeast No. 15). In contrast, Association Yeast No. 6 was isolated from a prize-winning sake from this very brewery, in 1935—a tremendous mark of status. No. 6 yeast was long second in popularity only to the ubiquitous No. 7, and is still one of the strains sold by the Association today.

新政酒造株式会社　Aramasa Shuzō Kabushiki-gaisha

秋田県秋田市大町6–2–35　〒010–0921

☎ 0188–23–6407

6. Asa-biraki:
Junmai Ginjō Yume Akari

あさ開：純米吟醸、夢灯り

- Grade: *junmai ginjō* (55%)
- SMV: −1
- Acidity: 1.3
- Amino acids: 1.0
- Alcohol: 14.8%
- ¥1,456

Made from a charmingly-named local eating rice variety, *hitome-bore*— "love at first sight"! Highly fragrant, with an extremely light touch on the tongue. Sweet but crisp, and very delicate. The pastel sunset on the label lends a distinctive mood.

From the leading producer in Iwate Prefecture. Their untraditional label designs show the firm has a clear eye on new markets for their sake. This go-ahead aproach is also clear in their recently-built brewery, which houses state-of-the-art equipment, a high-tech computer-supervised section and a separate line for traditional hand-brewing in buildings that echo the beauty of old-fashioned sake breweries.

株式会社あさ開　Kabushiki-gaisha Asa-biraki

岩手県盛岡市大慈寺町10–34　〒020–0828

☎ 019–652–3111

7. Aya-giku: Iro wa Nioedo

綾菊：色はにをえど

- Grade: *honjōzō* (55%, 65%)
- SMV: +2
- Acidity: 1.4
- Amino acids: 1.1
- Alcohol: 15.3%
- ¥1,900, ¥950 (720 ml)

The name of this sake, rather cumbersome-looking in English, is a mnemonic device for remembering the old *iroha* arrangement of the phonetic alphabet. Sweetish aroma has rose elements. On the sweet side for +2; otherwise the neutral balance makes for a drinkable, unassuming brew. Made from *Oseto* sake rice, almost exclusively produced locally in Kagawa Prefecture.

Other breweries may agree that *ji-zake* should mean "sake produced using local rice," but few observe this rule even when brewing with the annual national trade contest in mind: "Gold prize" sakes are almost invariably made from *Yamada Nishiki* rice from Hyōgo Prefecture. Aya-giku sakes made from *Oseto* have broken this mold to take gold medals on many occasions.

綾菊酒造株式会社

Aya-giku Shuzō Kabushiki-gaisha

香川県綾歌郡綾上町山田下3393−1

〒761−2400

☎ 087−878−2222

P

Pasteurization

All sake has been pasteurized (heat-treated) except that specifically designated "*nama*" (生, "live" or "raw"). It is heated to over 60° C (140° F), which kills off all enzymes and any surviving yeast. *Nama* sake still contains these in an active state, and they can spoil the flavor and aroma of the sake. For this reason, extra care should be taken in the storage of *nama-zake*. It should be kept refrigerated, and drunk as quickly as possible when the seal is broken. (There are no preservatives in any sake, so even pasteurized sake should be carefully kept. Still, it is far less prone to spoil than *nama*.)

The process of heat-treating, known in English as pasteurization, and in Japanese as *hi-ire* (火入れ), was already in use in sake brewing some 300 years before Pasteur discovered it!

8. Biwa no Chōju:
Junmai Ginjō

琵琶の長寿：純米吟醸

- Grade: *junmai ginjō* (55%)
- SMV: +4
- Acidity: 1.7
- Amino acids: 1.6
- Alcohol: 15.4%
- ¥2,913, ¥1,340 (720 ml)

Forcefully dry sake with a rather subdued nose, lent depth by strong acidity in harmony with other flavors. Powerful beginnings melt to an unexpectedly soft finish. Excellent companion to tempura dishes. Made from the *Tamazakae* sake rice, developed locally in the 1960s, and much used by this firm.

⌂ Very small brewery making full-flavored brews with a devoted following in the capital. Named for Lake Biwa, Japan's largest body of fresh water. Also the first brewery where I got my hands dirty.

池本酒造有限会社　Ikemoto Shuzō Yūgen-gaisha

滋賀県高島郡今津町今津221　〒520−1621

☎ 0740−22−2112

9. Bizen no Sake Hitosuji:
Nama Ginjō Akaiwa Omachi

備前の酒一筋：生吟醸 赤磐雄町

- Grade: *ginjōshu* (50%)
- SMV: +3
- Acidity: 1.5
- Amino acids: 1.3
- Alcohol: 15−16%
- ¥650 (300 ml)

Out of the fridge, this brew is rather two-dimensional (astringency and dryness in a comfortless combination). As it approaches room temperature, the fragrance and subtle organic complexity of *Omachi* sake rice blossom deliciously. Let it warm a little to show its best.

⌂ Brewery situated in the heart of prized *Omachi* rice territory; in cooperation with local farmers, the firm has long been actively involved in its problematical production.

利守酒造株式会社　Toshimori Shuzō Kabushiki-gaisha

岡山県赤磐郡赤坂町762−1　〒701−2200

☎ 08695−7−3117

10. Chiyo Kotobuki: Sakigake

千代寿：魁（さきがけ）

- Grade: *junmaishu* (62%)
- SMV: +4
- Acidity: 1.4
- Amino acids: 1.4
- Alcohol: 15.3%
- ¥1,893

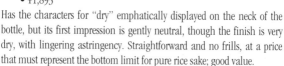

Has the characters for "dry" emphatically displayed on the neck of the bottle, but its first impression is gently neutral, though the finish is very dry, with lingering astringency. Straightforward and no frills, at a price that must represent the bottom limit for pure rice sake; good value.

千代寿虎屋酒造合資会社

Chiyo Kotobuki Toraya Shuzō Gōshi-gaisha

山形県寒河江市南町2丁目1番16号　〒991–0032

☎ 0237–86–6133

Q

Quiz

Q: Which of the following really exists (or existed)—

a) "Goblin-killer sake," b) "Black sake," c) "Goldfish sake"?

A: All three! *Onigoroshi* (goblin killer) was a term originally used to describe really grim sake, vicious enough to fell *oni* goblins. This term came to be used, with caustic humor, as a brand name for a number of products. Nowadays it is associated with very dry brews. Black sake (*kuroki*, written with characters meaning—surprise!—"black" and "sake") is one of the two specially-made brews consumed by the emperor in a number of rituals dating from the Heian period (794–1185). The other is *shiroki*, "white sake." These were in service in the 1993 wedding of the current emperor's son, the crown prince. "Goldfish sake" (*kingyo-zake*) was an ironic name for the grossly diluted sake sold in the war years. At that time, sake was taxed when made, so it could be diluted to whatever degree the market would bear at the retail stage. In the lean wartime years, some were so enthusiastic in this pursuit that it was said that a goldfish could happily swim about in the resulting watery liquor!

11. Daishichi: Junmai Kimoto

大七：純米生酛

- Grade: *junmaishu*
- SMV: +2
- Acidity: 1.5
- Amino acids: 1.4
- Alcohol: 15.0–15.9%
- ¥2,621

Made by the ancient (and now very rare) *kimoto* method. Pungent sake with an unusual, almost acrid bouquet. Central to its full flavor is an interesting interplay of sweet and bitter elements leading to a hearty, sweet finish. Solid but not stodgy.

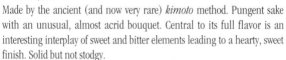 The notoriously laborious *kimoto* method is practiced by only a handful of breweries, but 70% of Daishichi sake is made this way. Indeed, this firm is probably the venerable technique's most famous practitioner.

大七酒造株式会社　Daishichi Shuzō Kabushiki-gaisha

福島県二本松市竹田1–66　〒964–0902

☎ 0243–23–0007

12. Daruma Masamune: Jūnen Koshu

達磨正宗：10年古酒

- Grade: *junmai* & *honjōzō* (70%)
- SMV: changes with age
- Acidity: changes with age
- Amino acids: changes with age
- Alcohol: 18%
- ¥4,857

This firm boasts an amazing range of venerable *koshu* (aged sake) dating from the 1970s onward. These are sold both in blends and in "vintages" offering the idiosyncratic delights of a single season's sake. Time capsules for the palate. Two of the fine vintage sakes are Shōwa Rokujū-nen Jōzōshu (brewed in the sixtieth year of the reign of emperor Showa [Hirohito], 1985 by western reckoning) and Shōwa Gojū-nen Jōzōshu, from BY (brewer's year) 1975. The former's color is a striking acid yellow, rather like lime cordial. Powerful *koshu* aroma has a strong woody flavor with sherry overtones. Basically sweet, but all five flavors are busily active. The result is harmonious, with a rounded mellowness that is the delight of highly-aged sake. The 1975 *koshu* is darker, gingery-brown in color. Nose is still more pungent. Combination of acidity and sweetness is very noticeable, but a strong dry/bitter underpinning gives a different direction than the predominant sweetness of younger *junmaishu*.

As wine lovers know so well, one of the poignant pleasures of a vintage is its transience. While the firm informs me that stock of both these products is almost exhausted, these classics are worth noting. However, the Jūnen Koshu, pictured here, is a (relatively) easily available alternative and is the *kura*'s perennial ten-year-old blend.

合資会社白木恒助商店　Gōshi-gaisha Shiraki Tsunesuke Shōten
岐阜県岐阜市門屋5–1　〒501–2521
☎ 058–229–1008

13. Den-shu: Junmai Yamahai

田酒：純米山廃

- Grade: *junmaishu* (55%, 60%)
- SMV: +3
- Acidity: 1.6
- Amino acids: ——
- Alcohol: 15.6%
- ¥2,816

Solid and dry in the mode of more familiar *junmaishu* (below), with a cedarlike, woody nose and a touch of pale straw color. Liquor clings lovingly to the sides of the glass. Clean-lined, but flavorsome, with a delicate astringent note. I prefer the fineness of the caramel/wood elements before it warms up. Shipped annually at year's end, and rather rare.

14. Den-shu: Junmaishu

田酒：純米酒

- Grade: *junmaishu* (55%, 60%)
- SMV: +3
- Acidity: 1.5
- Amino acids: ——
- Alcohol: 15.6%
- ¥2,525

A perennial favorite, well-built and firmly dry; a real drinker's sake with plenty of rice flavor. Very straightforward first impression complemented by shy vanilla hint. In my book, better near room temperature or slightly warmed.

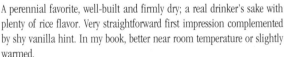

🏠 This brewery is in Aomori, the northern extremity of the main island of Honshu. The small output is the product of a large workforce; handmade sake rarely boasts this many hands. The name Den-shu is comprised of the characters for "rice field" and "sake": their brews exhibit the flavor of the main ingredient to an extent that justifies the name completely.

株式会社西田酒造店　Kabushiki-gaisha Nishida Shuzōten
青森県青森市油川大浜46　〒038−0059
☎ 0177−88−0007

15. Dewa-zakura: Ōka Ginjōshu

出羽桜: 桜花吟醸酒

- Grade: *ginjōshu* (50%)
- SMV: +5
- Acidity: 1.2
- Amino acids: ——
- Alcohol: 15.5%
- ¥2,505, ¥495 (300 ml)

Unmistakable fingerprint is the massive *ginjō* bouquet for which this is well-known: more floral even than the label with its pink cherry blossom petals. This uses Association No. 10 yeast, which is widely used in *ginjō* brewing in the northern prefectures, though rarely to produce such a powerful fragrance as this. Floral rather than fruity, though there is a touch of pear, and perhaps melon. Soft-feeling on the tongue, and has a transparency of flavor to match the clarity of the colorless liquor, which has a bitter focus. Extremely popular standard; often used to show sake newcomers what *ginjō-ka* is.

16. Dewa-zakura: Kare Sansui

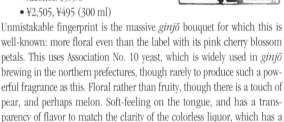

出羽桜：枯山水

- Grade: 55%
- SMV: +5
- Acidity: 1.3
- Amino acids: ——
- Alcohol: 15.5%
- ¥2,945

This is aged three years before shipping, but it has none of the dark, smoky *hine-ka* flavors that are anathema to lovers of the clean and fresh. What it does have is the roundness, the depth, and a lack of sharp edges, all of which are the strengths of mature sake. The liquor is exceptionally clear for its age; its austerity of line when cold gains in volume when slightly warmed. For me, definitely at its best as *nuru-kan*. The label retains the cherry blossom motif of other Dewa-zakura products. Their pale pink is set in an ascetic pattern (rather like the clouds found on temple screens), and the label is printed on plain white paper with a pale red border, creating an affecting austerity. Unlike its popular sister product (above), this may take some finding.

If this tasted like mud, I would still love it for the poetry of its name, which is taken from that style of gardening which, sadly, becomes merely "dry landscape" in English (poetry being, as Robert Frost said, what gets lost in translation). In it you find colossal rivers flowing between awesome mountain ranges—sculptured in a few narrow yards from rocks and moss and the gravel that forms the mighty currents of great rivers.

出羽桜酒造株式会社　Dewa-zakura Shuzō Kabushiki-gaisha
山形県天童市一日町1丁目4–6　〒994–0044
☎ 023–653–5121

17. Fuchū Homare: Junmai Daiginjō Watari-bune

府中誉：純米大吟醸、渡船

- Grade: *junmai daiginjō* (35%)
- SMV: +3
- Acidity: 1.3
- Amino acids: 1.1
- Alcohol: 16.5%
- ¥4,860 (720 ml)

Watari-bune is the name of a sake rice. This variety fell out of use many years ago and was revived by this firm, currently its only user. It is a relative of the sought-after *Omachi* variety, and its complex organic flavors show a strong family likeness. Expansive, boisterous *ginjō* with an apple bouquet that makes for flamboyant, distinctive sake. The rice is produced with the close cooperation of local farmers, whom the brewer honors by listing their names on every box.

府中酒造株式会社　Fuchū Shuzō Kabushiki-gaisha
茨城県石岡市国府5–9–32　〒315–0014
☎ 0299–23–0233

18. Fuku Nishiki: Sato

富久錦：里

- Grade: *junmaishu* (65%)
- SMV: +2.0
- Acidity: 1.7
- Amino acids: 1.6
- Alcohol: 15.4%

• ¥1,893

Plenty of action on the palate, with a pronounced bitterness complemented by lively, refreshing acidity that leaves a tingle on the tongue.

19. Fuku Nishiki:
Junmai Nama-zake

富久錦：純米生酒
• Grade: *junmaishu* (60%)
• SMV: +2.0
• Acidity: 1.8
• Amino acids: 1.7
• Alcohol: 15–16%
• ¥520 (300 ml)

Typical fragrance of unpasteurized sake, *kōji-bana*, well exemplified. In this case, a flowery (perhaps rose) bouquet combines with a smell of sweetcorn and something like smoked banana, if such a thing exists. Full, cheerful acid is the centerpiece. Fairly sweet, altogether jolly.

Striking label designs with a prize-winning logo make this an easy brand to spot on the shelf. All of Fuku Nishiki's sakes are *junmai*.

富久錦株式会社　Fuku Nishiki Kabushiki-gaisha
兵庫県加西市三口町1048　〒675–2223
☎ 0790–48–2111

20. Gekkeikan:
Yūmai-zukuri, Jōsen

月桂冠：融米造り、上撰
• Grade: *junmaishu* (68%)
• SMV: +6
• Acidity: 1.2
• Amino acids: 1.2
• Alcohol: 15.3%
• ¥1,890, ¥1,870 (1.8-liter carton), ¥950 (900 ml carton), ¥600 (500 ml), ¥365 (300 ml)

Fruit of a radical new brewing method wherein rice is not steamed in the traditional fashion, but reduced to a gruel-like consistency to enable saccharification to proceed apace. (Exact details of the technique are a trade secret.) Proper rice flavor of *junmai* comes through firmly. Dry, with well-balanced acid and astringency. Light, but not thin, and its success in the marketplace speaks for itself.

21. Gekkeikan: Roman, Ginjō Hizōshu

月桂冠：浪漫、吟醸秘蔵酒

- Grade: *ginjōshu* (58%)
- SMV: −2
- Acidity: 1.45
- Amino acids: 1.85
- Alcohol: 16.7%
- ¥3,400 (720 ml)

The nose recalls nuts and fruitcake, with a touch of secondhand bookshop. There is also a surprising (albeit faint) echo of the citrus-fresh aroma of young sake. The lightness of the color (a pale yellow) and the liquor are also exceptional for sake aged ten years. (Ten is actually the age of the youngest brew in the blend; many ingredients in the mix are older still.) Unexpected dryness has a woody feeling; there is a bitter/sweet stage in the middle and an acerbic dry finish.

♠ "Gekkeikan" means "laurel wreath," and the firm's Olympian presence is undisputed. At the turn of the century, it became the first brewery to sell bottled sake (forestalling the then customary dilution of sake in the keg by retailers), and has been at the forefront of numerous other developments. The firm has been the number one producer since the 1960s, and offers everything from the fruits of new technology to traditional handmade sakes. Not known for resting on their laurels.

月桂冠株式会社　Gekkeikan Kabushiki-gaisha
京都府京都市伏見区南浜町247　〒612−8045
☎ 075−623−2001

22. Ginban: Honjōzō (Jōsen)

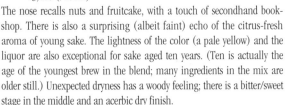

銀盤：本醸造（上撰）

- Grade: *honjōzō* (50%)
- SMV: +5
- Acidity: 1.3
- Amino acids: 1.2
- Alcohol: 15%
- ¥1,835

Unusual bouquet with buttery elements; also reminds me of lemonade. Round rice flavor lent focus by a light bitter edge. Light-bodied, particularly in the beginning. Taste burgeons at the finish, leaving a dry impression on the palate. Excellent value.

♠ Firm early to automate. Even their bottom-of-the-range "regular" sake is made from rice polished to 60%, indicative of exceptionally

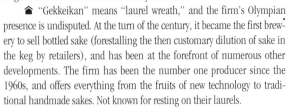
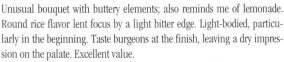

high standards. Savings made by low production costs (mechanization and fewer staff) are used to great effect in terms of raw materials. This is how machine-made sake should be.

銀盤株式会社　Ginban Kabushiki-gaisha
富山県黒部市荻生4853–3　〒938–0801
☎ 0765–54–1181

23. Ginrei Gassan: Dewa 33

銀嶺月山：DEWA 33

- Grade: *junmai ginjō* (≦55%)
- SMV: +1
- Acidity: 1.3
- Amino acids: 1.2
- Alcohol: 15.5%
- ¥1,000 (500 ml)

Fresh-tasting, with a splendid cleanness of edge: the sweetness is full on the palate, the effect of breadth enhanced by equilibrium with a complimentary dryness. Soft, bright acidity caps the fresh, youthful feeling. Crisp and charismatic. The Dewa 33 tag denotes a product belonging to a range promoted by Yamagata Prefecture. Each of the participating breweries has made a *junmai ginjō* using the sake rice developed in the prefecture and "Yamagata yeast."

月山酒造株式会社　Gassan Shuzō Kabushiki-gaisha
山形県寒河江市大字谷沢769–1　〒990–0521
☎ 0237–87–1114

24. Gokyō: Junmaishu

五橋：純米酒

- Grade: *junmaishu* (60%)
- SMV: +1.5
- Acidity: 1.6
- Amino acids: 1.7
- Alcohol: 15.5%
- ¥2,330

The aroma contains rice elements with a slightly musty touch of unripe pear. While cold, a strong bitter flavor is followed by an astringent finish, with a flavor-in-the-mouth (*fukumika*) that hints at the smoke and caramel typical of matured sake. I find that many pure rice brews with prominent astringent edges blossom if decanted, and this is no exception. As well as gaining a nutty mellow dimension as its temperature rises, it feels rounder on the palate as the sweetness becomes more evident. A gentle floral note emerges in the nose (my wife suggests hyacinth). Where this sake shows its true mettle, however, is with food, particularly oilier dishes, which it compliments with a flowering of sweet, rounded flavor one would never imagine from the sake alone.

One of the quirks of the Japanese is their tendency to give everything a ranking. So, with no question of debate, there are the Three Great Mountains, the Three Most Beautiful Views, the Three Great Gardens, and inevitably, the Three Famous Bridges. One of these is the source of this company's brand name, Gokyō. The characters are those for "five" and "bridges," referring to the five beautiful spans of the Kintaikyō bridge over the Nishikigawa river. This, I am told, is the source of the water used by the firm for brewing.

酒井酒造株式会社　Sakai Shuzō Kabushiki-gaisha
山口県岩国市中津町1–1–31　〒740–0027
☎ 0827–21–2177

25. Hama Chidori: Junmai Daiginjō

浜千鳥：純米大吟醸

- Grade: *junmai daiginjō* (40%)
- SMV: +2
- Acidity: 1.4
- Amino acids: 1.2
- Alcohol: 16–17%
- ¥7,800, ¥3,900 (720 ml)

Bouquet is oddly reminiscent of baking cakes. Gentle acid and shy sweetness in the beginning give way to a fine astringency. The final dryness is pronounced, but not so as to undermine the delicacy of the overall effect. Intriguing confectionery bouquet is more prominent close to room temperature. This seems to be a characteristic of Hama Chidori sakes in general. Subtle, repays attention.

株式会社釜石酒造商会
Kabushiki-gaisha Kamaishi Shuzō Shōkai
岩手県釜石市小川町3–8–7
〒026–0045
☎ 0193–23–5613

26. Hana-hato: Kijōshu

華鳩：貴醸酒

- Grade: *kijōshu* (65%)
- SMV: −44.7
- Acidity: 3.5
- Amino acids: 2.9
- Alcohol: 16.7%
- ¥1,800 (500 ml)

Kijōshu, "noble-brewed sake," is startlingly different from the standard. The color is dark caramel. The nose has a dark, fragrant pungency similar to that of sake aged over many years without refrigeration. Sherry comes to mind; also mince pies, black treacle, Christmas pudding. Same rich, dark, sweet combination—complemented by a voluptous sourness. On the tongue, has a thick, rich texture. Cornucopia of flavors and aromas is most persistent. Not to be hurried.

This Hiroshima firm was pioneer in the peculiar and pungent field of *kijōshu*.

榎酒造株式会社　Enoki Shuzō Kabushiki-gaisha
広島県安芸郡音戸町南隠渡2–1–15　〒737–1205
☎ 0823–52–1234

27. Haru-shika: Chō Karakuchi

春鹿：超辛口

- Grade: *junmaishu* (58%)
- SMV: +12
- Acidity: 1.6
- Amino acids: 1.5
- Alcohol: 15–15.9%
- ¥2,555, ¥1,408 (720 ml), ¥515 (300 ml)

Fleeting sweetness is flushed away by earthy dry flavor, with a lingering astringency. The technical problems of brewing a +12 *junmai* make this a rarity. Indubitably dry, but a different dryness than that of alcohol-added sakes of a similar meter value. Nose has an intriguing mushroom-and-chili-pepper feel.

Highly successful, this product accounts for well over half the firm's total output. and is reportedly the most popular single brand of import sake in the United States.

28. Haru-shika:
Haku-teki, Jimyōshu

春鹿：白滴、而妙酒

- Grade: *junmai ginjō* (60%)
- SMV: +5
- Acidity: 1.3
- Amino acids: 1.4
- Alcohol: 15–16%
- ¥2,331, ¥1,166 (720 ml), ¥467 (300 ml)

Nuts and unripe fruit in the bouquet. Dry with a crisp acid tang and a mellow, nutty astringency to finish. Prime sake rice *Yamada Nishiki* polished to 60%, giving a clean, clear flavor with economy of line.

🏠 This brewery is situated in the heart of Nara. The ancient capital is symbolized by the deer that roam its parks and thoroughfares, and give their name to Haru-shika: "Spring Deer."

株式会社今西清兵衛商店
Kabushiki-gaisha Imanishi Seibei Shōten
奈良県奈良市福智院町24–1　〒630–8381
☎ 0742–23–2255

29. Hideyoshi:
Tokubetsu Junmaishu

秀よし：特別純米酒

- Grade: *junmaishu* (60%)
- SMV: +1
- Acidity: 1.5
- Amino acids: 1.4
- Alcohol: 15–16%
- ¥1,450 (720 ml)

Spicy, peppery, pungent nose hides a distant suggestion of banana. Initial sweetness is swept away by sturdy rice flavor and hefty acid. Satisfying fullness of flavor gives an impression of a higher percentage of alcohol than is the case. Lingering aftertaste is relatively gentle.

合名会社鈴木酒造店　Gōmei-gaisha Suzuki Shuzōten
秋田県仙北郡中仙町長野字二日町9　〒014–0207
☎ 0187–56–2121

30. Hira-izumi: Yamahai Junmaishu

飛良泉：山廃純米酒

- Grade: *junmaishu* (58%)
- SMV: +4
- Acidity: 1.9
- Amino acids: 1.5
- Alcohol: 15.2%
- ¥2,730, ¥1,560 (720 ml), ¥440 (200 ml)

Fine-lined, but powerful acidity is characteristic of the *yamahai* style. Pleasant, grainy bouquet with a nutty touch. Has rough edges when cold; these can be smoothed by warming, when it gains a gorgeous velvety softness and loses its lingering aftertaste.

31. Hira-izumi: Yamahai Honjōzō

飛良泉：山廃本醸造

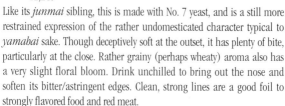

- Grade: *honjōzō* (60%)
- SMV: +3
- Acidity: 1.5
- Amino acids: 1.3
- Alcohol: 15.2%
- ¥2,240

Like its *junmai* sibling, this is made with No. 7 yeast, and is a still more restrained expression of the rather undomesticated character typical to *yamahai* sake. Though deceptively soft at the outset, it has plenty of bite, particularly at the close. Rather grainy (perhaps wheaty) aroma also has a very slight floral bloom. Drink unchilled to bring out the nose and soften its bitter/astringent edges. Clean, strong lines are a good foil to strongly flavored food and red meat.

🏠 One of the oldest *kura*, founded 1487.

株式会社飛良泉本舗　Kabushiki-gaisha Hira-izumi Honpo
秋田県由利郡仁賀保町平沢中町59　〒018–0402
☎ 0184–35–2031

32. Hitori Musume: Sayaka

一人娘：さやか

- Grade: *honjōzō* (55%)
- SMV: +8
- Acidity: 1.5
- Amino acids: 1.7
- Alcohol: 15.5%

• ¥2,088

Mild, ricey aroma, followed by parched, emphatically dry flavor. Dryness is reinforced by *shibumi* (astringency), then tempered with a very faint sweetness at the finish. The name means "clear" or "bright"; the taste is clear and crisp to match. Distinctive and strong, but beguilingly drinkable.

33. Hitori Musume: Ginjō Sayaka

一人娘：吟醸さやか

• Grade: *ginjō* (50%)
• SMV: +5
• Acidity: 1.5
• Amino acids: 1.6
• Alcohol: 15.0–15.9%
• ¥3,204

Strong and distinctive bouquet with the idiosyncratic dusty character peculiar to this firm. Dryness and *shibumi* both powerful, yet with an unexpected mildness.

⌂ This firm's sake is something of a peculiarity: this is that rare thing, a brewery which specializes in dry sake using soft water. What is more, the "Only Daughter" brand was determinedly dry even in the days when sweeter sake was the norm. Their unique brewing method (ingredients added to the mash in two stages as opposed to the conventional three) is presumably responsible for the quiet but distinct character that is their trademark.

株式会社山中酒造店　Kabushiki-gaisha Yamanaka Shuzōten
茨城県結城郡石下町新石下187　〒300–2706
☎ 0297–42–2004

34. Hoku-setsu: Daiginjō

北雪：大吟醸

• Grade: *daiginjō* (49–50%)
• SMV: +5
• Acidity: 1.3
• Amino acids: 1.3
• Alcohol: 15.6%
• ¥3,239, ¥1,905 (720 ml)

This firm offers about a dozen *daiginjō* products; this one is distinguished by the tag *Honjōzō te-zukuri karakuchi* (本醸造手造り辛口), or dry sake made by hand. It is rare to find a brew so uncompromisingly dry.

There is a moment of fragile sweetness to begin, and hints of astringency and bitterness, but they don't stand much of a chance in the face of such medicinal dryness. I'm tempted to think it would make a good hangover cure. The bouquet is rather prickly, and its pear-like character emerges a little more (as does the distant sweet note) as the sake is warmed.

☗ "Northern Snow," one of the half-a-dozen sake makers on the island of Sado, is a successful exponent of the light, smooth Niigata style of brewing which has made such a huge impact on the marketplace in recent years.

株式会社北雪酒造　Kabushiki-gaisha Hokusetsu Shuzō
新潟県佐渡郡赤泊村大字徳和2377–2　〒952–0706
☎ 0259–87–3105

35. Ichi no Kura: Junmaishu Yamahai Ki-ippon

一ノ蔵：純米酒、山廃生一本

- Grade: *junmaishu* (60%)
- SMV: +2 to +4
- Acidity: 1.6–2.0
- Amino acids: 1.7–1.9
- Alcohol: 15.0–15.9%
- ¥2,427, ¥1,165 (720 ml)

Feels much drier than SMV suggests; crisp at the finish, and light of line for *yamahai*. When hot, it is dominated by a rather obtrusive bitterness. Warm, it is comfortably mellow; the sweetness brought out by warming is a welcome counterbalance to the persistent dryness. Those who dislike the custom of warming sake should be converted at a blow.

36. Ichi no Kura: Aa, fushigi na o-sake

一ノ蔵：あ、不思議なお酒

- Grade: *junmaishu* (65%)
- SMV: –75 to –65
- Acidity: 5.5–6.5
- Amino acids: 0.5–0.7
- Alcohol: 8.0–8.9%
- ¥1,068 (720 ml), ¥520 (300 ml)

Name means "Ah, what a strange sake," and few will have any other reaction. Has an unmistakably winelike bouquet, and is in fact made with wine yeast. More similar to a sweet, white muscat wine than other *junmai* sakes. Low alcohol is a consequence of the choice of yeast, not dilution. Indeed a strange sake!

⌂ Ichi no Kura means "One Brewery." The name commemorates the founding of the present firm in the 1970s, when four breweries amalgamated to form one company.

株式会社一ノ蔵　Kabushiki-gaisha Ichi no Kura
宮城県志田郡松山町千石大欅14　〒987–1304
☎ 0229–55–3322

Until 1992, sake was grouped for tax purposes into first and second class, first class brews being the more expensive. Small breweries often preferred to waive the cost of the necessary assessment, giving rise to the odd situation that many outstanding sakes were ranked (by default) as second class. A spreading awareness that many "first class" products were utterly outclassed by such sakes (with the economic advantage of a lower tax bracket and thus a lower retail price) was an important factor in the *ji-zake* boom. Ichi no Kura's Mukansa ("Non-assessment") Junmai and Mukansa Honjōzō were an affirmation of this way of thinking. The grade-differentiated tax assessment has been discontinued, but these two popular brands retain the name even in these happily enlightened days.

---

37. Inaba-zuru: Junmai Ginjō, Gōriki

いなば鶴：純米吟醸、強力

- Grade: *junmai ginjō* (40%)
- SMV: +4
- Acidity: 1.5
- Amino acids: 1.2
- Alcohol: 16.5%
- ¥ 5,830, ¥2,910 (720 ml)

Name with characters meaning "strong" and "power" is not a reference to the flavor of the sake, but the name of a rare local sake rice, as rescued from dormant oblivion by this firm. Full-tasting but not as macho as the name suggests, with a soft feel on the tongue. Somewhat dry, with a tenacious finish. The rarity of the rice is reflected in the limited availability of the sake.

中川酒造合名会社　Nakagawa Shuzō Gōmei-gaisha
鳥取県鳥取市立川町2–305　〒680–0061
☎ 0857–24–9330

38. Iso Jiman: Ginjō Shiboritate, Nama-zake Genshu

磯自慢：吟醸しぼりたて、生酒原酒

- Grade: *ginjōshu* 55%
- SMV: +6
- Acidity: 1.3
- Amino acids: 1.1
- Alcohol: 17–18%
- ¥2,440 (720 ml)

Sold as a new sake, with a typically high bouquet, very *ginjō*, and perhaps a hint of pear, but undeniably fruity. The low acid level contributes to its sophistication. Begins with pearlike translucent fruitiness, followed by insistent dryness. The overall depth of flavor belies the light, clean first impression.

39. Iso Jiman: Honjōzō Shiboritate, Nama Chozō

磯自慢：本醸造しぼりたて、生貯蔵

- Grade: *honjōzō* (65%)
- SMV: +5.5
- Acidity: 1.2
- Amino acids: 1.3
- Alcohol: 15.6%
- ¥1,840

Touch of mushroom flavor, plus melon/pear, in the slightly smoky nose. At first, somewhat bitter; dry clarity complemented by retiring sweetness and a quiet tang. A shadowy fruity element adds extra dimension to the firm, dry/bitter axis which persists to the aftertaste.

⌂ One of the Shizuoka breweries that enjoys successful results with the prefecture's homemade yeast variety. The small output of complex, fragrant handmade sakes is in big demand.

磯自慢酒造株式会社　Iso Jiman Shuzō Kabushiki-gaisha
静岡県焼津市鰯ヶ島307　〒425–0032
☎ 054–628–2204

40. Iwa no I: Yamahai Ginjō, Ichidan Jikomi

岩の井：山廃吟醸、一段仕込

- Grade: *ginjōshu* (50%)
- SMV: −15
- Acidity: 2.5
- Amino acids: 2.2
- Alcohol: 15.5%

• ¥5,238, ¥2,571 (720 ml)

Deep bouquet has a suggestion of burnt caramel and cooking apples. Rather high levels for acids and amino acids might suggest coarse lines. The result of an unusual brewing method (apparently one-stage, as opposed to the normal three) is sweet, with voluptuous apply acid; round, thought-provoking and far from coarse.

岩瀬酒造株式会社　Iwase Shuzō Kabushiki-gaisha
千葉県夷隅郡御宿町久保1916　〒299–5102
☎ 0470–68–2034

41. Kamo Izumi: Shusen, Junmai Ginjōshu, Hon Jikomi

加茂泉：朱泉、純米吟醸酒、本仕込

• Grade: *junmai ginjō* (60%)
• SMV: +1.5
• Acidity: 1.6
• Amino acids: 1.4
• Alcohol: 16–17%
• ¥1,600 (720 ml)

Unabashed *hine-ka* (oft-maligned "aged-sake smell") noticeable as soon as the cap is pulled, even before pouring. Conventional *ginjō* bouquet subsumed by damp wood and mushrooms: tangy forest-floor aroma will separate sheep from goats at a sniff. Acidity takes center stage on the palate, with sweet (and slightly bitter) elements supporting. Room temperature is splendid, but you'd be mad if you didn't try it warmed, too. Strong-flavored *ginjō* products sometimes fall between two stools, but this retains a convincing *ginjō* elegance despite its big bones. How do they do it?

42. Kamo Izumi: Junmai Ginjōshu, Koshu

加茂泉：純米吟醸酒、古酒

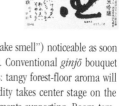

• Grade: *junmai ginjō* (60%)
• SMV: +1.5
• Acidity: 1.6
• Amino acids: 1.4
• Alcohol: 16.0–16.9%
• ¥3,000 (720 ml)

Color is rather mossy brown. According to the angle and the light, it sometimes offers a rather ghoulish greenish aspect. The complex *koshu* nose reminds me, in this case, of whisky-filled chocolate. For a brew so venerable (made in the 1988 season) the flavor is surprisingly light. Delicate sweetness is succeeded by an insistent dry note; a final, lingering astringency brings subtle woody, nutty tones.

🏠 Hiroshima firm famous for pure rice brews. Many products are shipped unfiltered after maturing, ensuring plenty of character, lively exchanges of opinions, and an enthusiastic following. The company's style is magnificently immune to fashion.

賀茂泉酒造株式会社　Kamo Izumi Shuzō Kabushiki-gaisha

広島県東広島市西条上市町2–4　〒739–0006

☎ 0824–23–2118

When I started drinking sake, Kamo Izumi's Shusen (and sister product, Ryokusen) soon became solid favorites. At that stage, though, I could speak almost no Japanese and read still less, so, until quite recently, I had no idea of the product names (which mean respectively Red and Green Spring). In my mind, they were effectively filed under "Red and Green Kamo Izumi." Non-readers of Japanese, despair not!

---

43. Kiku-hime: Yamahai Junmaishu

菊姫：山廃純米酒

- Grade: *junmaishu* (65%)
- SMV: +1
- Acidity: 1.7
- Amino acids: ——
- Alcohol: 16.5%
- ¥2,900, ¥1,400 (720 ml)

Lovely deep yellow color is well matched with a strong but mellow flavor. The grassy fullness of the pungent ricey aroma is matched by the tangy depth of robust *yamahai* flavor. Throughout, strong without harshness, capped finally by sweetness and astringency emerging from the rice taste. Despite the exceptionally meaty acid, retains harmony across a range of temperatures, with a slight bitter-chocolate aftertaste.

44. Kiku-hime: Yamahai Junmai Genshu

菊姫：山廃純米原酒

- Grade: *junmai* (65%)
- SMV: ——
- Acidity: ——
- Amino acids: ——
- Alcohol: 19.4%

• ¥3,500

Released twice yearly, and strictly restricted to these seasonal sales. Very much a question of taste; not for the timid. Unpasteurized, *yamahai*, pure rice, undiluted, unfiltered—a recipe for a monster sake. Those who favor the light and airy should keep their ten-foot poles handy. The bouquet has a quality of citruslike freshness; hits the palate with a *whoomph*, and follows up with a huge, tangy *whoosh*. Difficult to find and impossible to forget.

⌂ "Chrysanthemum Princess" sakes are some of the most sought-after of all. Results of exceptionally exacting standards for raw materials (100% sake rice) are appreciated by adoring fans. The range of *yamahai* products is held up by many as the benchmark for the genre.

菊姫合資会社　Kiku-hime Gōshi-gaisha

石川県石川郡鶴来町新町夕8　〒920–2126

☎ 07619–2–1234

45. Kiku no Shiro: Daiginjō

菊の城：大吟醸

• Grade: *daiginjō* (40%)
• SMV: +4
• Acidity: 1.4
• Amino acids: 1.0
• Alcohol: 17.0–17.9%
• ¥3,884 (720 ml)

Fine-lined but full; classic, fruity *ginjō*. The aroma is suggestive of peaches, though it gives an impression of much more tang. The richly-layered flavors combine to give an unusually powerful effect for the *daiginjō* class.

株式会社菊の城本舗　Kabushi-gaisha Kiku no Shiro Honpo

熊本県菊池市大字隈府95　〒861–1331

☎ 0968–25–2009

46. Kiku-zakari: Junmai Ginjō

菊盛：純米吟醸

• Grade: *junmai ginjō* (48%)
• SMV: +4
• Acidity: 1.5
• Amino acids: 1.1
• Alcohol: 16.5%
• ¥4,400, ¥2,200 (720 ml)

The russet color of the label finds a pale echo in the color of the liquor. The bouquet is an intriguing complex of grass and stone with a slight smoky touch of sweet apple. On the palate, full *junmai* breadth of flavor combines splendidly with unimpeachable *ginjō* elegance; an altogether wonderful buoyancy of flavor. Nuts and caramel, fruit and smoke.

🏠 This is one of a number of breweries to have diversified into beer brewing in the wake of the recent reform of licensing laws. Where Japanese beer drinkers formerly had a choice of domestic producers so limited they could be counted on the fingers of one hand, there are now well over a hundred producers of micro-brewed beer. This firm's offering is called Hitachino Nest Beer, and uses the punchy slogan "Nest is Best."

木内酒造合資会社　Kiuchi Shuzō Gōshi-gaisha
茨城県那珂郡那珂町鴻巣1257　〒311–0133
☎ 029–298–0105

47. Kin-sen: Hitoyo-zake

金泉：一夜酒

- Grade: *junmai daiginjō* (40%)
- SMV: +3
- Acidity: 1.2
- Amino acids: 1.2
- Alcohol: 16–17%
- ¥3,000

Powerful *ginjō* bouquet is a perfumed amalgam of fruits—melon, pear, banana—which conceal a greener, more herbal note, perhaps due to *Omachi* rice. A rather strong bitter note dominates as the temperature rises; at its best well-chilled. Soft, fresh combination of light tang and fine toffee-apple sweetness is pleasing.

🏠 Small Hiroshima brewery with a growing reputation for high-octane *ginjō* sake. Most brewery owners leave the fearsomely hard work of the actual brewing to the *tōji* and his staff, but the master brewer here is none other than the owner's eldest son, still in his thirties. "Golden Fountain" produces almost nothing but labor-intensive *ginjōshu*, a masochistic tour de force.

堀本酒造株式会社　Horimoto Shuzō Kabushiki-gaisha
広島県豊田郡安芸津町三津4333　〒729–2402
☎ 0846–45–0016

48. Kita no Nishiki: **Hizō Junmaishu**

北の錦：秘蔵純米酒

- Grade: *junmaishu* (55%)
- SMV: +3
- Acidity: 1.6
- Amino acids: 1.8
- Alcohol: 17.5%
- ¥ 2,500, ¥1,300 (900 ml)

Made from *Miyama Nishiki* sake rice and laid down before sale. Aroma is an unusual mix, with mushroom/toadstool elements and smoky/woody hints. Insistent dry and bitter flavors conceal shy sweetness with odd sour, woody notes. Over-chilling may stifle the strange and intriguing mix of flavors.

🏠 Though young by national standards, its 1880 founding makes this the oldest company presently brewing on the northern island, Hokkaidō.

小林酒造株式会社　Kobayashi Shuzō Kabushiki-gaisha
北海道夕張郡栗山町錦3–109　〒069–1521
☎ 01237–2–1001

49. Koku-ryū: **Junmai Ginjō**

黒龍：純米吟醸

- Grade: *junmai ginjō* (55%)
- SMV: +3
- Acidity: 1.4
- Amino acids: 1.3
- Alcohol: 15.5%
- ¥2,700, ¥1,350

Extremely full, fruity flavor, pearlike with odd liquorice notes in bouquet and taste. Aromatic and intriguing, flowering on the palate; full middle, crisp, dry finish. Always complex, always spicy.

The name means "Black Dragon"; the dragon theme is borrowed from the nearby Kuzu-ryū ("Nine-headed Dragon") river. This river also gives its name to a big-grained sake rice variety, currently produced only in Fukui Prefecture.

黒龍酒造株式会社　Koku-ryū Shuzō Kabushiki-gaisha
福井県吉田郡松岡町春日1–38　〒910–1133
☎ 0776–61–0038

50. Koshi no Homare: Tokubetsu Junmaishu

越の誉：特別純米酒

- Grade: *junmaishu* (55%)
- SMV: +2
- Acidity: 1.6
- Amino acids: 1.8
- Alcohol: 15.9%
- ¥2,621, ¥1,311 (720 ml)

Shy nose has mild rice and faint flowery (hay) elements. Sweet and tangy on the tongue at first, light of body but not thin. Almost colorless. Dryish close has a certain ricey pungency. Modest but charming.

原酒造株式会社　Hara Shuzō Kabushiki-gaisha

新潟県柏崎市新橋5–12　〒945–0056

☎ 0257–23–6221

51. Ko-tsuzumi: Tenraku

小鼓：天楽

- Grade: *daiginjō* (45%)
- SMV: +3.5
- Acidity: 1.1
- Amino acids: 0.8
- Alcohol: 16.5%
- ¥10,000, ¥5,000 (720 ml)

Visually mouthwatering, the presentation—gold and black box, custom-made black frosted bottle—leaves the contents with a lot to live up to. The classic *ginjō* nose—grapes and a fresh, strawberry note—is the first sign that the sake itself has no intention of being overshadowed. The flavor is very transparent, an initial moment of sweetness fading into a drier finish with a bitter aftertaste. Light and fine—the order of the day. The unpasteurized version is sadly hard to find, but I find the *nama* tang brings a very flattering extra dimension. Oddly, I find that the virtues of the *nama* blur as it warms; the pasteurized version certainly looses nothing from the increasing presence of round, sweet elements as it nears room temperature.

A striking range of coordinated designs give Ko-tsuzumi products a distinctive identity, instantly recognizable at several paces. The various sakes also share an enviable elegance of balance. What is more, this cultured company boasts a haiku poet as president:

酒庫に米蒸す音の朝月夜

Sakagura ni kome musu oto no asa zuki yo

Sound of rice steaming

In the sake brewery:

The moonlit night before daybreak

—Shōkoshi Nishiyama

株式会社西山酒造場　Kabushiki-gaisha Nishiyama Shuzōjō
兵庫県氷上郡市島町中竹田1171　〒669–4302
☎ 0795–86–0331

52. Kudoki Jōzu: Junmai Ginjō

くどき上手：純米吟醸

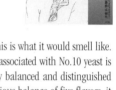

- Grade: *junmai ginjō* (50%)
- SMV: +1
- Acidity: 1.2
- Amino acids: 0.8
- Alcohol: 15.0–15.8%
- ¥2,913

If there were such a thing as a "ricefruit," this is what it would smell like. Has peach notes. The elegant style of sakes associated with No.10 yeast is well represented. Mild and toothsome, finely balanced and distinguished by an exquisite acidity. Thanks to a harmonious balance of five flavors, it exists in the twilight zone between sweet and dry.

🏠 The name is generally rather leeringly supposed to suggest someone with good pick-up technique, but the boss here told me it was in fact chosen by his wife (a student of history) in homage to the notorious ability of medieval warlord Hideyoshi Toyotomi to manipulate people's actions to his advantage—another sense of *kudoku*.

The labels in the style of a Japanese woodblock print (*ukiyo-e*) make Kudoki Jōzu easy to spot. One of the small but growing number of breweries where the *tōji* (chief brewer) and president are one and the same person. Perhaps "superman" is a better expression.

亀の井酒造株式会社　Kamenoi Shuzō Kabushiki-gaisha
山形県東田川郡羽黒町大字戸野字福の内1　〒997–0103
☎ 0235–62–2307

53. Kuro-matsu Kenbishi (Kenbishi): Tokusen

剣菱 (黒松剣菱)：特撰

- Grade: *honjōzō* (70%)
- SMV: −1 to 0
- Acidity: 1.8–2.0
- Amino acids: 1.9–2.1
- Alcohol: 16.5%
- ¥2,235

The pungent nose has a sharp fragrance; there must be a wild flower that smells like this. Sturdily sweet for the first moment on the palate, then the other flavors chime in: sourness and a strong, lingering dry edge, with astringency and a woody bitterness. Warming brings out the best in the wealth of flavors—sweet, sour, and a hint of cocoa. Plenty of character and bursting with flavor.

🏠 One of the nation's biggest makers, and also one of the oldest. Records show that it has been around for five hundred years or so, but the exact date of foundation is unknown. (The company was originally situated in Itami, moving to Nada only well into this century.) It is renowned for its traditional stance, both *yamahai moto* and *futa kōji* (see Chapter 3, Making Sake) said to contribute to its characteristic style. The famous trademark represents a stylized sword and shield.

剣菱酒造株式会社　Kenbishi Shuzō Kabushiki-gaisha
兵庫県神戸市東灘区御影本町3–12–5　〒658–0046
☎ 078–811–0131

54. Mado no Ume: Kaden

窓乃梅：花伝

- Grade: *ginjōshu* (50%)
- SMV: +4
- Acidity: 1.1
- Amino acids: 1.4
- Alcohol: 15.5%
- ¥2,670, ¥1,359 (900 ml), ¥1,165 (720 ml)

Refined sake of the light, smooth type described with the word *tanrei* (淡麗) in Japanese. This expression is dangerously prone to be misused as a codeword for "featureless," but here it is used to describe a positive virtue rather than a hollow blandness. Slightly dry. Well rounded, with a mild balance giving an exceptionally elegant effect. Generously priced considering the highly polished rice used.

The evocative name of the brewery means "the plum by the window," in commemoration of a picturesque story about a plum blossom wafting through a window into a fermentation tank, and the exquisitely fragrant sake that was the result.

窓乃梅酒造株式会社　Mado no Ume Shuzō Kabushiki-gaisha
佐賀県佐賀郡久保田町大字新田1640, 1833　〒849–0203
☎ 0952–68–2001

R

Rice and water are the two main raw materials of sake. Although eating rice can be (and is) used in sake making, the best kinds are the specially designated sake rice varieties.

Among the many strains of sake rice (*sakamai*) are some particularly large-grained varieties grown (and in many cases developed) especially for brewing. These are known as *kōtekimai* (好適米) in Japanese. A true brewer's rice of this sort is distinguished by a soft opaque white center called *shinpaku* (心白), meaning "white heart," and usually has a larger, softer grain than other varieties. The fat grain can be polished very highly and still leave a good-sized core of white rice for use in brewing. This is obviously of most importance in the making of *ginjō*-type sake, where the rice is polished to at least 60% of its original size. In fact, most *ginjō* products are made from true brewer's rice.

The type called *Yamada Nishiki* is widely considered to be the best-suited of all for brewers' needs, though there are dozens of varieties, all with particular characteristics which affect the pattern of fermentation and the flavor of the sake.

Sake rice is labor-intensive from an agricultural point of view. Where standard eating rice varieties grow to about 90 centimeters, some strains of brewer's rice stretch to 120 centimeters, the additional height making them much more prone to devastation by the destructive typhoons which strike Japan every year. If fertilizers are used, the stems grow still longer and are more vulnerable, so farmers are forced to accept low yields for such varieties. To add insult to injury, many of these are late-harvesting strains. Unsurprisingly, many farmers balk at the extra labor and risk involved. In one or two English texts on sake, I have seen it suggested that two-thirds of all sake in Japan is made with *Yamada Nishiki* rice. If only! The sad truth is that demand for brewer's rice far exceeds the actual supply.

55. Manzai-raku: Yuki no Kura

萬歳楽：雪の蔵

- Grade: *honjōzō* (63%)
- SMV: +1 to +3
- Acidity: 1.3–1.4
- Amino acids: 1.3–1.5
- Alcohol: 14.0–14.9%
- ¥1,748

On the sweet side, and with a pleasant fruity note lending an elegant feeling. This and *ginjō* fragrance make it a bargain at this price. Picturesque name means "brewery in the snow."

56. Manzai-raku: Kiku no Kura

萬歳楽：菊の蔵

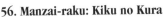

- Grade: *junmaishu* (60%)
- SMV: 0 to +3
- Acidity: 1.7–2.0
- Amino acids: 1.5–1.8
- Alcohol: 14.0–14.9%
- ¥1,893

Light of body, with delicate sweetness and astringency: a general lightness of touch uncommon in pure rice sake. Close is crisp, clean, and final. Very low-priced *junmai*. Brand name "Chrysanthemum brewery" refers to the "Chrysanthemum Sake" tag given to sake from this area, already renowned for its quality in the Muromachi period (1333–1573).

株市会社小堀酒造店　Kabushiki-gaisha Kobori Shuzō ten
石川県石川郡鶴来町本町1–747　〒920–2121
☎ 07619–3–1171

57. Masu-izumi: Gentei Daiginjō

満寿泉：限定大吟醸

- Grade: *daiginjō* (50%)
- SMV: +5
- Acidity: 1.3
- Amino acids: ——
- Alcohol: 17–18%
- ¥7,000, ¥3,200 (720 ml)

It is common to divide superior *ginjō* sakes into two schools, *aji* (flavor) *ginjō* and *kaori* (aroma) *ginjō*. To make a sake in the *ginjō* style that delights both the nose and the palate is supremely difficult, and a better example of success than this I have rarely tasted. This depth of fruity flavor in combination with such a notably powerful nose is a true tour de force.

The No. 14 yeast mainly used by this brewery is a relative of the classic No. 9 *ginjō* yeast.

株式会社桝田酒造店　Kabushiki-gaisha Masuda Shuzōten
富山県富山市東岩瀬町269　〒931–8358
☎ 0764–37–9916

58. Masumi: Junmai Daiginjō, Sanka

真澄：純米大吟醸、山花

- Grade: *junmai daiginjō* (45%)
- SMV: +3
- Acidity: 1.3
- Amino acids: 1.1
- Alcohol: 16%

¥4,850, ¥2,430 (720 ml), ¥970 (300 ml)

Wine bottle with gold labeling makes for a product easily spotted by non-readers of Japanese. The unrepentantly flowery, powerful *ginjō* bouquet contrasts with the bold and bitter shadows of the flavor.

59. Masumi: Honjōzō, Nama-zake

真澄：生酒

- Grade: *honjōzō* (60%)
- SMV: +3
- Acidity: 1.4
- Amino acids: 1.1
- Alcohol: 15%
- ¥1,170 (720 ml), ¥485 (300 ml)

Straightforward and solid, the *kōji-bana* nose of young and unpasteurized sake is complemented by a tinge of almond/melon flavor off the palate. The label bears vague English phrases and, most importantly, the basic rule for all *nama-zake*: "Should be kept refrigerated." The bottle design has an appealing, nostalgic simplicity.

Long-time sake drinkers will find Masumi products comfortingly familiar. The yeast that gives character to this company's brews is the source of Association No. 7 yeast—*the* most widely used nationwide (still used by around half of all the nation's breweries), and the template of contemporary non-*ginjō* sake. Masumi sake has a feeling of unshakable, down-to-earth reliability.

宮坂醸造株式会社　Miyasaka Jōzō Kabushiki-gaisha
長野県諏訪市元町1–16　〒392–0006
☎ 0266–52–6161

60. Midori-kawa: Hokujō, Ginjō

緑川：北穣、吟醸
- Grade: *junmai ginjō* (50%)
- SMV: +4.5
- Acidity: 1.5
- Amino acids: 1.4
- Alcohol: 16.0–16.9%
- ¥4,560, ¥2,330 (720 ml)

Subtle, dry, and rounded, with grassy notes to the aroma. The rather rare sake rice *Hokuriku* No. 12, polished to *daiginjō* levels, yields a sake that is fine but not thin. The overall effect owes more to grasses than fruit, with the organic feeling that distinguishes Midori-kawa sake. A mild astringency persists to the last. Sister product Hokujō Honjozō is made from the same rice polished to 60% and priced at ¥3,500.

緑川酒造株式会社　Midori-kawa Shuzō Kabushiki-gaisha
新潟県北魚沼郡小出町大字青島4015–1　〒946–0043
☎ 02579–2–2117

61. Miyo-zakae: Konya wa Saikō!

御代栄：今夜は最高！
- Grade: *junmaishu*
  (see below) (65%)
- SMV: 0
- Acidity: 1.2
- Amino acids: 1.1
- Alcohol: 15–16%
- ¥1,500 (900 ml)

Unusual blend of *junmai* and *ginjō*. A somewhat sharp alcoholic edge to the nose conflicts pear/melon with fruitiness more evident on the tongue. Sweet and soft with a bitter aftertaste, and a free rope (hanging from the neck of the bottle) with every bottle.

Highly specific playful marketing and amusing names distinguish this company. Special sakes for Father's Day, Mother's Day, Valentine's Day. They even offer a product called Tanjōbi Omedetō—"Happy Birthday"! I've been waiting for years for a pretext to buy the ceramic ninja full of sake. The firm also apparently has an interest in Australia's only sake brewery.

北島酒造株式会社　Kitajima Shuzō Kabushiki-gaisha
滋賀県甲賀郡甲西町針756　〒520–3231
☎ 0748–72–0012

62. Nishi no Seki: Shizuku Sake

西の関：滴酒

- Grade: *daiginjō* (40%)
- SMV: +4
- Acidity: 1.3
- Amino acids: 1.1
- Alcohol: 17.5%
- ¥3,500 (720 ml)

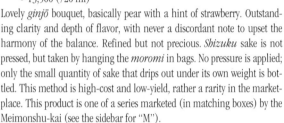

Lovely *ginjō* bouquet, basically pear with a hint of strawberry. Outstanding clarity and depth of flavor, with never a discordant note to upset the harmony of the balance. Refined but not precious. *Shizuku* sake is not pressed, but taken by hanging the *moromi* in bags. No pressure is applied; only the small quantity of sake that drips out under its own weight is bottled. This method is high-cost and low-yield, rather a rarity in the marketplace. This product is one of a series marketed (in matching boxes) by the Meimonshu-kai (see the sidebar for "M").

63. Nishi no Seki: Junmai

西の関：純米

- Grade: *junmaishu* (60%)
- SMV: −3
- Acidity: 1.32
- Amino acids: 2.3
- Alcohol: 15.7%
- ¥2,486, ¥1,068 (720 ml)

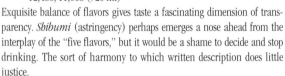

Exquisite balance of flavors gives taste a fascinating dimension of transparency. *Shibumi* (astringency) perhaps emerges a nose ahead from the interplay of the "five flavors," but it would be a shame to decide and stop drinking. The sort of harmony to which written description does little justice.

⌂ Nishi no Seki is renowned and respected as a pioneer in the marketing of *ginjō* sake.

萱島酒造有限会社　Kayashima Shuzō Yugen-gaisha
大分県東国東郡国東町綱井392–1　〒873–0513
☎ 0978–72–1181

64. Niwa no Uguisu: Daruma Label Daiginjō

庭の鴬：達磨ラベル大吟醸

- Grade: *daiginjō* (40%)
- SMV: +5.5
- Acidity: 1.3
- Amino acids: 1.0
- Alcohol: 15.3–15.6%
- ¥5,000, ¥2,500 (720 ml)

Refreshing aroma has pear and peach notes with a pinewood piquancy. Same pearlike element in the flavor. No extremes of taste, though an unaggressive bitterness lingers. The whole effect is very young and green; sappy, if there is such a word. Highly distinctive label design is a personal favorite. The Daruma of the label is the Zen monk of legend, Bodhidharma, the founder of Zen who is said to have spent nine years practicing *zazen* (seated meditation) facing a wall. The ubiquitous red, round (and legless!) Daruma doll commemorates the story and brings luck.

🏠 Tiny firm with extraordinary ratio of staff to volume of production; the essence of hand-brewing. Lovely name (more euphonious than its translation!) means "the garden's bush-warbler."

合名会社山口酒造場　Gōmei-gaisha Yamaguchi Shuzōjō
福岡県三井郡北野町今山534–1　〒830–1122
☎ 0942–78–2008

65. Otoko-yama: Kimoto Junmai

男山：生酛純米

- Grade: *tokubetsu junmaishu* (60%)
- SMV: +4
- Acidity: 1.6
- Amino acids: 1.6
- Alcohol: 15–16%
- ¥2,233, ¥1,165 (900 ml)

Dry base with a neutral balance of sweet, sour, and bitter elements, capped with a slightly astringent flourish. Idiosyncratic character associated with *kimoto* style is most understated. This is apparently one of the top-selling import sakes in the United States.

🏠 Properly "Hokkai Otoko-yama," to distinguish it from other users of the "Man Mountain" tag. (A sake of this name became famous in the Edo period (1603–1868), provoking a bandwagon effect whereby a number of breweries adopted the name, presumably hoping for reflected glory).

男山株式会社　Otoko-yama Kabushiki-gaisha

北海道旭川市永山2条7丁目　〒079–8412

☎ 0166–48–1931

Seasonal brewing

Long ago, sake was made from the autumn equinox to the spring equinox (still national holidays in Japan), and named for the time of production.

shinshu	新酒	"new sake"
		↓
ai-zake	間酒	"intermediate sake"
		↓
kanmae-zake	寒前酒	"pre-cold sake"
		↓
kan-zake	寒酒	"cold sake"
		↓
haru-zake	春酒	"spring sake"

Centuries ago, experience taught brewers that the best sake was that known as *kan-zake*: sake brewed in midwinter. As time went by, technical advances made it possible to brew larger batches, and brewers were able to restrict their activities to the coldest days of the year without reducing their output. This pattern is known as *kan-zukuri* (寒造り), cold-weather (winter) brewing. In firms that make *ginjō* sake, the very coldest months are still the time set aside for the laborious brewing of the finest sake of the year, and the pattern of brewing established in the Edo period (1603–1868) continues. Many companies (my own employer included) still brew exclusively in the winter, according to this traditional pattern. However, many large firms now run refrigerated plants, a policy that has changed the seasonal nature of sake brewing. Production can be carried on year-round, spreading outlay and liberating the firm from the thorny problems of seasonal hiring practices (see the sidebar for "U"), which bedevil the traditional system.

66. Ōyama: Junmaishu

大山：純米酒

- Grade: *junmaishu* (60%)
- SMV: +8
- Acidity: 1.2
- Amino acids: 1.0
- Alcohol: 15.3%
- ¥2,230

Crystal clear transparency foretells lightness of body. The now-you-smell-it, now-you-don't hint of vanilla/banana in the aroma provides a rarefied fruitiness.

67. Ōyama: Tameiki Toiki

大山：ため息といき

- Grade: *junmai daiginjō* (40%)
- SMV: +5
- Acidity: 1.4
- Amino acids: 1.0
- Alcohol: 15.3%
- ¥2,910 (720 ml)

Name signifies "breath of a sigh." Effect is suitably breezy. Aroma is fruity without a doubt, but what fruit? I waver between melon and pear. Dryness is lent a dimension of softness from constant, translucent sweetness. Fine but not thin.

🏠 Computerizing in the early 1970s, Ōyama exploits contemporary technologies in making its clean, reliable, and perenially popular sakes.

加藤嘉八郎酒造株式会社

Katō Kahachirō Shuzō Kabushiki-gaisha

山形県鶴岡市大山3–1–38　〒997–1124

☎ 0235–33–2008

68. Ōzeki: One Cup Ōzeki

大関：ワンカップ大関

- Grade: —
- SMV: 0
- Acidity: 1.4
- Amino acids: ——
- Alcohol: 15.4%
- ¥214 (180 ml)

Since its introduction in 1964, One Cup has had a revolutionary impact on marketing. Ready-to-drink and handy for Japan's ubiquitous vending machines, it has inspired swarms of imitators; now accounts for one third of Ōzeki's huge turnover. A household name. The vending machines are set to be phased out in a couple of years, which may cut into its sales.

⌂ Firm takes its name from the second-highest rank in sumo wrestling, and is now a major sponsor of the national sport. When the name was adopted a little over a century ago, the currently supreme rank of *yokozuna* only existed unofficially, so the moniker symbolized top dog, not the No. 2 spot it does today!

大関株式会社　Ōzeki Kabushiki-gaisha
兵庫県西宮市今津出在家町4–9　〒663–8227
☎ 0798–32–2111

69. Rihaku:
Junmai Ginjō, Chō Tokusen

李白：純米吟醸、超特撰
- Grade: *junmai ginjō* (55%)
- SMV: +4
- Acidity: 1.6
- Amino acids: 1.1
- Alcohol: 15–16%
- ¥3,107

Mild *ginjō* nose has melon/pear hints, with a diverting smoky edge. Impact of rather high acidity forms an expansive combination with the formidable dry flavor that pushes through to the finish. Deep flavors combine in a full, appetizing taste that doesn't cloy; the level in the bottle sinks very quickly. The very clean, palate-clearing finish also contributes to this effect.

70. Rihaku: Junmai Ginjō, Nama
李白：純米吟醸、生
- Grade: *junmai ginjō* (59%)
- SMV: +3
- Acidity: 1.6
- Amino acids: 1.1
- Alcohol: 15–16%
- ¥650 (300 ml)

Unusual nose has elements of burnt caramel and smoked cheese (less bizarre an effect than it seems on paper!). As always with Rihaku, full-bodied acidity is central. Flavorful, with a mild sweetness and plenty of depth. The *fukumika*, the after-aroma perceived in the nose (flavor-in-the-mouth), has the toasty character that seems to be common to this firm's *nama* products.

⌂ Rihaku is the Japanese name of Chinese poet Li Po, almost as famous for his drinking as his writing, proving by the nature of his fame his dictum: "The Saints and Sages of old times are all stock and still, / Only the mighty drinkers of wine have left a name behind."

I have been instructed to record my wife's appreciative endorsement of Rihaku sake.

李白酒造有限会社　Rihaku Shuzō Yūgen-gaisha
島根県松江市石橋町335　〒690–0881
☎ 0852–26–5555

71. Sanshō-raku: Junmai Ginjō

三笑楽：純米吟醸

- Grade: *junmai ginjō* (60%)
- SMV: +5
- Acidity: 1.5
- Amino acids: 1.5
- Alcohol: 15.8%
- ¥1,748 (720 ml)

Ripe-apple sweetness gains depth from a gentle but pervasive acidity. Grainy nose. Pulls off the trick of being fresh and full and finishing cleanly. Breadth of flavor is as satisfying as one could wish; toothsome tang is a highlight.

三笑楽酒造株式会社　Sanshō-raku Shuzō Kabushiki-gaisha
富山県東礪波郡平村上梨678　〒939–1914
☎ 0763–66–2010

72. Setchū-bai: Honjōzō

雪中梅：本醸造

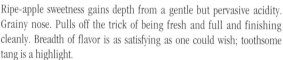

- Grade: *honjōzō* (63%)
- SMV: –3.5
- Acidity: 1.3
- Amino acids: 1.4
- Alcohol: 15.9%
- ¥2,300

Smooth from start to finish. Sweet and seamless, though the finish brings an unexpected, mild dryness. Edgeless, luxurious, and silky on the tongue. Impeccable.

⌂ "Plum in the Snow" brewery suffers from same glut of demand as still more preposterously famous Koshi no Kanbai (also in Niigata). These firms' products are so sought after that their prices suffer an extraordinary inflationary effect. On leaving the brewery, they do the rounds of the middlemen, who pass them on after taking their cut. Consequently, they arrive on many retailers' shelves at several times the starting price. The Japanese fondness for famous names does nobody any favors here.

株式会社丸山酒造場
Kabushiki-gaisha Maruyama Shuzōjō
新潟県中頸城郡三和村大字塔ノ輪617　〒942–02
☎ 0255–32–2603

73. Shichi-fukujin: Junmaishu

七福神：純米酒

- Grade: *junmaishu* (65%)
- SMV: +2.0
- Acidity: 1.7
- Amino acids: 1.6
- Alcohol: 15.2%
- ¥2,050, ¥970 (720 ml)

Low priced but not low on flavor; less fruity than the *ginjō* sakes for which the same No. 9 yeast is widely used, with a nuttier, soft flavor. Splendid value at room temperature or a touch below: its very gentle *shibui* (astringent) note is also flattered by considerate warming.

74. Shichi-fukujin: Daiginjō Tezukuri

七福神：大吟醸てづくり

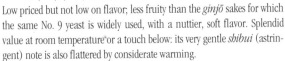

- Grade: *daiginjō* (50%)
- SMV: +6
- Acidity: 1.3
- Amino acids: 1.2
- Alcohol: 15.8%
- ¥3,400 ¥1,750 (720 ml)

From the slight but agreeable nose to the subtle outlines of its flavor, this is a well-bred affair, with enough character to stand up for itself without accompanying food. Dry and tangy elements lead the way, increasingly complemented by a touch of sweetness, a pleasant surprise considering its

+6 SMV. A balanced sake, easy on the palate and the wallet. I am told that the bargain price is a relic; when this product came on the market a long time ago—this firm began selling *ginjō* sake the year I was born—it *was* very high priced, and so raising the price has always seemed rather pushy to its makers. What nice people.

Another point of departure is the label's *two* dates. The more recent is the standard shipping date; the other gives the actual date of production. This excellent practice deserves to be more widely followed. In this case, the sake is aged for two years before shipping, a decision that certainly contributes to the character of the sake, and that the consumer would be unaware of under the normal labeling system.

🏠 "Shichi-fukujin" means the "Seven Lucky Gods," the seven deities of fortune whose depictions are as familiar a sight in Japan as Father Christmas in the West. (Nowadays the latter is also no stranger in Japan, although I have yet to come across him on a sake bottle.)

菊の司酒造株式会社
Kiku no Tsukasa Shuzō Kabushiki-gaisha
岩手県盛岡市紺屋町4–20　〒020–0885
☎ 019–624–1311

T

Tōji

The word *tōji* (杜氏) is widely misused in Japanese. Very often, it is used to mean simply "a brewer (of sake)." However, there are several brewers in a brewery, but only one *tōji*. A better gloss would be "master brewer." The *tōji* is the boss. He plans the brewing schedule, he determines the methods used, and final responsibility for the success or failure of production rests with him. His work requires acute senses, technical knowledge, and a gift for dealing with people, since teamwork is an indispensible ingredient of success in brewing. (I say *he* and *his* because, to the best of my knowledge, there are no female *tōji* as of this writing. I have heard of a woman who has the qualifications, but I was also told that the chief brewer in the company in question is still, as yet, a man. More and more women are taking up positions in breweries, however, so I look forward to being able to revise this entry in the future.)

75. Shige-masu:
Daiginjō, Hako-iri Musume

繁桝：大吟醸、箱入娘

- Grade: *daiginjō* (40%)
- SMV: +5
- Acidity: 1.3
- Amino acids: 1.0
- Alcohol: 17–18%
- ¥3,400 (720 ml)

Aroma is not strong, but the fruity undertone gives an impression of depth. At first straightforward, the dry flavor with complex fruity notes blossoms on the palate. Firm acid, bitter-astringent flavors act lightly on the balance: the final aroma in the nose has a touch of liquorice; plenty of food for thought.

"Hako-iri Musume" translates gruesomely as "Daughter in a Box." The phrase in fact refers to a precious, cosseted daughter.

株式会社高橋商店
Kabushiki-gaisha Takahashi Shōten
福岡県八女市大字本町2–22–1　〒834–0031
☎ 0943–23–5101

76. Shimehari-tsuru: Jun

〆張鶴：純

- Grade: *junmai ginjō* (50%)
- SMV: +3
- Acidity: 1.4
- Amino acids: 1.3
- Alcohol: 15.7%
- ¥2,900, ¥1,450 (720 ml)

Dry, without a trace of harshness, a fine resonant balance of sweetness and translucent acid. Slight vanilla elements to the bouquet. Warms to give a faintly woody feeling. This brewery uses *Gohyakuman-goku*, Niigata Prefecture's standard sake rice, and one of the most widely used in brewing nationwide.

宮尾酒造株式会社
Miyao Shuzō Kabushiki-gaisha
新潟県村上市上片町5–15　〒958–0873
☎ 0254–52–5181

77. Shin-kame: Junmai, Kassei Nigori-zake

神亀：純米、活性にごり酒

- Grade: *junmaishu* (60%)
- SMV: +4 to +7
- Acidity: 1.9
- Amino acids: around 1.2
- Alcohol: 17.0–17.9%
- ¥3,200, ¥1,600 (720 ml), ¥1,150 (500 ml), ¥670 (300 ml)

"Pure rice, active, cloudy sake," says the label, an optician's delight with lots of small print. The first section is a warning: if the sake is stored in a warm place, the cap will shoot off because of the gas produced by the still-living yeast. Next comes an explanation of how to go about opening the bottle. The most important point is not to shake it. Crack the seal with the merest of touches, and you will be rewarded by a "*shoo*"—the sound of the escaping gas. Open the cap in the normal way, and your bottle of sake will seethe and fizz and make a mess of your clothes. Do it right, and you can impress your friends as the sediment (that sat so quietly at the base of the bottle) suddenly erupts to the surface. Fireworks in a bottle, if you like. Sorry, I forgot: the fragrance is a sweet-seeming, candy-floss kind of thing and the flavor, considering the more than 17% alcohol and all that rice floating about, is unexpectedly fine. The impact of the gas—its fizz and its tingle—insists on center stage, bringing bitterness as it attacks the tongue.

⌂ The Shin-kame brewery is famous for making 100% pure rice sake.

神亀酒造株式会社　Shin-kame Shuzō Kabushiki-gaisha
埼玉県蓮田市馬込1978　〒349–0114
☎ 048–768–0115

78. Shira-taki: Jōzen Mizu no Gotoshi

白瀧：上善如水

- Grade: *ginjōshu* (59%)
- SMV: +3
- Acidity: 1.3
- Amino acids: 1.3
- Alcohol: 14–15%
- ¥2,524, ¥1,262 (720 ml), ¥583 (300 ml)

Hugely successful product accounts for almost half of the company's sales. The clear glass bottle and modern feeling of the label and packaging make for instant recognition. Representative of the ultra-light style of the Niigata region, with a spectacular flowery bouquet.

　白瀧酒造株式会社　Shira-taki Shuzō Kabushiki-gaisha
　新潟県南魚沼郡湯沢町大字湯沢2640　〒949–6101
　☎ 0257–84–3443

79. Shi-tennō: Chōshun

四天王：長春

- Grade: *daiginjō* (40%)
- SMV: +5
- Acidity: 1.4
- Amino acids: 1.0
- Alcohol: 16–17%
- ¥6,000, ¥3,000 (720 ml)

Flowery *ginjō* nose conceals an unconventional smoky undertone. Altogether light and fine with a firm finish, astringency at last giving way to final bitter/dry flavors. *Eki-ka jikomi* brewing technology is a relatively new methodology, generally associated with attempts to cut labor costs (by automation). Its use in making *ginjō* is unusual, but clean edges prove its feasibility. This firm also makes a deluxe version of Chōshun, stored in the larger 18-liter bottles reserved for the finest sake until mature, then rebottled in the standard 1.8-liter size and sold at ¥10,000.

　🏠 The characters for the name of the firm mean "Sweet-strong brewery." Shi-tennō (meaning the "Four Emperors") is a reference to the Buddhist guardian deities, one guarding each of the cardinal points of the compass.

　甘強酒造株式会社　Kankyō Shuzō Kabushiki-gaisha
　愛知県海部郡蟹江町大字蟹江本町字海門96番地　〒497–0033
　☎ 0567–95–3131

80. Sui-gei: Junmai Ginrei

酔鯨：純米吟麗

- Grade: *junmai ginjō* (50%)
- SMV: +7
- Acidity: 1.7
- Amino acids: 1.0
- Alcohol: 16.0–16.9%
- ¥2,720, ¥1,650 (720 ml)

Delicate fruity nose has resiny, evergreen edge. Clean, but with plenty of character; light, green-fruity feeling expands to a sharp dry finish, which softens as the sake warms in the glass.

81. Sui-gei: Tokubetsu Junmaishu, Chikuju

酔鯨：特別純米酒、竹寿
- Grade: *junmaishu* (60%)
- SMV: +6.5
- Acidity: 1.5
- Amino acids: 1.2
- Alcohol: 15.0–15.9%
- ¥2,330, ¥970 (720 ml)

Only the barest trace of aroma rising from the glass—followed by an ebullient fragrance in the mouth; the trademark of *aji* (flavor) *ginjō* sake. Crisply dry and light of body, with a delicate acidity and a pleasant astringency. Pure rice sake made from high-grade white rice has *ginjō*-level refinement and clean finish. Overchilling a grave error.

☖ One of my favorite names; "Sui-gei" means "Drunken Whale"! Around sixty percent of the output is *ginjō* class.

酔鯨酒造株式会社　Sui-gei Shuzō Kabushiki-gaisha
高知県高知市長浜566–1　〒781–0270
☎ 0888–41–4080

82. Sumiyoshi (Taruhei): Kin Sumiyoshi

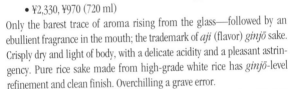

住吉（樽平）：金住吉
- Grade: *junmaishu* (60%)
- SMV: +5
- Acidity: 2.0–2.1
- Amino acids: 1.85–1.95
- Alcohol: 16.1%
- ¥3,107, ¥1,553 (900 ml)

Extraordinarily deep gold color and beefy aroma presages a strong rice flavor which is its dominant feature. A drink to get your teeth into. Richness of flavor is due primarily to aging in barrels made of famous cedar from Yoshino, Nara Prefecture. Idiosyncratic and uncompromising—tends to produce strongly polarized opinions!

☖ Brewery is justly famous for its various *taru-zake*s, all with deep flavor from the keg and unusually high acidity. Some of the most distinctive sakes of all.

樽平酒造株式会社　Taruhei Shuzō Kabushiki-gaisha
山形県東置賜郡川西町中小松2886　〒999−0122
☎ 0238−42−3101

U

Unions

Sake brewers' unions are centered around the home region of their members, taking their name from the old names for their home districts; Izumo for modern-day Shimane Prefecture, Echigo for Niigata, and so on. The Tanba and Tajima groups from Hyōgo Prefecture have long been renowned; the Nanbu union, from Iwate Prefecture, is currently the largest.

Traditional brewing takes place only in the winter. This made it an ideal source of winter income for the fishermen, and, more frequently, farmers of rural Japan, who found their land snowbound and unproductive every winter. For centuries, the men of the fishing and farming villages have left their homes for the brewing season, and each region developed its own prized skills and secrets.

Sadly, though, the present generation of brewers from the old unions may be the last. As the population of rural communities dwindles, agriculture (and, by extension, the sake industry) is facing an acute manpower shortage. The relatively few young people in these regions are no doubt also discouraged by the traditional pattern of winters spent away from home and family, not to mention the long hours and heavy labor that are still facts of life in many small concerns. So, with the average age of *kurabito* nationwide over sixty, and breweries going out of business due to labor problems every year, it seems certain that the industry will continue to face severe challenges in the near future.

83. Suwa Izumi: Daiginjō, Ōtori

諏訪泉：大吟醸、鵬

- Grade: *daiginjō* (40%)
- SMV: +3
- Acidity: 1.4
- Amino acids: 1.2
- Alcohol: 16.5%
- ¥7,402, ¥3,398 (720 ml)

Bouquet is fresh and full but not heavy, with elements of rose hiding amongst fruit. Flavor blossoms sweetly on the palate, harmonizing impeccably with the fine *ginjō-ka*. A delectable tang is followed by a dryish finish, a gentle astringency all the while playing its part in the inimitable balance. Its classic status is no surprise.

84. Suwa Izumi: Junmaishu

諏訪泉：純米酒
- Grade: *junmaishu* (60%)
- SMV: +2.5
- Acidity: 1.6
- Amino acids: 1.3
- Alcohol: 15.3%
- ¥2,136, ¥1,068 (720 ml)

Aroma is a slight but clear rice fragrance. First impression on the palate is straightforward, with a roundness lent by a mild but prominent acidity. Free of the musty character sometimes found in dryer *junmai* sake. Clean, fresh lines harbor tingly astringency and undertones of mushroomlike flavor.

諏訪酒造株式会社　Suwa Shuzō Kabushiki-gaisha
鳥取県八頭郡智頭町大字智頭451　〒689–1402
☎ 0858–75–0618

85. Taki Jiman: Hayase

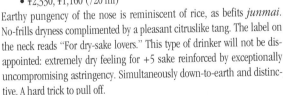

瀧自慢：滝水流（はやせ）
- Grade: *junmaishu* (60%)
- SMV: +5 to +8
- Acidity: 1.5
- Amino acids: 1.2
- Alcohol: 15–16%
- ¥2,330, ¥1,160 (720 ml)

Earthy pungency of the nose is reminiscent of rice, as befits *junmai*. No-frills dryness complimented by a pleasant citruslike tang. The label on the neck reads "For dry-sake lovers." This type of drinker will not be disappointed: extremely dry feeling for +5 sake reinforced by exceptionally uncompromising astringency. Simultaneously down-to-earth and distinctive. A hard trick to pull off.

瀧自慢酒造株式会社　Taki Jiman Shuzō Kabushiki-gaisha
三重県名張市赤目町柏原141　〒518–0464
☎ 0595–63–0488

86. Taki Koi: Junmai Ginjō, Hikami

瀧鯉：純米吟醸、氷上

- Grade: *junmai ginjō* (60%)
- SMV: +2
- Acidity: 1.6
- Amino acids: 1.6
- Alcohol: 15%
- ¥2,667, ¥1,500 (720 ml)

One of those lovely names that bring an extra dimension to drinking sake: *taki* is "waterfall," *koi* is "carp." The flavor is distinguished by a young, green-feeling astringency, in tune with the color—pale yellow, with a greenish cast. One of those pure rice brews that, for me, is so much more approachable around room temperature, rather than straight out of the fridge. The astringency is complemented by a sweetness that smooths the edges and draws out a sharp, spicy note. The name of the product, Hikami, comes from the region of Hyōgo Prefecture where the rice for this sake was organically grown.

⌂ This is a relatively small company in the Nada district, the home of many of the giant makers. "There's *ji-zake* in Nada, too," as they once remonstrated with me.

木村酒造株式会社　Kimura Shuzō Kabushiki-gaisha
神戸市東灘区御影石町1-1-15　〒658-0045
☎ 078-851-0260

87. Tama Ōgi: Junmai Ginjō

玉扇：純米吟醸

- Grade: *junmaishu* (60%)
- SMV: +2
- Acidity: 1.5
- Amino acids: 1.3
- Alcohol: 15–16%
- ¥4,500, ¥2,300 (720 ml)

Made from two rice varieties, classic sake rice *Omachi* and *Shinsenbon*. Rice flavor is supreme from start to finish. Bouquet is also dominated by grainy rice with a touch of fruit, and an unusual undertone, rather ashy in character. Indefatigable rice flavor forms a long finishing partnership with strong acid. Acidity is high, and the result is strong-tasting but surprisingly gentle. Depth and power, but unexpectedly light body makes for a very satisfying, drinkable sake.

Not long after writing this, I was saddened to discover that this brewery in Hiroshima Prefecture had closed its doors. I have left this entry as an example of a sad, ongoing phenomenon: every year sees breweries closing their doors, each of them taking with it a unique flavor that can never be recovered or replicated. R.I.P.

玉扇酒造株式会社　Tama Ōgi Shuzō Kabushiki-gaisha

88. Tateyama: Junmai Ginjō

立山：純米吟醸

- Grade: *junmai ginjō* (58%, 60%)
- SMV: +3.9
- Acidity: 1.3
- Amino acids: ——
- Alcohol: 15.0–15.9%
- ¥3,400

Beefy, dry sake has a clear flavor of rice and a refreshing acid touch. Despite depth of flavor, it goes the distance, never becoming cloying. Elegant enough to please the *ginjō* fan, and solid enough for the pure-rice lover. One of those sakes where the standard 1.8-liter bottle seems just the right size, and one of my wife's top three.

🏠 The official company name is seldom-remembered Ginrei Tateyama, referring to the spectacle of sun reflecting off the snow-covered peak of Tateyama—one of Japan's "Three Great Mountains." The firm has two breweries, supervised by father-and-son *tōji*.

立山酒造株式会社　Tateyama Shuzō Kabushiki-gaisha
富山県砺波市中野220　〒939–1322
☎ 0763–33–3330

89. Tatsu-riki (Daiginjō): Kome no Sasayaki (YK35)

龍力 (大吟醸)：米のささやき

- Grade: *daiginjō* (35%)
- SMV: +4
- Acidity: 1.5
- Amino acids: 0.9
- Alcohol: 17–18%
- ¥10,000, ¥5,000 (720 ml)

Fruity bouquet with a grassy edge. Bitter elements interact well with central acidity, the mark of many Tatsu-riki products. This is a fine, spacious-feeling *ginjō*. The meaning of YK35: Y = *Yamada Nishiki* sake rice, K = the classic No. 9 *ginjō* yeast (originally from Kumamoto Prefecture), 35 = rice polishing ratio of 35%. This formula traditionally accounts for a large portion of gold medal–winning sakes in the annual trade contests (though new yeasts now challenge No. 9's monopoly). Using nothing but premium brewer's rice, this firm aims at nothing less than the title "the Romane Conti of the sake world."

株式会社本田商店　Kabushiki-gaisha Honda Shōten
兵庫県姫路市網干区高田361–1　〒671–1226
☎ 0792–73–0151

90. Tedori-gawa: Meiryū Tedori-gawa, Daiginjō

手取川：名流手取川、大吟醸

- Grade: *daiginjō* (40%)
- SMV: +4 to +5
- Acidity: 1.0–1.2
- Amino acids: 0.8–0.9
- Alcohol: 15–16%
- ¥2,428

Very reasonably-priced *daiginjō*. Some people look at me as if I were blaspheming when I suggest that some *ginjō* sakes taste splendid served warm. This, for me, is one example. Gently warmed, it gains a flattering mellow dimension. Served chilled, it is dry—almost austere—with just a touch of conciliatory sweetness at the finish.

🏠 Brewery takes its name from the nearby river, which also supplies the water used in brewing.

株式会社吉田酒造店　Kabushi-gaisha Yoshida Shuzōten
石川県松任市安吉町41　〒924–0843
☎ 076–276–3311

91. Tengu-mai: Yamahai Shikomi, Junmaishu

天狗舞：山廃仕込、純米酒

- Grade: *junmaishu* (60%)
- SMV: +3
- Acidity: 1.8
- Amino acids: 2.0
- Alcohol: 15.9%
- ¥2,761, ¥1,333 (720 ml)

Pale, grassy color. When chilled, *yamahai* acid and astringent/dry elements are prominent. Rounder and smoother near room temperature. Powerful taste best complemented by fried or oily food, when fatty flavors and the harsher features of the sake melt alchemically into a transfigured softness.

株式会社車多酒造　Kabushiki-gaisha Shata Shuzō
石川県松任市坊丸町60–1　〒924–0823
☎ 076–275–1165

92. Tosa-tsuru: Honjō Karakuchi

土佐鶴：本醸辛口

- Grade: *honjōzo* (65%)
- SMV: +10
- Acidity: 1.4
- Amino acids: 1.2
- Alcohol: 15–16%
- ¥2,041, ¥972 (720 ml), ¥701
  (500 ml), ¥450 (300 ml)

Prominent nose has a fruity, ripe-melon character. Central to flavor is the
+10 dryness, which manages to be simultaneously forceful and mild. First
impression is of a very earthy sake, but the elegance of balance is unexpectedly subtle; acid and astringency lend a depth not always found in
dry sakes. Paper wrapping has a nostalgic feel, but also serves the purpose
of protecting the sake from light.

93. Tosa-tsuru: Ginjōshu Global

土佐鶴：吟醸酒グローバル

- Grade: *daiginjō* (40–50%)
- SMV: +5
- Acidity: 1.3
- Amino acids: 1.0
- Alcohol: 16–17%
- ¥1,943

Looking rather like a brandy bottle, this is, nonetheless, state-of-the-art
Japanese sake. Perhaps "Global" refers to the fact that the date on the bottle is given in both the Western and the Japanese reckoning (by the number of years of the current emperor's reign). Whatever the concept, the
result is a convincing *ginjō*, with a tight, sharp flavor profile, a crisp finish and a pronounced pear-cum-melon nose. A sound low-cost introduction to the pricey world of *ginjō* sake.

Tosa is the old name for Kōchi Prefecture, on the island of Shikoku.
The region is renowned for dry sake and startling drinking games, and is
also known for *bekuhai*, a type of drinking cup that cannot be put down
without draining it, either because of a rounded or conical base, or
because of a hole in the botttom. Need I say more? (*Tsuru* means "crane.")

土佐鶴酒造株式会社　Tosa-tsuru Shuzō Kabushiki-gaisha

高知県安芸郡安田町1586　〒781–6400

☎ 08873–8–6511

94. Tsukasa Botan: Senchū Hassaku

司牡丹：船中八策

- Grade: *junmaishu* (55–60%)
- SMV: +8
- Acidity: 1.4
- Amino acids: 1.2
- Alcohol: 15.0–15.9%
- ¥2,865, ¥1,456 (720 ml)

Crisp and clinical, with a grassy astringency. A retiring sweetness sits quietly behind the dominant dry central theme. A throaty edge culminates in an immaculate clean finish. Instantly recognizable for the chili-pepper red calligraphy of the label. Like Tosa-tsuru, a representative of the Kōchi tradition of dry sake.

司牡丹酒造株式会社　Tsukasa Botan Shuzō Kabushiki-gaisha

高知県高岡郡佐川町甲1299　〒789–1201

☎ 0889–22–1211

Vending machines

The Japanese love gadgets, and vending machines are no exception. At times, there seems to be one on every street corner. Climb Mount Fuji itself, and you will not escape them. From machines around the nation, you can buy beer, soft drinks, eggs, pornography, CDs, batteries, flowers, and, of course, sake. The vending machines that sell alcohol are set to close up shop at 11 P.M., apparently to protect the morals of youth.

However, the alcohol vending machines are to be phased out in a few year's time. This will undoubtedly save a great deal of electricity, though whether it will have an equally redeeming influence on the nation's young people I cannot say. The one group of people on whom it will have a considerable and immmediate effect are the retailers who have come to rely on the machines as an important tool of their trade.

95. Tsuki no Wa: Tokubetsu Junmaishu

月の輪：特別純米酒

- Grade: *junmaishu* (55%)
- SMV: +4
- Acidity: 2.1
- Amino acids: 1.4
- Alcohol: 15.4%
- ¥2,425, ¥1,261 (720 ml)

Unusual herby nose, with a briny tang. Dare I say seaweed? SMV suggests a sweeter sake, but the feeling is dryish with a gentle but determined astringency. Distinguished by a light and limpid acidity. Less noticeable is a certain underfelt sweetness.

🏠 Small brewery endowed with truly lovely buildings that have housed its activities since foundation in 1886. Overall, subtle, intricate, and organic sakes repaying thought.

月の輪酒造店　Tsuki no Wa Shuzōten
岩手県紫波郡紫波町高水寺向畑101　〒028–3303
☎ 019–672–2503

96. Ugo no Tsuki: Dai Ginjō, Nama

雨後の月：大吟醸、生

- Grade: *daiginjō* (40%)
- SMV: +5.5
- Acidity: 1.3
- Amino acids: 1.0
- Alcohol: 17.2%
- ¥6,000, ¥3,000 (720 ml)

The rice is Hiroshima *Omachi*, but there is more fruit than the grassy notes common in *Omachi* sake. The aroma is fruity and spicy. Flavor unfolds quickly on the tongue with that *nama* tingle and a splendid, full, sweet-and-sour complex. As it warms, mild sweetness spreads out, bringing a touch of a sweet strawberry scent. There are some light nutty elements in the middle, and a bitter tingle which lingers on. Excellent.

🏠 Small brewery produces full, soft-flavored sake. What a beautiful name, too: Ugo no Tsuki means "moon after rain."

相原酒造株式会社　Aihara Shuzō Kabushiki-gaisha
広島県呉市仁方本町1–25–15　〒737–0152
☎ 0823–79–5008

97. Ume Nishiki: Taiyō no Ginjō

梅錦：太陽の吟醸

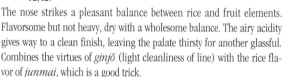

- Grade: *junmai ginjō* (55%, 60%)
- SMV: +3
- Acidity: 1.5
- Amino acids: ——
- Alcohol: 15.3%
- ¥2,427

The nose strikes a pleasant balance between rice and fruit elements. Flavorsome but not heavy, dry with a wholesome balance. The airy acidity gives way to a clean finish, leaving the palate thirsty for another glassful. Combines the virtues of *ginjō* (light cleanliness of line) with the rice flavor of *junmai*, which is a good trick.

梅錦山川株式会社　Ume Nishiki Yamakawa Kabushiki-gaisha
愛媛県川之江市金田町金川14　〒799–0194
☎ 0896–58–1211

Water and wells

Sake is mainly water, so it is obviously a crucial ingredient. The most famous water of all is *Miyamizu*, which occurs naturally only in a tiny part of the Nada region of Hyōgo Prefecture. By an almost miraculous series of favorable geological conditions, the water is ideally suited to brewing. Its amazing qualities were first recognized in the eighteenth century, and it was one of the main factors in the rise of the Nada breweries to dominance. (Around a third of all sake produced in Japan comes out of Nada.)

Formerly, great sakes were born first and foremost of fine water. Nowadays, however, even breweries in regions with iron-heavy water (which is disastrous for brewing) can correct matters by filtration and other treatments, effectively synthesizing *Miyamizu* (rather as British brewers talk about "Burtonizing" water—after the famous brewing town of Burton-on-Trent). Nonetheless, pollution is an increasingly severe problem. More and more manufacturers are choosing a supply of filtered water. Even if the company's well currently supplies wonderful water (as it may have done for generations), the sad fact is that the danger of pollution is ever-present.

98. Ume no Yado: Daiginjō, Omachi

梅乃宿：大吟醸、雄町

- Grade: *daiginjō* (40%)
- SMV: +4
- Acidity: 1.4
- Amino acids: 1.1
- Alcohol: 16.2%
- ¥6,000, ¥3,000 (720 ml)

When I first started drinking sake, I soon learned to love Ume no Yado as a sake that didn't cloy, with new and complex flavors unfolding in shifting combinations over the course of a bottle. Even after seven years of brewing the stuff, I still think this is our *daiginjō*'s greatest strength. This *Omachi* version (we also have a sister product made from *Yamada Nishiki* rice) is a quite unconventional *ginjō*—the standard, fruity *ginjō-ka* subsumed by the grassy, herbal characteristics deriving from the *Omachi* rice variety. Takes at least a couple of glasses to get the measure of; overchilling guaranteed to spoil the fun.

99. Ume no Yado: Honjōzō

梅乃宿：本醸造

- Grade: *honjōzō* (60%)
- SMV: +4
- Acidity: 1.4
- Amino acids: 1.2
- Alcohol: 15.5%
- ¥1,700

Perfectly acceptable cold, but thorough research by the author has shown this to be best appreciated warmed (preferably at the end of a long working day in a cold sake brewery in midwinter). Hot, it is racy with fierce dry edge; warm, a glowing sweetness soothes and coddles weary body and soul. Aged two years and more before sale, giving a mellow roundness to the flavor.

Since no one would believe protestations of objectivity, I won't make any. This is where I work, and the products of the sweat of my brow taste pretty good to me. Considering our methodology and the high grade of raw materials used, our range is a bargain.

🏠 The name comes from a spectacularly gnarled and twisted plum tree (*ume*) in the boss's garden, said to be almost three hundred years old. This was visited intermittently by a bush warbler, rather in the fashion of an inn—*yado*.

梅乃宿酒造株式会社　Ume no Yado Shuzō Kabushiki-gaisha
奈良県北葛城郡新庄町東室27　〒639–2102
☎ 0745–69–2121

100. Ura-gasumi: Karakuchi

浦霞：辛口

- Grade: *honjōzō* (65%)
- SMV: +5
- Acidity: 1.3
- Amino acids: 1.3
- Alcohol: 15.4%
- ¥2,140

Karakuchi is "dry," and the taste is as free of frills and fanfare as the name. Masterful economy of line: dry is dry, but smooth is smoother, a certain bitterness asserting itself within the flawless balance. With its understated class, it is one for the drinker, not the taster, and excellent value.

🏠 Miyagi Prefecture's Ura-gasumi is well known to sake connoisseurs for its famous *ginjō*, Zen, and a range of charismatic sakes. It is also one of the elite group of *kura* that can claim to be the birthplace of one of the Association yeasts. In 1966, No. 12, isolated from Ura-gasumi *ginjō*, went on sale as the last of the Association yeasts to derive from a specific brewery.

株式会社佐浦　Kabushiki-gaisha Saura
宮城県塩釜市本町2–19　〒985–0052
☎ 022–362–4165

101. Waka Ebisu: Gizaemon

若戎：義左衛門

- Grade: *junmai ginjō* (60%)
- SMV: +3
- Acidity: 1.5
- Amino acids: 1.4
- Alcohol: 15.8%
- ¥2,330, ¥1,160, ¥275 (180 ml)

Rounded balance of the five flavors, the unostentatious *ginjō* nose, and smooth body combine in a drinkable sake without edges. Good example of the *aji ginjō* ("flavor *ginjō*") type, where emphasis is on harmony and depth of flavor rather than the spectacular, flowery *ginjō* bouquet. Also fine lightly warmed. Mellow, mellow.

102. Waka Ebisu: Kanjukushu

若戎：完熟酒

- Grade: *junmaishu*
- SMV: +3
- Acidity: 1.5
- Amino acids: 1.4
- Alcohol: 15.8%
- ¥2,620, ¥1,285 (720 ml)

Yamahai sake aged for twelve months before shipping; has an evergreen sharpness to its aroma. First dry and rather harsh impression gives way to a complex acidulous middle. The tail has a faint sweet quality, similar to very ripe fruit.

合名会社重藤酒造場

Gōmei-gaisha Shigefuji Shuzōjō

三重県名賀郡青山町阿保1317

〒518–0226

☎ 0595–52–1153

X

Xeixu, *xinxu*, and *xochu* may look like Chinese place names, but are in fact sake-related terms. They are, respectively, renderings of the Japanese words *seishu*, *shinshu*, and *shōchū*—whose meanings the interested may discover elsewhere in these pages. They come from a Japanese-Portuguese dictionary published in 1603, a pioneering work of such importance that it was translated into other languages for the use of scholars as late as the 1860s. It contains a quantity of information about sake brewing that speaks volumes for its thoroughness.

Apart from the "X-words" above, terms in the seventeenth-century volume that the reader will also find in the present book include *coxu* (*koshu*), *coji* (*kōji*), *moto*, *moromi*, and *casu* (*kasu*). The modern reader is hard-pressed to find such a depth of information (a problem *The Insider's Guide* seeks to correct). The dictionary is also of importance to scholars of sake history, for whom it is a prized source of information in a period otherwise poorly documented.

103. Wakatake-ya Denbei:
Fuku-iku Genroku no Sake

若竹屋伝兵衛：馥郁元禄之酒

- Grade: *junmaishu* (85%)
- SMV: −30
- Acidity: 3.0
- Amino acids: 4.0
- Alcohol: 17.5%
- ¥3,500, ¥1,600 (720 ml)

Extraordinary sake reportedly made according to methods recorded in documents dating to the Genroku period (1688–1704). Color is the same dark brown as the bottle! Thick, almost treacly texture gives a creamy/oily feel on the tongue. The chocolaty aroma has its counterpart in the flavor, a dark chocolate with sour notes. Not as colossally sweet-tasting as its startling SMV suggests; altogether unusual.

合資会社若竹屋酒造場

Gōshi-gaisha Wakatake-ya Shuzōba

福岡県浮羽郡田主丸町大字田主丸706–1　〒839–1233

☎ 09437–2–2175

104. Waka-tsuru (Hisui Waka-tsuru): Kijōshu

若鶴(翡翠若鶴)：貴醸酒

- Grade: *kijōshu* (70%)
- SMV: −44
- Acidity: 3.0
- Amino acids: 2.7
- Alcohol: 16–17%
- ¥3,000 (720 ml)

Relatively translucent rust color. The aromas are bitter cocoa and chocolate, with pungent sour cherry and unripe plum, a suggestion of a fresher, citrus tang, and a whiff of ammonia. The liquor is slick on the tongue, but less oily than many *kijōshu*. The sweet chocolate/caramel of the flavor join with a surprisingly sharp tang and a fresh, almost green quality. Chocolate flavors linger longest.

若鶴酒造株式会社

Waka-tsuru Shuzō Kabushiki-gaisha

富山県砺波市三郎丸208　〒939–1308

☎ 0763–32–3032　Fax 0763–32–1251

Yeast

In days past, the yeast used in sake brewing was of the kind known in Japanese as *ie tsuki kōbo*—"house yeast," if you like. Natural yeasts found in the air and growing on the timbers of the building were used to convert sugars in the mash into alcohol. The problem with this hit-and-miss method is that there are good yeasts and bad, and there was no way of guaranteeing a safe fermentation. In 1906, the Japanese Brewer's Association began to sell pure yeast cultures. The first of these were isolated from prize-winning breweries' *moromi*. Later on, strains developed with the aid of new biotechnological techniques were added to the roster. Nowadays, the Japanese Brewer's Association continues to market high-quality pure yeast strains, and these are extremely widely used. The most popular strains are Association No. 7, and, for high-grade *ginjō* sakes, Association No. 9, though brewers in northerly areas frequently prefer No. 10. A *ginjō* yeast from Akita became the latest addition to the Association's portfolio (as No. 15) in 1996.

Recent years have seen the growing use of other yeast varieties apart from the Association's standard range. Some prefectures have developed their own regional speciality, of which Nagano and Shizuoka are perhaps the best-known examples. Some firms use strains developed in their own laboratories.

One of the most important developments in this area has been the popularization of strains which do not produce foam (which is described on page 49). This means that brewers are spared the time-consuming task of cleaning the remains of the foam off the walls of the tank after it recedes. It also allows the producer to increase the size of each batch by around a third—the amount of space otherwise taken up by the foam at its peak. The non-foam (*awa-nashi*) Association strains are designated with 01 after the number of its parent. So the foam-free version of No. 9 is No. 901, of No. 10, 1001, and so on.

The importance of a good yeast cannot be overestimated. Every yeast strain has a particular character, both in terms of the taste and flavor of the sake, and in its behavior during fermentation. The fragrance of sake is strongly affected by the choice of yeast. Research into new strains proceeds apace and is likely to provide provocative developments in coming years.

105. Yama-tsuru: Ori-zake

山鶴：おり酒

- Grade: *junmaishu* (55%)
- SMV: +3
- Acidity: 1.5
- Amino acids: 1.4
- Alcohol: 15.5%
- ¥2,800, ¥1,300 (720 ml)

Relatively few companies sell *ori-zake* with its fine sediment. Naturally, the flavor peculiar to *moromi* (sake before pressing) is obvious. People tend to love it or hate it. This example has the soft, fat, full flavor common in sake made by *tōji* from Hyōgo's Tajima region.

106. Yama-tsuru: Junmai Ginjō, Nama-zake

山鶴：純米吟醸、生酒

- Grade: *junmai ginjō* (55%)
- SMV: +3
- Acidity: 1.5
- Amino acids: 1.5
- Alcohol: 16.5%
- ¥570 (300 ml)

The typical *kōjibana* flavor of *nama* is exceptionally prominent, as is true of much of this firm's sake, unpasteurized and otherwise. The taste is full, soft, and round, with a deep, pungent sweetness.

⌂ "Mountain Crane" brewery is a very small scale *kura*. Brewing takes place in highly compact, state-of-the-art buildings designed by architect and sake lover Jirō Shinoda.

中本酒造株式会社　Nakamoto Shuzō Kabushiki-gaisha
奈良県生駒市上町1067　〒630–0131
☎ 0743–78–0005

107. Yorokobi no Izumi: Kyokuchi (Omachi) Nama

歓の泉：極至（雄町）生

- Grade: *daiginjō* (40%)
- SMV: +5
- Acidity: 1.4
- Amino acids: 0.8
- Alcohol: 17.3%
- ¥6,800, ¥2,910 (720 ml)

Complex herbal/fruity bouquet sets the tone. Luxurious fullness of flavor with all the subtle range of the organic, grassy herbal tones *Omachi* rice offers. "Kyokuchi" means "zenith"; *Omachi* fans will certainly agree. Sister product is made from prize *Yamada Nishiki* rice. Still more luxurious is Kiwami Naka-gumi, truly the cream of the cream.

108. Yorokobi no Izumi:
Asahi, Junmai Ginjō, Nama

歓の泉：朝日、純米吟醸、生

- Grade: *junmaishu* (55%)
- SMV: +3
- Acidity: 1.2
- Amino acids: 1.0–1.1
- Alcohol: 15.5%
- ¥ 2,430, ¥1,270 (720 ml)

Rather high percentage of alcohol gives a richness of flavor as backdrop. Bouquet is fruity with a citrus bite and a nutty overtone. Taste is much more assertive than retiring nose. Appropriately elegant *ginjō* balance, with all five flavors robustly present and correct. Dryness/bitterness perhaps outlast the rest, but the center of the flavor is its fruity character, with depth to hold the interest.

中田酒造有限会社
Nakada Shuzō Yūgen-gaisha
岡山県倉敷市呼松町888　〒712–8053
☎ 086–455–8601

109. Yuki no Matsushima:
Chō-kara

雪の松島：超辛

- Grade: *honjōzō* (60%)
- SMV: +20
- Acidity: 1.6
- Amino acids: 1.4
- Alcohol: 18.2%
- ¥2,427

Claims to be Japan's driest sake. Chilled, it certainly feels it—searing dryness fading to a ricey aftertaste on the palate and in the nose. This said, the first touch on the palate is unexpectedly sweet. Mysteriously mellow as it approaches room temperature. Pale straw color. As it warms still further, a strong astringent note joins with re-emerging dryness.

🏠 Matsushima ("Pine Island") is one of Japan's most famous beauty spots. The firm boasts a selection of unusually dry brews; also markets a *daiginjō* confidently named "Excellent."

宮城酒類株式会社　Miyagi Shurui Kabushiki-gaisha
宮城県仙台市泉区明通3–8　〒981–3206
☎ 022–378–7532

Z

Zymotic

Splendid word, isn't it, "zymotic"? Right up there with "oxymoron" and "tintinnabulous." It means "of, by, or referring to fermentation," gives me a "Z-word," and provides a chance to describe "multiple parallel fermentation," a highly unusual feature of the chemistry of sake brewing.

The simplest way of obtaining alcohol (outside of popping a few coins into a vending machine) is the method used in making wine. Natural sugar (glucose) in the grape is converted by yeast (which is also found naturally on fruit) directly into alcohol and carbon dioxide, a pattern known as "simple fermentation."

The case of brewing beer is more difficult since there are no simple sugars in the barley grains used. In the process called malting, enzymes convert starch in the grain into sugars. This is known as saccharification, and is hard to say when drunk. Once the malting process is finished (to cut a long story very short), then yeast is added, and the conversion of sugar to alcohol takes place. This process of two consecutive stages is called multiple fermentation.

Rice, like barley, contains no sugar. The key to sake making is the conversion of starch in the rice grain to sugar by a mold (*Aspergillus oryzae*). This is known as *kōji*. The remarkable part is that both the conversion of starch to sugar and of sugar to alcohol take place simultaneously in the fermenting mash. This unique balancing act is called multiple parallel fermentation, which is at least as difficult to say as saccharification. It is still easier said than done, however. The brewer must maintain the mash in a condition suitable for both the needs of the yeast *and* saccharification, a feat of bio-chemical acrobatics that leaves little leeway for incidental concerns like days off or sleep.

This highly unusual pattern of fermentation is also why it is possible for the *tōji* alone, of the world's brewers, to make a beverage of around 20% alcohol by fermentation. Imagine the sugar that the yeast has converted into alcohol: if this were all present in the mash from the beginning, the yeast's metabolic functions would be suppressed, and it would be impossible for fermentation to proceed. In rice mash, however, the enzymes from the *kōji* convert starch into sugar little by little over the twenty days (or even a month or more) of the fermentation, giving the yeast a steady supply of nutrition—from which the yeast all the while gradually produces alcohol. Any number of problems can derail this delicately balanced process. For example, if the steamed rice is too soft, the enzymes from the *kōji* turn starch into sugar faster than the yeast can consume it. In this case, the brewer will be left with a batch of unexpectedly sweet sake, since the yeast's activity will be stifled too quickly, leaving a residue of unfermented sugars. In the opposite case (very hard steamed rice) the yeast will use up the little available sugar in no time, and the resulting sake is likely to be excessively dry. The brewer's skill in handling this balance is the crucial factor in making a successful sake.

III

SAKE AT
THE SOURCE

7

Izakaya Bars and Restaurants in Japan

O ne sign of a serious sake establishment is how they treat their supply: stock should be kept refrigerated and away from strong light. An additional headache for restaurateurs is looking after open bottles. Like wine, sake oxidizes once exposed to the air, so conscientious places do their best to avoid the accumulation of half-empty bottles. This is sometimes a problem where the shop has a bigger selection than they can really care for effectively—not solely a question of numbers, but also of turnover. It's a sad thing to fork out the hard-earned, only to find yourself drinking sake that saw its finest hour days or weeks ago.

Life and funds being short, I have not, unfortunately, been able to do a nationwide survey of places to drink and buy sake. I first got mixed up with sake in Osaka, and Osaka and the Kansai area are the best represented as a result. Occasional forays to Tokyo allowed me to sample what the capital has to offer, so I am able to share a few recommendations there. As for the rest of the country, I'm afraid I have very little first-hand drinking experience to draw on, so bar/restaurant entries are correspondingly scarce. Those who live in regions with no relevant entries should refer to the section on retailers, which is slightly more comprehensive, geographically speaking. Retailers will usually be happy to point you in the direction of a bar or restaurant offering good sake.

A listing in brackets after the name of the place in question is the speciality of the establishment. For example: Honmakai (sushi) would be a listing for the sushi shop Honmakai. Where no comment is made, the shop is an *izakaya*, a term that encompasses cozy drinking establishments where food, beverages, and conversation are dolled out in equally appealing portions. Those readers with experience of Japanese nightlife, however brief, will already be familiar with them.

My focus on sake exacerbates the inevitably thorny question of how to rate the cost of the victuals. In places with a wide selection, prices may start at a few hundred yen per glass, and go right on up to several thousand yen for the same measure. As a result, the price guidelines offered are, necessarily, only the roughest of rough estimates. I have envisioned an evening out with a light meal and two or three *go* (360–540 milliliters) of quality sake. The rare places that offer sound sake at such a price that ¥3,000 per person will see you through all but the most immoderate session are marked with a single yen sign (¥). Top of the range establishments—where ¥10,000 per head or under is probably only possible if you're a dieting teetotaler—rate ¥¥¥¥.

Price ratings for bars and restaurants

¥ — Cheap, and, if you're lucky, cheerful. ¥3,000 per head certainly possible.

¥¥ — Around ¥5,000 a throw.

¥¥¥ — May reach five figures.

¥¥¥¥ — Go out to blow out.

■ MAJOR CITIES

KOBE

Espoir Hiraoka (retailer/*tachi-nomiya*)   エヌポワ　ヒラオカ

The Hiraokas run a little *tachi-nomiya* a minute's walk from their shop in Kōbe's Honmachi, mercifully spared by the Great Hanshin Earthquake that devastated the city in 1995. One of those rare places where you can enjoy *ginjō* sake at downtown prices.

> 5–2–15 Motomachi-dōri, Chūō-ku, Kobe 650–0022
> 神戸市中央区元町通5–2–15　〒650–0022
> ☎ 078–341–2563
> 5–9 P.M., closed Sundays
> NEAREST STATION: Nishi Motomachi, Hanshin line
> ¥

Ginjō (*tachi-nomiya*)   吟醸

At the time of writing, this is a *tachi-nomiya* (a shop to stand and drink at the counter) by west exit No. 1 of the Nagata subway station, housed in a temporary-looking, prefab kind of affair. In its pre-earthquake incarnation, this was a top class *izakaya* with shrinelike status amongst many Kansai sake lovers and brewers. Ginjō was maturing, promoting, and selling *ginjō* sake way before most people had even heard of it. For the moment, you can drink 180 milliliters of top-class *daiginjō* for ¥1,000. Lower grades start at ¥350 per glass. This is surely too good to last.

Wakore Nagata Sogo Bldg., 7F, 7–27 Yonban-chō, Nagata-ku, Kobe 653–0003

神戸市長田区四番町7–27 ワコーレ長田相互ビル1階　〒653–0003

☎ 078–579–3275

4:30–9:30 P.M., closed Sundays and holidays

NEAREST STATION: Nagata, Yamate subway line

¥

KYOTO

Aburachō　油長

Primarily a retailer, but concealing a little counter—space for about a dozen customers—in its airy interior. Here, if you have the stamina, you may sample the pride of every brewery in Fushimi—about two dozen makers in all. Simple food selections are also available. You may either select three sakes yourself, or choose one of the sets designed by the management. Your order is served in baby tasting cups, complete with blue "snake's eye" rings in the bottom, delivered on a wooden palette. The various sets come with a theme: you can compare sakes made from three different varieties of sake rice, or three different grades, for example. They start from ¥600.

780 Higashi-ōte-chō, Fushimi-ku, Kyoto 612–8053

伏見区東大手町780　〒612–8053

☎ 075–601–0147, fax 075–621–5050

10 A.M.–10 P.M. (last order 9:30 P.M.), closed Tuesdays

NEAREST STATION: Fushimi-Momoyama, Keihan line, Momoyama Goryō-mae, Kintetsu line

¥

Daigen (retailer/*tachi-nomiya*)　大源

Next to the counter in this charming family-run sake shop hang *noren* curtains. They announce the existence of a little *tachi-nomiya* (a shop with a counter to stand and drink at). For a few hundred yen you can buy a glass of sake, or some nuts or dried squid, or any of the other snacks beloved of Japanese drinkers. This particular shop is unusual, first, for its architectural beauty (the long counter is set in a narrow room with an extraordinarily high ceiling, the space scored by rough-hewn timber beams that are one of the glories of old Japanese houses), and secondly for offering its lucky customers a rare chance to taste fine sake—all the way to *ginjō* level—at *tachi-nomiya* prices. (Starting from ¥300, and with *ginjō* class sake for ¥500 for 180 milliliters.) I wish it were in my neighborhood.

18 Nishi-kawa-chō, Nishi-kyōgoku, Ukyō-ku, Kyoto 615–0852

右京区西京極西川町18　〒615–0852

☎ 075–313–0273

6–9 P.M., closed Sundays

NEAREST STATION: Nishi-Kyōgoku, Hankyū line

¥

Deai Jaya Osen　　出逢ひ茶屋 おせん

Food is in the classic Kyoto *o-banzai* style. (This has nothing to do with the "three cheers" war cry—which literally means "ten thousand years," incidentally.) It denotes a choice of fresh home-cooked dishes, presented in a mouthwatering display on the counter before you. Sake starts from an approachable ¥600 per glass; about a dozen varieties await your attention in the refrigerated coolers behind the counter. Apart from the prepared food of the day, there is a repertoire of other dishes cooked to order; the tempura is excellent.

Kaburenjō Kita, Ponto-chō, Nakagyō-ku, Kyoto 604–8002

中京区先斗町歌舞練場北　〒604–8002

☎ 075–231–1313

5–11 P.M., closed Wednesdays

NEAREST STATION: Sanjō, Keihan line

¥¥

Suginoko Tei　　すぎのこ亭

Handily situated near Sanjō Ōhashi. The business card advertises *ji-zake* and *maboroshi no shōchū*. *Maboroshi* means a dream, and is a favorite word in the vocabulary of Japanese sales people. The Japanese seem to be more prone than most to the mystique of the rare—and therefore sought-after. Persuade the consumer that your product—sake, *shōchū* spirit, whatever—is a dream, a mirage, a rarity, and your fortune is made. Which is not to knock this establishment, which offers a wide range of sake and *shōchū*, good examples of which are not so common in this part of Japan; drinkable dreams, at a most reasonable price.

Takata Building, 1F, 105 Nakajima-chō, Kawaramachi-dōri, Sanjō Higashi-iru, Nakagyō-ku, Kyoto 604–8004

河原町通三条東入中島町105タカタビル1階　〒604–8004

☎ 075–255–0050

5–11 P.M., closed first and third Sundays

NEAREST STATION: Sanjō, Keihan line

¥¥

Suikō 酔香

Take off your shoes to go in, and relax with an unsurpassed range of carefully tended sakes—and fine food. A few minutes' walk away is Matsuo Shrine, where the resident deity is none other than the god of sake. The 130-plus varieties of sake are kept to a standard that is a credit to the shadow of Matsuo-sama. Many of the offerings are unique to Suikō, personally selected by owner Horii-san on his perennial wanderings around Japan's breweries. Many more have been lovingly matured in-house before they reach the customer. Sake from ¥600 (180 milliliter) upwards. Food includes *yakitori* (two skewers for ¥300), ¥700 *somen* noodles, *sashimi* starting at ¥1,000, and much else according to the season and the particular offerings of the day. Though certainly not a cheap evening out, food and drink of this quality at this price is a first-class bargain. The management ask customers not to come wearing strong perfume, as it obstructs the clientele's enjoyment of the fragrant sakes on offer. Those weary of sake (is such a thing possible?) will find a fine selection of predominantly German wines. Horii-san is also a wine enthusiast—or is "fanatic" the word I'm looking for?

Silk Coat Arashiyama 1F, 14–4 Yakushi Shita-chō, Arashiyama, Nishikyō-ku, Kyoto 616–0026

西京区嵐山薬師下町14–4シルクコート嵐山1階　〒616–0026

☎ 075–864–0505, fax 075–864–0607

6 P.M.–2 A.M. (last order), closed Mondays

NEAREST STATION: Matsuo, Hankyū line

¥¥¥

Tanba 居酒屋 たんば

This is a smallish *izakaya* in the Fushimi brewing district. The homey, Japanese-style interior is a clutter of knicknacks, Buddha figurines, kites, boxes and bottles, pottery, and endless sake labels. There is also a quantity of sumo paraphernalia. The menu is good, fresh, inexpensive *izakaya* fare: *yakitori*, sashimi, deep-fried blowfish, clams cooked in sake, and so on. The sake list comprises a couple of dozen famous names, mainly priced at a very affordable ¥450 per glass. For ¥1,000, you can try the *o-tameshi* set: small glasses of three contrasting types of sake to compare.

3–475, Shinmachi, Fushimi-ku, Kyoto 612–8041

伏見区新町3–475　〒612–8041

☎ 075–621–0971

5 P.M.–midnight, closed Thursdays

NEAREST STATION: Fushimi-momoyama, Keihan line

¥½

Udatsu-ya　うだつ屋

Charmingly situated in an old-fashioned converted dwelling. The interior is in the same mode, and the Mama-san presides in kimono. The atmosphere has that particular intimacy which female proprietors of *izakaya* are so skillful at engendering. The music is, unexpectedly, jazz, which is somehow very refreshing in such extremely Japanese surroundings. The focus of the food is *oden*, that versatile hot pot which can be a rough or ready standby in a laborer's bar, or an elegant dish of subtle flavors, as the occasion demands. Here it is available in its upmarket manifestation, from ¥300 a piece. Homemade spring rolls, shrimp balls, and a number of other dishes are also available. Sake is served in glass decanters, 180 milliliters at a time, averaging about ¥1,000. Sometimes establishments offering this kind of atmosphere can prove a shock to the wallet; this is a good place to enjoy the charm without leaving a pound of flesh lighter—maybe just an ounce or two.

> Shinmachi-kami, Kitayama, Kita-ku, Kyoto 603–8105
> 北区北山新町上　〒603–8105
> ☎ 075–493–3935
> 6 P.M.–midnight, closed Sundays and holidays
> NEAREST STATION: Kitaōji or Kitayama, Karasuma subway line
> ¥¥½

NAGOYA

Romantei　浪漫亭

The large urnlike structures inside the restaurant are modeled on a *kamado*, the traditional Japanese cooking area with large cast iron pots set in an earthen or store hearth. Food here is prepared out back in more contemporary surroundings, but the *kamaba* does have a role to play. Don't be surprised when the lights go down and drums and gongs ring out in the gloom. You are about to be treated to an indoor fireworks display on a scale which is quite alarming given the size of the room. (Every evening at 7 and 9.) Excellent sake and food are good value for money, as the enthusiastic and youthful clientele attests.

> Ark Building, B1F, 3–22–7 Nishiki, Naka-ku, Nagoya-shi 460–0003
> 中区錦3–22–7　アークビル地下1階　〒460–0003
> ☎ 052–961–7622, fax 052–961–1480
> 5 P.M.–midnight (Fridays and Saturdays to 1 A.M., holidays to 11 P.M.), closed Sundays
> NEAREST STATION: Sakae, Higashama subway Line
> ¥¥

OSAKA

Ajikatsu 味勝

Cheerful place with a voluble clientele of homeward-bound businessmen, where I spent many a happy hour over many a fine glass of sake when I still lived in the big city. Sake starts from ¥500 a glass.

2–14–18 Kyōmachibori, Nishi-ku, Osaka 550–0003

西区京町堀2–14–18 〒550–0003

☎ 06–6445–8103

5–10 P.M., closed Saturdays, Sundays, holidays

NEAREST STATION: Awaza, Sennichi-mae subway line or Chūō line

¥¥

Ebisu-ya えびす屋

Set in the back streets behind Midōsuji, Osaka's arterial thoroughfare, Ebisu-ya has a hard-core clientele of salarymen since almost no one actually lives in the area. Early in the evening, it's about as lively as a night-watchman's lunchbreak; later on, it is boisterously busy, though where the switch happens I can never quite pinpoint. No one gets out sober. Fresh fish dishes (not all raw) a specialty.

4–6–15 Hiranomachi Chūō-ku, Osaka 541–0046

中央区平野町4–6–15 〒541–0046

☎ 06–6203–4003

11:30 A.M.–1:30 P.M., 5–10:30 P.M., closed Sunday, holidays

NEAREST STATION: Honmachi, Midōsuji subway line

¥¥

Fuji (*okonomiyaki*) ふじ

Okonomiyaki, yakisoba, and a variety of other dishes, all cooked on the metal grill in front of the customer. Not a vast number of brands here, but tastefully selected. Also open for lunch. The location of the shop makes it ideal for the restoration of spirits of those demoralized by a visit to the Osaka Immigration office, five minutes' walk away.

1–2–9 Uchi-hirano-chō, Chūō-ku, Osaka 540–0037

中央区内平野町1–2–9 〒540–0037

☎ 06–6941–9801

11:30 A.M.–2 P.M., 5:30–11 P.M., (Saturdays 6–11 P.M.), closed Sundays, holidays

NEAREST STATION: Tenmabashi, Tanimachi subway line

¥¥

Ji-zake Tengoku Shōya   地酒天国 翔家 (阿部野店)

To call a bar a "sake paradise" (*tengoku*) might seem fanciful, but consider that the wonderful, seedy Osaka arcade in which it is situated glories in the name "Abeno Ginza," and a touch of hyperbole seems only fitting. Large, but not impersonal. A helpful sake menu features pictures of offerings, numbering over a hundred. A welcome (but unusual) touch is a selection of *koshu,* highly aged sake. They have another branch in Nanba.

Meigaza Building, Abeno Ginza-dōri, 1F, 1–7–47 Abenosuji,

Abeno-ku, Osaka 545–0052

阿倍野区阿倍野筋1–7–47あべの銀座通り名画座ビル1階

〒545–0052

☎ 06–6633–1474, fax 06–6633–1498

4:30–11 P.M. (Sundays and holidays to 10:30 P.M.)

NEAREST STATION: Tennōji, JR, Kintetsu, and various subway lines

¥

Mugitarō   麦太郎

Lurking next to a pachinko parlor around a corner from the self-consciously cute "Edo no Machi." (In the basement of the D • D House building, this is an olde worlde affair, with nice fountains and things.) There are maps posted here and there, but I always need at least two circuits before finding the place. Among the sixty thoughtfully-chosen sakes, familiar labels are to be seen, but a number of rare finds are usually lurking. Wide range of prices (from ¥500 a glass) is reassuring. Mugitarō has been serving fine sake for over fifteen years.

D • D House, B1F, 1–8–1 Shibata, Kita-ku, Osaka 530–0012

北区芝田1–8–1　D.Dハウス地下1階　〒530–0012

☎ 06–6376–2828

5–11:30 P.M., closed third Monday

NEAREST STATION: Umeda, Hankyū line and various subway lines

¥¥

Tanbaya   丹波屋

This shop fills like magic around six as everyone piles in on their way home from work to stoke up on good food—and sake of a quality all too rarely found in workaday *izakaya* like this. Classic drinking snacks like crab brains (*kani miso*) and salt pickled thingummies (*shio kara*) are good and cheap here. Sake starts from the ¥300 range (per glass). Aside from the brands advertised on the walls, the Master (Yamamoto-san) has lots and lots of goodies tucked away in his coolers.

1–1–40 Shikanjima, Konohana-ku, Osaka 554–0014

此花区四貫島1–1–40　〒554–0014
☎ 06–6461–6675, fax 06–6463–4026
4–11 P.M., closed Thursdays and third Wednesday
NEAREST STATION: Chidoribashi, Hanshin line
¥

Tōmorokoshi (*teppanyaki*, iron-plate grill)　とうもろこし

About 150 kinds of *ji-zake*. The rather unusual mood of the decor suggests a café more than a pub. An original and extensive menu includes several cheese-heavy items for those suffering from withdrawal symptoms. Regulars can keep a personal copy of the sake menu to remember what they have drunk. Prices are not displayed, so it's wise to check to avoid unpleasant surprises. Master Suchi-san is a workaholic, and stays open until the last customer gives up. I did most of my early, revelationary drinking here.

1–14–15 Takakura-chō, Miyakojima-ku, Osaka 534–0011
都島区高倉町1–14–15　〒534–0011
☎ 06–6924–3612, fax 06–6927–9789
6 P.M.–2 A.M
NEAREST STATION: Miyakojima, Tanimachi subway line
¥¥

Toriten (*yakitori*)　鳥てん

Cunningly designed to confuse the inebriated by being in multiple locations. All the branches are in the "Hi Hi Town" complex, across the road from Kintetsu Station/Department Store. This sake is mainly *honjōzō*, *junmai* class (which keeps costs down), though higher grades are also represented. Usual range of *izakaya* dishes.

6–3–31 Uehonmachi, Tennōji-ku, Osaka 546–0001
天王寺区上本町6–3–31　〒546–0001
☎ 06–6773–3827 (main branch), ☎ 06–6773–6522 (south branch, tel/fax)
3–10:30 P.M. (last order 9:50 P.M.), closed second Monday
NEAREST STATION: Tanimachi 9-chōme, Sennichi-mae and Tanimachi subway lines; Uehonmachi, Kintetsu line
¥

Uchōten (*yakitori*)　宇鳥天 西天満店

Very unassuming little shop, tucked away in the business district of Nishitenma. All the good things that this deceptively simple style of food offers, and a selection of sake which is sound without being dull, starting from ¥450 per glass.

5–15–14 Nishitenma, Kita-ku, Osaka 530–0047

北区西天満5–15–14　〒530–0047

☎ 06–6315–8594

5–11 P.M., closed Sundays, holidays

NEAREST STATION: Higashi-Umeda or Minami-morimachi,
Tanimachi subway line

¥

Yamasan (*oden*)　　山三 ミナミ店

Don't judge a sake by the label, or an *izakaya* by the shop front.
Disguised as a cheap *râmen* noodle shop lurking in the shadows of the
Kabuki Theater, Yamasan is a cheerful, hectic *nomiya* with a thought-
provoking selection of exceptional sakes chosen by the boss, a qualified
sake taster and recipient of honors in a number of sake-tasting contests.
Small and bustling; not for large groups (i.e., more than two or three
people).

4–2–9 Nanba, Chūō-ku, Osaka 542–0076

中央区難波4–2–9　〒542–0076

☎ 06–6643–6623

5:30 P.M.–midnight, closed Sundays, holidays

NEAREST STATION: Nanba, various subway lines

¥

TOKYO

Aka Oni　　銘酒居酒屋 赤鬼

This area, five minutes from Sangenjaya Station, is a welter of *izakaya*,
Japanese-style "snacks," and watering holes of every description. It is a
district that retains something of the flavor of the old days, with its narrow
streets, the old-fashioned arcade on the main road, and the excellent rick-
ety Setagaya line. On a recent visit, I saw an elderly and unaccompanied
Alsatian, clearly a local character, being greeted by passersby while it
waited patiently for the light to change; the proprietor of a rice shop looking after business while playing the flute; and a ghostly pale, elderly lady
cradling a clearly blind, alarmingly fat, and obviously enormously con-
tented mongrel in a kind of sling arrangement. With all this in five minutes' stroll, it can be seen that this is a corner with more local color to the
square foot than many. Perfectly at home here is Aka Oni.

The master of the "Red Devil" takes his sake seriously. Of course you
might think it's his business, but Takizawa-san is devoted above and
beyond, to the extent of enrolling in Tokyo Agricultural University and

graduating from the renowned brewing science department—in his spare time! There is a broad and varying selection of excellent sake from a stock numbering three figures, with *nama* the focus. Prices for sake start at ¥600 per glass. It comes served in a slightly smaller version of the tasting cups with their characteristic pattern of blue circles in the bottom. Food is lovingly prepared and various. "Roasted tuna cheek" (*maguro no hoppeta yaki*) sounds somewhat bizarre in English, but is succulent and delicious in any language.

I am fond of the delicacies listed in the old and battered menu under *Aka Oni no Chinmi* ("Red Devil's Rare Tastes"). The excellent *soba* noodles handmade daily by the boss himself are currently most popular, I was unsurprised to hear. It is not a large establishment, so it may be wise to book.

2–15–3 Sangenjaya, Setagaya-ku, Tokyo 154–0024

世田谷区三軒茶屋2–15–3　〒154–0024

☎ 03–3410–9918, fax 03–3487–6279

5:30 P.M.–12:30 A.M. (last order 11:30 P.M.), closed Sundays, holidays

NEAREST STATION: Sangenjaya, Tōkyū Shintamagawa line

¥¥½

Dengyobō　傳魚坊

Sake is the *kami-sama* here, and a jealous god into the bargain. So unbending is the policy that this is possibly the only restaurant in Japan with no beer. Those who like something fizzy to wash off the dust before getting down to serious sake business are met with a fragrant, carbonated cocktail of blended *ginjō* sake.

In the courtyard garden inside the restaurant area is a *suikinkutsu*, an elegant adornment for formal gardens beloved of the Edo period (1603–1868), of which examples are now sadly few. It is essentially a large earthenware pot, inverted and buried. Water trickles over the rim of a stone basin, between the pebbles on the surface, and then drips into the subterannean chamber formed by the pot. As each drop falls it creates an exquisite sound, reverberating in the peculiar acoustics of the space. The bell-like tones are said to resemble the sound of the *koto*, a traditional stringed instrument. The characters of the word *suikinkutsu* are those for water, *koto*, and a cave.

Such constructions require a setting of great tranquility for their appreciation. Dengyobō is a tranquil haven, and the harp-like tones of the *suikin-kutsu* are not the only exquisite rarity on the premises. All the sake here is *daiginjō* class. Many of the wide range are custom-brewed, and not on sale elsewhere. The theme is *shinsei daiginjō*, a kind of ultra-*ginjō* made only from perfect grains of rice (cracked grains are discarded). The food, which arrives at a civilized and stately pace, is of a similar level. Order by course, from ¥5,000 upwards. If you choose the "Clever" course (¥10,000 + sake) or the leave-it-to-us *o-makase* course (¥15,000 + sake) and call a halt before the last dish arrives, the difference (according to the number of dishes untouched) will be deducted from your bill. Come with plenty of time and enough cash not to worry about the bill.

1–9 Yotsuya Wakaba, Shinjuku-ku, Tokyo 160–0011

新宿区若葉1–9　〒160–0011

☎ 03–5269–6696, fax 03–5269–6698

5:00–11:00 P.M. (reservation needed), closed Sundays

NEAREST STATION: Yotsuya, JR Chūō–Sōbu lines and Marunouchi and Nanboku subway lines

¥¥¥¥

Donjaka　呑者家

Vinyl-and-*tatami*-seated *izakaya*, very cheap and raucously cheerful. They do a bargain line in *kiki-zake* sets—three glasses of different grades of the good stuff to compare for a ridiculously low ¥650. Single orders of sake come in glass toothmugs from ¥550 upwards. Sound sake at this price is heavenly; pretty much everything else about the place veers more towards the earthly or downright earthy. Quite a wide range of low-priced *izakaya* food, including thought-provoking items like fried almonds and cheese. This place is a good excuse for missing the last train. It's not that big, so if you want to go in force, go a couple of doors down, descend the staircase wallpapered with sake labels, and you will find Dora. This offers more of the same as (and is even more noisy than) Donjaka, a kind of Hard Rock with sake, and very roomy. There are three sister shops nearby.

Main branch

3–9–10 Shinjuku, Shinjuku-ku, Tokyo 160–0022

新宿区新宿3–9–10　〒160–0022

☎ 03–3341–2497 (tel/fax)

5 P.M.–6:00 A.M.!

NEAREST STATION: Shinjuku Sanchōme, Marunouchi and Toei Shinjuku subway lines

¥

Hoshino　ほし野

A most unassuming and modest little place, of the kind it is nice to have in the neighborhood. Unless you're very lucky, though, you'll be hard-pressed to find a range of sake like this nearby. A 180-milliliter serving of

pure rice sake is a most wallet-friendly ¥600. A glass of one of their selection of *daiginjō* sakes will set you back a little more, starting from ¥800.
Their signboard advertises blowfish and eel; they also have *sashimi* and
yakitori, which is ¥140 a skewer.

> 3–22–2, Higashi-Ueno, Taitō-ku, Tokyo 110–0015
>
> 台東区東上野3–22–2　〒110–0015
>
> ☎ 03–3834–3460, fax 03–3828–0456
>
> 5–11 P.M., closed Sundays and holidays
>
> NEAREST STATION: Ueno, JR Yamanote and Keihin Tōhoku lines
> and Ginza subway line
>
> ¥¥½

Ichi no Chaya　一ノ茶屋

Master Sakuragi-san is author of numerous books on the subject of sake.
An authority as well as an author, he will only countenance sake that falls
within the exacting range of his holy trinity: unpasteurized, *junmai*,
ginjō. He was also the first person ever to bring a number of now famous
brands to the capital. Among the names introduced by him is Ume no
Yado—the brewery I work for. Fine food, and superb *nama* sake selected
by Sakuragi-san on his periodic rounds of the country's breweries.

> 2–21–10 Kanda-awaji-chō, Chiyoda-ku, Tokyo 101–0063
>
> 千代田区神田淡路町2–21–10　〒101–0063
>
> ☎ 03–3251–8517, fax 03–3258–6009
>
> 5–11 P.M., closed Saturday, Sunday, holidays
>
> NEAREST STATION: JR Ochanomizu (Chūō/Sōbu line). Subways:
> Ogawamachi (Shinjuku line), Shin Ochanomizu (Chiyoda line),
> Awaji-chō (Marunouchi line).
>
> ¥¥¥

Ikesu　いけす

I can vouch for the quality of food and drink here, having enjoyed both on
many occasions. Since I always go there for the post-meeting celebration
of the annual bash of the sake club run by the boss, I have never been as a
paying guest, and so cannot give a ¥ rating myself. The boss tells me that
about ¥3,000 does the trick for most.

> 3–10–6 Myōjin-chō, Hachiōji-shi, Tokyo 192–0905
>
> 八王子市明神町3–10–6　〒192–0905
>
> ☎ 0426–48–1118, fax 0426–42–1508
>
> 5–11 P.M., closed Sundays, holidays
>
> NEAREST STATION: Hachiōji, JR Chūō line
>
> ¥¥½

Ji-zake-ya   地酒屋

Kabukichō is named for the traditional kabuki theater there. This was once a rip-roaring popular entertainment, but is now patronized mainly by old ladies and hard-core culture vultures. Notwithstanding the associations of the address, though, the area is now more of a home to subcultures than high culture. All varieties of flesh-peddling establishment are represented, along with more respectable manifestations of nightlife. The area has also reportedly become a center of activity for Triad gangs. The young are there in force, crowding doorways and squares, and hardly an undyed head of black hair in sight. On the edge of this mass of activity is Ji-zake-ya, an old-fashioned *aka-chōchin* ("red lantern," from the traditional marker for an *izakaya* and not to be confused with the red lights up the road, which have quite a different significance). The shop-front has seen better days, and the inside is not as young as it was, either. About the only new part of the decor are the paper tags displaying the names of sake varieties on offer, which should tell you what Ji-zake-ya's priorities are, if the name hasn't gotten the point over already. I can't imagine people come here for the food. Sake comes in a *tokkuri* decanter, either *ichi-gō* or *ni-gō* (180 or 360 milliliters). Prices range from ¥600 to ¥2,600; the selection is *honjōzō* upwards. The interior is really quite gloomy; long-time drinkers will find it very nostalgic. There are cheaper places, there are certainly cleaner places, but for a glass or two of sake to end the evening, fair enough.

Dai 3 Hirasawa Building, 1F, 2–46–7 Kabuki-chō, Shinjuku-ku, Tokyo 160–0021

新宿区歌舞伎町2–46–7第三平沢ビル1階　〒160–0021

☎ 03–3205–3690

6 P.M.–1 A.M., closed second Sunday

NEAREST STATION: Shinjuku, various lines

¥¥

Sakanatei   酒菜亭

The sign on the portal warns non-sake drinkers to abandon hope (well, not to come in, actually). You're not supposed to have more than one beer; still, it's not the hushed mass of connoisseurs the rather pompous warning on the door suggests. The interior combines traditional Japanese and naked-concrete modern. A balanced selection of sake ranges from familiar stand-bys to more out-of-the-way offerings. Food is also safely above average. *Sashimi* arrives with *wasabi* root and one of those nice sharkskin graters.

Koike Building, 4F, 2–23–15 Dōgenzaka, Shibuya-ku, Tokyo 150–0043

渋谷区道玄坂2–23–15小池ビル4階　〒150–0043

☎ 03–3780–1313, fax 03–3464–8986

5:30–11:30 P.M. (last order 11 P.M.), closed Sundays, holidays

NEAREST STATION: Shibuya, various lines

¥¥½

Sakanaya　酒菜屋

In the thronging heart of Ikebukuro's entertainment quarter, you will find this place at the top of a staircase lined with empty sake bottles like an hour guard. More bottles crowd the shelf halfway up. Mind your head as you duck through the little half door which is the way in, and you will be met with the sight of still more bottles lining the walls of the restaurant itself. Lots of bottles; hundreds of them. There are lots of bottles in the fridges too. The menu lists well over a hundred varieties, and Sakanaya is sufficiently packed to mean that they can keep this huge selection in good condition. (A quick turnover means no half-empty bottles hanging around with the contents oxidizing, a problem all too common in places with a big range of sake.) At first glance, it has rather the feeling of one of the ubiquitous *izakaya* chains, but I'm glad to say the food, though very reasonably priced, is far from being of that bland, conveyor-belt-and-microwave variety. They offer a wide choice, with daily recommendations on blackboards. Also don't forget to look at the listings on the little bamboo mat you will find rolled up on the table, or you'll miss such bargains as *ika no ichiya boshi*—a "hung-for-a-night" squid you can grill to your taste on the *hibachi* brazier they will provide you with. For ¥650!

The sake prices seem too good to be true, with *honjōzō* starting at less than ¥300 a glass, *junmai* from ¥370, and *ginjō* beginning under ¥400. Sister shops do business in Ueno and two other Ikebukuro locations.

1–35–8 Nishi-Ikebukuro. Toshima-ku, Tokyo 171–0021

豊島区西池袋1–35–8　〒171–0021

☎ 03–3590–9560

5–11:30 P.M. (Saturdays to 11 P.M.)

NEAREST STATION: Ikebukuro, various lines

¥½

Sake no Ana　銀座らん月 酒の穴

I've been in some holes in my time, but the "The Sake Hole" is definitely not one of them. Smack in the middle of the Ginza, but not horrifically priced like many establishments in the area. Prices are by the *ana* (穴), a mysterious unit of currency equal to ¥100. A 180-milliliter serving of sake costs 5 *ana* for *honjōzō*, 6 for *junmaishu*, 12 or 16 for *ginjō*. *Nama* brews are served in 300-milliliter bottles at ¥1,200 or ¥1,500 (sorry, 12 or 15 *ana*). The counter area is backed by air-conditioned shelves of bottles. You will be asked if you want your sake warm or cold. The cold stuff comes in a jug set in crushed ice. Each place has a copper apparatus for warming sake. If, like me, you enjoy the shifts of flavor with temperature, this is a rare treat. Reliable offerings of the Meimonshu-kai, an association of producers and retailers, form the bulk of the range here. A number of the big makers (Kikumasa, Kenbishi, Kamozuru) are represented, which speaks for a welcome openness of mind. Food is refreshingly inventive Japanese. These prices for this level of fare would be good news anywhere in Tokyo: in the Ginza it seems miraculous. Their flexible style of serving sake is simply splendid, allowing play and study according to individual taste. A big hand for Sake no Ana.

Ginza Rangetsu, B1F, 3–5–8 Ginza, Chūō-ku, Tokyo 104–0061
中央区銀座3–5–8らん月地下1階　〒104–0061
☎ 03–3567–1133, fax 03–3562–5697
11:30 A.M.–11 P.M. (Sundays and holidays to 9 P.M.)
NEAREST STATION: Ginza, various subway lines
¥¥½

Sawamura　酒処 澤村

The shop is laid out in standard fashion: half-a-dozen tables, and a row of seats at the counter looking into the glass case holding the raw materials for the food offerings. Over one corner of the counter hangs a slightly shaggy brown globe. This object is made of cedar needles, and one is to be seen in front of pretty much any brewery in Japan. These *sugi-dama* come from the shrine in Nara Prefecture which houses the sake god, and were once visual signboards in a pre-literate age. In a bar today, they are a good omen. When you unfold the paper wrapper for your chopsticks, you will find its reverse covered with a list of over fifty breweries, from Hokkaidō to Kyūshū, whose sakes are on offer. If you read the small print, you will discover that there are two or three different types from each of the breweries, from limited-edition *daiginjō*s and venerable *koshu* down through to *honjōzō* class. This is just on the menu; a footnote advises that rarities and seasonal offerings are also available. You will look far for such a wide selection of quality sake. The food is high-grade with the freshness which is the key to superior Japanese cuisine. The sake is served in 1.5- or 3-*gō tokkuri*. The smaller 270-milliliter order will likely cost in the region of ¥4,000, though bear in mind that there are many precious things on the menu which will set you back considerably more. The *washi* wrapper for your chopsticks (a fund of information) exhorts the customer to inquire freely about price or anything else. I would suggest that a small group is ideal. More than four is probably pushing it. A little pricey.

1–11–1 Dōgenzaka, Shibuya-ku, Tokyo 150–0043
渋谷区道玄坂1–11–1　〒150–0043
☎ 03–3464–8870, fax 03–3751–4192
5–11:30 P.M., closed Sundays, holidays
NEAREST STATION: Shibuya, various line
¥¥¥ ½

Shōnaihama　庄内浜

An aging sign proclaiming "beautiful sake" sits above a frontage of bamboo equally hoary. This place has been here for twenty-five years, and is a welcome contrast to the bland modern developments that surround it. Opening the sliding door in the wall, one looks for a staircase leading to the expected second story. What you see, however, is what you get; space for only a handful of customers. You can fill every seat, throw in the couple who run the place, and you will still be in single figures. Behind the counter a number of sake bottles are displayed, mainly famous names, also in single figures. The actual stock in the refrigerator somewhere out in back may break the two-figure barrier: I'm not sure. Twenty-five years in the trade is perhaps not that unusual, but I know of few *izakaya* which can claim to have been serving *ginjō* for more than two decades. To say that they are not jaded by their long career is an understatement; they seem to be having the time of their lives.

4–8–7 Ginza, Chūō-ku, Tokyo 104–0061
中央区銀座4–8–7　〒104–0061
☎ 03–3564–1389, fax 03–3552–0165
5:30 P.M.–midnight, closed Sundays and holidays
NEAREST STATION: Ginza, various subway lines
¥¥¥ (¥2,000 charge)

Yakitori Binchō　炭火焼鳥 備長

Yakitori is cooked over *binchō-tan*, the *ginjō* of charcoals, where the customers at the counter can watch and drool. Orders are by the skewer, or by a range of courses. The menu is handwritten, so it may require a little perseverance to read the names of the sixty or so sakes. With such a sound and interesting selection, leaving the choice to the staff should be safe enough. Prices range from ¥500 to ¥1,200 per glass. One or two additional treasures are available as the "manager's selection." Draft beer comes in ceramic mugs. Those looking for a little more character than the repetitive standards of the Big Four can choose from the varying range of *ji-bîru*, micro-brewed beers, in the American idiom. The shadowy interior is in a kind of moody Japanese style. Three cheers for good food and fine sake at a fair price. Sister shops are to be found in Hongō, Yokohama, and Kobe.

> Marina Building, 2F, 3–10–5 Roppongi, Minato-ku, Tokyo 106–0032
> 港区六本木3–10–5マリーナビル2階　〒106–0032
> ☎ 03–5474–0755, fax 03–5474–0757
> 6 P.M.–midnight (last order 11 P.M.), closed year end to New Year's Day
> NEAREST STATION: Roppongi, Hibiya subway line
> ¥¥

■ PREFECTURES

HIROSHIMA

Kimura (Kyoto cuisine)　木むら

Sake here is all *junmai* (pure rice), stringently chosen to complement Kimura-san's marvelous homemade food. The sake is served in lovely handmade glass *tokkuri* that arrive in earthenware bowls full of ice water. Mmm. The counter is loaded with beautiful plates and bowls full of the day's fare. She must spend all day cooking. Dining out rarely comes better.

> 2–8–14 Mikado-chō, Fukuyama-shi 720–0805
> 福山市御門町2–8–14　〒720–0805
> ☎ 0849–27–0808
> 5–10:30 P.M., closed Sundays and holidays
> NEAREST STATION: JR Fukuyama
> ¥¥½

Yume-hachi (*yakitori*)　夢八

The interior blends standard Japanese elements with some contemporary touches to pleasant effect. The dozen-or-so sakes on the menu are changed with the seasons. For those who want something a bit stiffer, there is rather good *shōchū* in the large ceramic pots on the counter. *Yakitori* is the main fare, but don't miss the excellent *zaru-dōfu*, tofu served in a bamboo basket.

3–8 Nobuhiro-chō, Fukuyama-shi 720–0064

福山市延広町3–8　〒720–0064

☎ 0849–22–9412

5–11 P.M. (Sundays and holidays to 10 P.M.)

NEAREST STATION: JR Fukuyama

¥¥

NARA

Rakubō　楽房

The menu announces a range of sake hailing from Hokkaidō to Okinawa. *Nihonshu* from the length of the archipelago—brands numbering in the seventies—finds its place here beside a smaller selection of *shōchū* spirits and Okinawa's contribution to the world's roster of intoxicants, *awamori*. This is all too rare a find in this part of Japan. Not all the sake makes it into the limited space of the menu; you will find monthly selections on a separate card, and a look in the big coolers or at the bottles on the undulating counter may give you more ideas. Prices for sake start at a most reasonable ¥400 per glass: *ginjō* comes at ¥1,200. You may choose to sit at the undulating counter, but if you find the spooky green illumination on the ceiling unsettling, the small tables of the tatami-matted *zashiki* area may suit you better. Good food comes by the dish or by the course. (For example, ¥2,500 gets you the B course—a starter, sashimi, eight kinds of skewered tidbits (from familiar *tsukune* ground chicken to delicious originals like *shiso* leaf wrapped in sliced beef), and *onigiri* riceballs.

Pasuteru Building, 2F, 9 Tsunofuri-chō, Nara-shi 630–8224

奈良市角振町9パステルビル2階　〒630–8224

☎ 0742–26–4021

5–11 P.M., closed Sundays

NEAREST STATION: JR Nara

¥¥

Ryōzanpaku　梁山泊

Very pleasant Japanese-style interior, with seats at the counter where you can watch your food being cooked, or *zashiki* seating of the foreigner-friendly kind with a pit to stretch the legs in. Sake comes in an Aladdin's lamp kind of glass server in mystifying 230- and 270-milliliter measures. Prices start at ¥1,050. Alternatively, you may choose to take a bottle (720 milliliters for ¥6,600 and upwards). Well-worn, atmospheric, and offering that rare service, an English sake list.

13 Nishi-jōdo-chō, Nara-shi 630–8345

奈良市西城戸町13　〒630–8345
☎ 0742–26–2523
5–11 P.M., closed Sundays
NEAREST STATION: JR Nara
¥¥¥

OSAKA

Kisugi (*kushiyaki*)　きすぎ

Stays open until the small hours. Unusual policy of serving sake at room temperature works well with many of the *junmai* brews available.

1–16–2 Mizuo, Ibaraki-shi 567–0891
茨木市水尾1–16–2　〒567–0891
☎ 0726–34–7021
5 P.M.–4 A.M.
NEAREST STATION: Ibaraki, Hankyū line
¥¥

8

Brewery-Run Antenna Shops

Some breweries own drinking establishments. Since they are in the nature of an advertisement, one imagines that they should have the best any firm has to offer. Some carry rare varieties not on sale elsewhere. The following list offers a sampling of these brewery-related establishments. Numbers in parentheses refer to recommendations in the Sake Sampler.

HYŌGO PREFECTURE

Shinryūgura (Tatsu-riki, 89)　親竜蔵
　　125 Minami Ekimae-chō, Himeji-shi 670–0962
　　姫路市南駅前町125　〒670–0962
　　☎ 0792–88–8630
　　11 A.M.–10 P.M., closed Sundays
　　NEAREST STATION: JR Himeji

Tatsu-riki (89)　多津利起
　　Himeji Eki Festa, 210 Minami Ekimae-chō, Himeji-shi 670–0962
　　姫路市南駅前町210姫路駅フェスタ　〒670–0962
　　☎ 0792–21–3574
　　11:30 A.M.–9 P.M., closed third Thursday
　　NEAREST STATION: JR Himeji

KŌCHI PREFECTURE

Sui-geitei (Sui-gei, 80, 81)　酔鯨亭
　　1–17–25 Minami-harimaya-chō, Kōchi-shi 780–0833
　　高知市南はりまや町1–17–25　〒780–0833
　　☎ 0888–82–6577
　　11:30 A.M.–2 P.M., 5–10 P.M., closed Sundays

NEAREST STATION: JR Kōchi

Torisei (Makers of the Shinsei brand)　鳥せい本店

186 Kami-aburakake-chō, Fushimi-ku, Kyoto 612–8047

伏見区上油掛町186　〒612–8047

☎ 075–622–5533

11:30 A.M.–10 P.M., closed Mondays (open when Monday is holiday)

NEAREST STATION: Fushimi-momoyama, Keihan line; or
Momoyama Goryō-mae, Kintetsu line

NAGOYA

Tama no Hikari　玉乃光酒蔵　大名古屋ビル店

Dai Nagoya Building, B1F, 3–28–12 Meieki, Nakamura-ku,
Nagoya-shi 450–0002

中村区名駅3–28–12　大名古屋ビル地下1階　〒450–0002

☎ 052–561–1812

4:30–9:30 P.M. (last order 9 P.M.), closed Sundays, holidays

NEAREST STATION: JR Nagoya, various lines

OSAKA AND VICINITY

Namakura (Makers of Ama no Zake: 2, 3)　なまくら

Novaty Nagano Nankai, 1F, 5–1 Nagano-chō, Kawachi-Nagano-shi,
586–0014

河内長野市長野町5–1ノバティー長野南海1階　〒586–0014

☎ 0721–56–0056

4–10 P.M., closed first and third Wednesdays

NEAREST STATION: Kawachi-nagano, Nankai Kōya Line

Tama no Hikari　玉乃光酒蔵　梅田店

2–11–8 Sonezaki, Kita-ku, Osaka 530–0057

北区曽根崎2–11–8　〒530–0057

☎ 06–6313–6776

11 A.M.–2 P.M., 4–10 P.M. (Saturdays to 9 P.M.), closed Sundays,
holidays

NEAREST STATION: Umeda, various subway lines

TOCHIGI

Azumarikishi　東力士酒蔵

3–1–13 Baba-dōri, Utsunomiya-shi 320–0026

宇都宮市馬場通り3–1–13　〒320–0026

☎ 028–633–3027
4:30–10 P.M., closed Sundays
NEAREST STATION: Utsunomiya, JR

TOKYO AND VICINITY

Mado no Ume (54) 窓乃梅酒蔵
Yamada Building, B1F, 8–11–13 Ginza, Chūō-ku, Tokyo 104–0061
中央区銀座8–11–13山田ビル地下1階　〒104–0061
☎ 03–3571–3914
5:30–11 P.M., closed Saturdays, Sundays
NEAREST STATION: Ginza, various subway lines

Mamagotoya (Sawa no I) ままごと屋
2–748 Sawai, Ōme-shi, Tokyo 198–0172
青梅市沢井2–748　〒198–0172
☎ 0428–78–9523
10 A.M.–5 P.M., closed Mondays (Tuesday if Monday is a holiday)
NEAREST STATION: Sawai, JR Ōme line

Shōchikubai no Sakagura (Shōchikubai) 松竹梅之酒蔵
7–8–15 Ginza, Chūō-ku, Tokyo 104–0061
中央区銀座7–8–15　〒104–0061
☎ 03–3571–2631
11:30 A.M.–1:30 p.m, 5–11:00 P.M. (Saturdays to 10 P.M.), closed
Sundays
NEAREST STATION: Ginza, various subway lines

Tama no Hikari 玉乃光忠臣蔵　八重洲仲通り店
Yasu Building, 1F, 1–8–9 Yaesu, Chūō-ku, Tokyo 103–0028
中央区八重洲1–8–9八洲ビル1階　〒103–0028
☎ 03–3274–0998
4:30–11 P.M., closed Sundays and holidays
NEAREST STATION: Tokyo, various lines

Taruhei (82) 樽平
8–7–9 Ginza, Chūō-ku, Tokyo 104–0061
中央区銀座8–7–9　〒104–0061
☎ 03–3571–4310
5–10 P.M. (last order), closed Sundays, holidays, third Saturday
(except Dec. and Jan.)
NEAREST STATION: Ginza, various subway lines

Tengu-mai (91)   天狗舞

Kōno Building, B1F, 1–11–11 Nishi Shinjuku, Shinjuku-ku, Tokyo 160–0023

新宿区西新宿1–11–11　河野ビル地下1階　〒160–0023

☎ 03–3342–4560

5–10:30 P.M., closed Sundays, holidays

NEAREST STATION: Shinjuku, various lines

Yūkun Sakagura (Yūkun)   有薫酒蔵

1–4–14 Yaesu, Chūō-ku, Tokyo 103–0028

中央区八重洲1–4–14　〒103–0028

☎ 03–3271–8231

5–10 P.M., closed holidays and weekends (except last Saturday of the month)

NEAREST STATION: Tokyo, various lines

9

Retailers in Japan

Having decided *what* to buy, the next question is *where*? Though the situation is improving, the "average" sake shop may still have sadly little to offer. A basic criterion is storage; sake is highly sensitive to light and temperature, and dealers who care take pains to preserve their stock. Refrigeration is a must, and exposure to direct sunlight a bad sign. This is doubly true for *nama* sakes. A wide range of products is fun for browsing, but a few brands carefully tended is probably better than a vast stock gathering dust. Likewise, decent quality is always better than dodgy quantity, however exciting a list of dozens of brands appears. The local beer shop on the corner is more likely to offer some action than was the case only a few years ago, but specialist stores are inevitably that much more exciting. They are generally also very pleased to find someone interested, and often respond with information, and even occasional samples.

This list is comprised of retailers known to me personally, supplemented with a few that I have not visited myself but which are longstanding and trusted dealers in the sake trade by my employer, Ume no Yado.

■ MAJOR CITIES

For smaller cities, such as Hiroshima and Nara, please refer to prefectural listings.

KOBE CITY

This prefecture is home to many of the nation's brewing craftsmen, and to Yamada Nishiki, *king of sake rice strains. It is also the site of the Nada/Nishinomiya region, which accounts for around a third of all sake produced in Japan.*

Morishita Sake Ten   森下酒店

   7–1–1 Dainichi-dōri, Chūō-ku, Kōbe-shi 650–0064

   中央区大日通7–1–1   〒650–0064

   ☎ 078–221–4856

The owner here is a history freak. While visiting his beloved Nara many years ago, it struck him that Nara also had lots of sake breweries. A little research showed that most authorities hold Nara to be the original home of sake. Morishita-san tried sake from every brewery in Nara Prefecture—some sixty-odd at the time! At one stage he sold almost nothing *but* Nara sake. Now he carries *ji-zake* from all over Japan, but about a third of his stock is still from Nara. The shiny new shop was opened in June 1997 on the site of its predecessor, flattened by the Great Hanshin Earthquake of 1995. The *tachi-nomiya* pub adjacent is also run by the family, and apart from the usual range of drinks and simple snacks, it also offers any of the Nara sakes in stock, served by the shot.

Espoir Hiraoka   エスポワ　ヒラオカ

   5–2–15 Motomachi-dōri, Chūō-ku, Kōbe-shi 650–0022

   中央区元町通5–2–15   〒650–0022

   ☎ 078–341–2563, fax 078–371–3318

See Chapter 7, *Izakaya* Bars and Restaurants in Japan.

Iseda Sake Ten   伊勢田酒店

   75–1 Arise Igawadani-chō, Nishi-ku, Kōbe-shi 651–2113

   西区伊川谷町有瀬75–1   〒651–2113

   ☎ 078–975–1626

KYOTO CITY

Kyoto is one of Japan's most visited cities. Visitors come to see its phenomenal collection of beautiful temples, shrines, gardens, and castles. It is also a famed center for traditional arts and crafts, inclusive of sake brewing. Most of the breweries are in the Fushimi area, roughly between the Fushimi, Tanbashi, Momoyama Goryō-mae, and Chūshojima stations on the Kintetsu line, and Keihan's Tanbabashi and Fushimi Momoyama stations. A stroll round the area is a chance to see some of its many breweries, from modern factory plants to the lovely traditional kura *which grace its streets. Some firms run museums open to the public, notably Gekkeikan's Memorial Hall. (Admission is ¥300, including a little souvenir bottle of sake. A few minutes' walk from Kintetsu Momoyama Goryō-mae station.) See also entries under Kyoto in the prefectural listing.*

Aburachō　油長

Fushimiōte-suji Shōtengai Sanbangai Chūō Minamigawa

780 Higashi-ōte-chō, Fushimi-ku, Kyoto 612–8053

伏見区東大手町780　〒612–8053

☎ 075–601–0147

The Fushimi region is Japan's second largest brewing center, and Aburachō is smack in the middle of Fushimi. For more details, see the entry in Chapter 7, *Izakaya* Bars and Restaurants in Japan.

Nishijinya　西陣屋

252 Asukai-chō, Imadegawa-dōri Horikawa-higashi-iru,

Kamigyō-ku, Kyoto 602–0054

上京区今出川通堀川東入飛鳥井町252　〒602–0054

☎ 075–451–6590, fax 075–451–6599

Part of the "Sake Republic" group, which includes Kikuya and Sawada as well. An *izakaya* nearby is run by the same people.

Owariya　尾張屋

49–3 Kita-ōiri-chō Nishi-kyōgoku, Ukyō-ku, Kyoto 615–0881

右京区西京極北大入町49–3　〒615–0881

☎ 075–321–0670, fax 075–321–1786

Down the stairs is a rather excellent cellar. In it you will find lots of good sake and lots of good wine. If you wish, you may pay a ¥500 table charge and share your purchase with your friends on the spot. If you should be so inclined, you can also rent your own personal strongbox in which to keep your bottle of Romane Conti.

Liquors Daigen　リカーズ大源

18 Nishikawa-chō Nishikyōgoku, Ukyō-ku, Kyoto 615–0852

右京区西京極西川町18　〒615–0852

☎ 075–313–0273

See the entry for Daigen in Chapter 7, *Izakaya* Bars and Restaurants in Japan.

O-sake no Kyōwakoku Sawada　お酒の共和国サワダ

10 Nishi-kujō, Ōkuni-chō, Minami-ku, Kyoto 601–8449

南区西九条大国町10　〒601–8449

☎ 075–691–9366

Tominaga　トミナガ

478 Ōmiya-chō, Kaminoshimodachiuri-dōri Onmaedōri-nishi-iru,

Kamigyō-ku, Kyoto 602–8363

上京区上ノ下立売通御前通西入大宮町478　〒602–8363

☎ 075–464–0002, fax 075–465–1001

NAGOYA

Sake no Tsuboi　酒のつぼい

2–13 Shiotsuke-dōri, Shōwa-ku, Nagoya-shi 466–0022

昭和区塩付通2–13　〒466–0022

☎ 052–751–9908, fax 052–752–5746

Master Tsuboi-san and his friends have held a sake study session on Thursday—every Thursday—without fail, for over ten years!

OSAKA CITY

Osaka is western Japan's largest city, and freely and frequently lays claim to a distinct and colorful local dialect and character. People in the region also hold the area to be the true heart and home of sake brewing, though now only a handful of producers remain active. The Ikeda region, once one of Japan's leading brewing areas, was incorporated into greater Osaka but still boasts a number of quality sake outlets.

Isodaya　磯田屋

2–1–49 Uriwari, Hirano-ku, Osaka 547–0024

平野区瓜破2–1–49　〒547–0024

☎ 06–6790–4753, fax 06–6707–1778

Run doublehandedly by Mr. and Mrs. Isoda. Adjoining the shop is a room with seating for people in single figures, where customers can bring their own food and sample the sakes in the fridge, or take part in the cozy special events that are held there every few months.

Nakayama Sake Ten　酒蔵　なかやま

2–15–2 Honjōhigashi, Kita-ku, Osaka 531–0074

北区本庄東2–15–2　〒531–0074

☎ 06–6371–0145

A stone's throw from the apartment where I lived when I first arrived in Japan. If only I'd known!

Shimada Shōten　島田商店

3–5–1 Itachibori, Nishi-ku, Osaka 550–0012

西区立売堀3–5–1　〒550–0012

☎ 06–6531–8119

In the basement is a shady haven where the thirsty seeker-after-knowledge can taste from the open bottles in the fridge. *Miso* and *umeboshi* to clear the palate, books for the mind, sake for the soul. Owner Shimada-san or his staff may be there to assist. If not, follow these rules and enjoy:

1. One glass (filled to three-quarters) for ¥200. Use a fresh glass for each sake.
2. No smoking (or strong perfume).
3. No conversations unrelated to sake.
4. No drunken or rowdy behavior.
5. Payment is made by the number of glasses.

These rules reflect the obvious but sometimes-forgotten fact that this is not a bar. It is much cheaper to drink at a bar; this is more in the way of a chance to sample things before buying.

On the main road on the opposite side of the block (Amida-ike suji) is Meimonshu Sakaba, the tranquil watering-hole under related management; easily spotted by the *sugi-dama* (brown globe of cedar needles) hanging outside. The retail end of things is back off the main street.

Shimizu-ichi Shōten　　清水一商店

1–12–15 Tenjinbashi, Kita-ku, Osaka 530–0041

北区天神橋1–12–15　〒530–0041

☎ 06–6351–8124

This shop sits in the shadow of the *torii* gate belonging to Tenmangū shrine, the focus of Tenjin Matsuri, one of Japan's Big Three Festivals.

Wainfūdo Hayashi Shōten　　和飲風土　林商店

1–15–8 Kasugade Kita, Konohana-ku, Osaka 554–0021

此花区春日出北1–15–8　〒554–0021

☎ 06–6461–2317

The first four characters of the name make up an elaborate pun. The characters mean roughly "Japanese drinking style" and sound like the English for "wine, food" when pronounced in Japanese.

Meiji-ya　　明治屋

1–21–7 Jūsō-honmachi, Yodogawa-ku, Osaka 532–0024

淀川区十三本町1–21–7（十三東映前）　〒532–0024

☎ 06–6301–5765

Yamanaka Sake no Mise　　山中酒の店

1–10–19 Shikitsu Nishi, Naniwa-ku, Osaka 556–0015

浪速区敷津西1–10–19　〒556–0015

☎ 06–6631–3959

SAPPORO

Meishu no Yutaka   銘酒の裕多加

>   15–4–13 Kita Nijūgojō Nishi, Kita-ku, Sapporo-shi 001–0025
>   北区北二十五条西15–4–13   〒001–0025
>   ☎ 011–716–5174

TOKYO

Not only sake shops, but sake breweries can really be found all over Japan—there are more than a dozen even in the overpopulated, polluted capital. As a result of sheer market density, it is possible to find a wider selection of sake on sale in Tokyo than anywhere else. See also entries under Chiba, Saitama, and Tokyo in the prefectural listing.

Kōshūya Sake Ten   甲州屋酒店

>   5–1–15 Minami-nagasaki, Toshima-ku, Tokyo 171–0052
>   豊島区南長崎5–1–5   〒171–0052
>   ☎ 03–3954–2757, fax 03–3954–2040
>   Closed Sunday and holidays

This shop is credited with the introduction of many brands, once unknown, now famous, to the capital. The story of its pioneering late owner was recently published in comic book form by the inimitable *manga* artist and sake lover Hitoshi Takase. Several years back, they moved to an underground location, a most effective strategy for temperature control.

Maruseu Honma Shōten   マルセウ本間商店

>   2–41–22 Sasazuka, Shibuya-ku, Tokyo 151–0073
>   渋谷区笹塚2–41–22   〒151–0073
>   ☎ 03–3377–8281, fax 03–3377–8283

In one of those lovely old-fashioned neighborhood shopping streets, which were where everyone bought their groceries and caught up on the gossip before some fool introduced supermarkets to Japan.

Masushin Shōten   升新商店

>   2–23–2 Ikebukuro, Toshima-ku, Tokyo 171–0014
>   豊島区池袋2–23–2   〒171–0014
>   ☎ 03–3971–2704

The streamers that festoon the shop front advertising prices give the impression of a bargain basement kind of operation, but don't be misled. Inside is a jumbled Aladdin's cave of the finest sake.

YOKOHAMA

Akimoto Shōten　秋元商店

　5–1–11 Serigaya, Kōnan-ku, Yokohama-shi 233–0006

　港南区芹が谷5–1–11　〒233–0006

　☎ 045–822–4534, fax 045–823–7817

Marujū Sake ten　丸十酒店

　1–2–4 Maruyama, Isogo-ku, Yokohama-shi 235–0011

　磯子区丸山1–2–4　〒235–0011

　☎ 045–751–4957

Yamamoto Shōten　山本商店

　3–1–1 Okamura, Isogo-ku, Yokohama-shi 235–0021

　磯子区岡村3–1–1　〒235–0021

　☎ 045–751–4532

■ PREFECTURES

AICHI

Inoue Sake Ten　井上酒店

　2–3–3 Hagoromo, Ichinomiya-shi 491–0025

　一宮市羽衣2–3–3　〒491–0025

　☎ 0586–24–1264

AOMORI

Jin Sake Ten　神酒店

　1–15–23 Kitakanazawa, Aomori-shi 030–0855

　青森市北金沢1–15–23　〒030–0855

　☎ 0177–76–6089, fax 0177–76–6580

Miyashige Shuho　宮重酒舗

　20–3 Nijūrokunichimachi, Hachinohe-shi 031–0044

　八戸市廿六日町20–3　〒031–0044

　☎ 0178–43–0061, fax 0178–43–0062

CHIBA

Ōnagi Sake Ten　オオナギ酒店

　6–260 Makuhari-chō, Hanamigawa-ku, Chiba-shi 262–0032

　千葉市花見川区幕張町6–260　〒262–0032

　☎ 043–273–7730

Ōnagi-san's little shop was bigger until a chunk of it got cut off to widen the railway. Quality, not quantity.

Shimaya Sake Ten　シマヤ酒店

3–14–23 Mitsuwadai, Wakaba-ku, Chiba-shi 264–0032

千葉市若葉区みつわ台3–14–23　〒264–0032

☎ 043–252–3251, fax 043–252–4200

Hyperactive Shimakage-san's enterprises include the adjoining convenience store, *izakaya*, and workshops and salesrooms dealing in British-made and classic cars. There are 8,000 or so bottles in the wine cellar, but this is as a drop to the oceans of sake on the refrigerated shelves. Everything the sake-lover could wish for in prodigious abundance; the shady shop boasts such original (and effective) temperature-control strategies as walls made of refrigerators, and a roof-top garden complete with ornamental pond. Where else can you shop for sake with a half a dozen carp swimming overhead? Massive, and easily reached by monorail to Mitsuwadai station.

Masuyoshi Sake Ten　升吉酒店

3–131–2 Shin Matsudo, Matsudo-shi 270–0034

松戸市新松戸3–131–2　〒270–0034

☎ 047–343–7594, fax 047–343–7487

EHIME

Jizake Kōbō Kitachi Sake Ten　地酒工房 きたち酒店

1092 Kō Hiraoka Ikazaki-chō, Kita-gun 795–0303

喜多郡五十崎町平岡甲1092　〒795–0303

☎ 0893–44–2327

FUKUI

Ishikawa Sake Ten　石川酒店

2–4–12 Nishikida, Fukui-shi 918–8004

福井市西木田2–4–12　〒918–8004

☎ 0776–36–0206

FUKUOKA

Harashima Sake Ten　全国地酒処 ひらしま酒店

22–10 Higoromomachi, Yahatahigashi-ku, Kitakyūshu-shi 805–0042

北九州市八幡東区羽衣町22–10　〒805–0042

☎ 093–651–4082

Tsuchiyama Sake Ten   土山酒店

    2–9–8 Takanosu, Yahatanishi-ku, Kitakyūshū-shi 806–0047

    北九州市八幡西区鷹の巣2–9–8　〒806–0047

    ☎ 093–621–7527

Yamada Yoshitarō Sake Ten   山田芳太郎酒店

    2–9–8 Kyūmoji, Moji-ku, Kitakyūshū-shi 801–0854

    北九州市門司区旧門司2–9–8　〒801–0854

    ☎ 093–321–2892

FUKUSHIMA

Sugimoto Shōten   杉本商店

    1–4 Oyamacho, Fukushima-shi 960–8012

    福島市御山町1–4　〒960–8012

    ☎ 0245–34–1726

GIFU

Nakashimaya Sake Ten   中島屋酒店

    1–1 Yoshinomachi, Gifu-shi 500–8844

    岐阜市吉野町1–1　〒500–8844

    ☎ 058–262–2515, fax 058–262–2892

Sake no Masukan   酒のますかん

    9–18 Wakamiya-chō, Gifu-shi 500–8828

    岐阜市若宮町9–18　〒500–8828

    ☎ 058–262–3954

Wineland Komiyama   ワインランド コミヤマ

    2–1 Tetsumei-dōri, Gifu-shi 500–8879

    岐阜市徹明通2–1　〒500–8879

    ☎ 058–265–5264, fax 058–262–2621

GUNMA

Higashino Sake Ten   東野酒店

    832 Nanokaichi, Tomioka-shi 370–2343

    富岡市七日市832　〒370–2343

    ☎ 0274–64–2121, fax 0274–64–4103

HIROSHIMA

Hiroshima's fame sadly rests on its unlucky fate as the first city ever to suffer nuclear bombing. Sake lovers also know it as a famed brewing center, well known for gentle sakes due to the soft water. As of 1996, it is also home to the National Institute of Brewing Research, and is thus the site of the annual industry contest for new sake.

Sakashō Yamada   酒商ヤマダ

Currently run by the second and third generations of Yamadas. The interior of the store retains the aspect of a rather old-fashioned sake shop. This combines with a highly contemporary range of well-cared-for, exemplary sakes from around the country. Though splendid things from all corners of the archipelago are present in abundance, local brewers in particular have an enthusiastic ally here. The various refrigerated storerooms scattered around the corner are kept at varying temperatures according to the type of sake they contain. The storerooms, the Yamada family's lovely old house, and the shop itself, will sadly all fall to the developer's bulldozers in a few year's time, when the construction of the new Southern Hiroshima Route reaches the area.

2–10–7 Ujina-kaigan, Minami-ku, Hiroshima-shi 730–0011
広島市南区宇品海岸2–10–7　〒730–0011
☎ 082–251–1013, fax 082–251–6596

Sake no Maeda   酒のマエダ

On the left side of the main thoroughfare in front of the station is a great red *torii*—one of the gates that mark the approach to a shrine. Hence the name of the street—Miya-dōri—in which the ebullient Maeda-san keeps her cheerful shop. She has wide selections of pretty much everything: sake, beer, wine, whisky with and without an "e," and liqueurs. Still, sake accounts for the largest part of her business. The refrigerators that line the back wall of the shop are only part of the story; more sake and wines are kept in the cool cellar space. Sake no Maeda also boasts a very jolly sundial on the shop front.

7–6 Motomachi, Fukuyama-shi 720–0063
福山市元町7–6　〒720–0063
☎ 0849-23-1719

HOKKAIDO

Doi Shōten   土井商店

1-chōme Biei-chō-Nakamachi, Kamikawa-gun 071–0207
上川郡美瑛町中町1丁目　〒071–0207
☎ 0166–92–1516, fax 0166–92–3618

HYŌGO

Iseda Saka Ten　伊勢田酒店
　　2–4–1 Asagiri-chō, Akashi-shi 673–0866
　　明石市朝霧町2–4–1　〒673–0866
　　☎ 078–912–0655

ISHIKAWA

Sake no Numata　酒のぬまた
　　2–154 Yokogawa, Kanazawa-shi 921–8163
　　金沢市横川2–154　〒921–8163
　　☎ 076–247–2415, fax 076–247–2429

KAGAWA

Meijijō Honpo　明治城本舗
　　3–4–8 Honmachi, Sakaide-shi 762–0044
　　坂出市本町3–4–8　〒762–0044
　　☎ 0877–46–2623, fax 0877–45–4193

KAGOSHIMA

Marushin　マルシン
　　336 Higashi-mochida Aira-chō, Aira-gun 899–5421
　　始良郡始良町東餅田336　〒899–5421
　　☎ 0995–65–8370

KANAGAWA

Nishimura Sake Ten　西村酒店
　　1–18–2 Goten, Hiratsuka-shi 254–0061
　　平塚市御殿1–18–2　〒254–0061
　　☎ 0463–31–7425

Sugano Shoten　菅野商店
　　1–16–6 Ōfuna, Kamakura-shi 247–0056
　　鎌倉市大船1–16–6　〒247–0056
　　☎ 0467–46–2468, fax 0467–43–6676

KUMAMOTO

Araki　あらき
　　431–1 Shimomiyaji Jōnanmachi, Shimomashiki-gun 861–4204
　　下益城郡城南町下宮地431–1　〒861–4204
　　☎ 0964–28–6550, fax 0964–28–6831

KYOTO

Kikuya　菊屋
2–1 Takezono Otokoyama, Yawata-shi 614–8376
八幡市男山竹園2–1　〒614–8376
☎ 075–981–0553, fax 075–982–5544

Maruman Shōten　マルマン商店
92–4 Kita-yamada Terada, Jōyō-shi 610–0121
城陽市寺田北山田92–4　〒610–0121
☎ 0774–52–3582

MIE

Weinkeller Hashimoto　ヴァインケラー ハシモト
2938–1 Higashimachi, Ueno-shi 518–0861
上野市東町2938–1　〒518–0861
☎ 0595–21–0342, fax 0595–24–5468

MIYAZAKI

Saitō Sake Ten　さいとう酒店
865 Ōaza Hōji, Miyazaki-shi 880–0123
宮崎市大字芳士865　〒880–0123
☎ 0985–39–3152

NAGANO

Kitahara Sake Ten　北原酒店
2–8–22 Ōte, Matsumoto-shi 390–0874
松本市大手2–8–22　〒390–0874
☎ 0263–32–5713

Mitsui Sake Ten　三井酒店
6–14–5 Chūō, Ueda-shi 386–0012
上田市中央6–14–5　〒386–0012
☎ 0268–22–0245, fax 0268–28–5105

NAGASAKI

Shuraku Miyazono　酒楽　みやぞの
721–42 Hayamimachi, Isahaya-shi 854–0125
諫早市早見町721–42　〒854–0125
☎ 0957–28–2415

NARA

Nara is famous for its wealth of temples dating from its time as the nation's capital more than a thousand years ago. Less well-known is that it was in many ways the true cradle of sake, scene of the development and discovery of many techniques vital to the craft even today.

Fukumori Sake Ten   福森酒店

2–474 Sanjō-dōri, Nara-shi 630–0000

奈良市三条通2–474　〒630–0000

☎ 0742–22–2773

In the heart of Nara City, highly accessible for visitors to the ancient capital.

Kitora   西の京 地酒処 きとら

3–30 Gojō-chō, Nara-shi 630–8032

奈良市五条町3–30　〒630–8032

☎ 0742–33–2557, fax 0742–35–3377

Close to the great temples of Yakushiji and Tōshōdaiji.

Nobori Sake Ten   登酒店

555 Tainoshō-chō, Tenri-shi 632–0071

天理市田井庄町555　〒632–0071

☎ 0743–62–0218, fax 0743–63–0165

OKAYAMA

Tada Hiromitsu Shuho   多田博光酒舗

1–7 Higashichūō-chō, Okayama-shi 700–0835

岡山市東中央町1–7　〒700–0835

☎ 086–222–2748

OSAKA

Hyōtanya   ひょうたん屋

19–8 Kanda-chō, Higashi Osaka-shi 579–8058

東大阪市神田町19–8　〒579–8058

☎ 0729–87–1138, fax 0729–88–1718

Liquor Shop Matsumura   まつむら酒店

4–13–39 Fujiidera, Fujiidera-shi 583–0024

藤井寺市藤井寺4–13–39　〒583–0024

☎ 0729–55–2547, fax 0729–38–4611

Ogino　おぎの
> 3–5–2 Kotobuki-chō, Tondabayashi-shi 584–0031
> 富田林市寿町3–5–2　〒584–0031
> ☎ 0721–23–2245, fax 0721–25–1986

Ōtsuki Sake Ten　大月酒店
> 5–10–35 Kishibe Kita, Suita-shi 564–0001
> 吹田市岸部北5–10–35　〒564–0001
> ☎ 06–387–9178, fax 06–387–9175

Sake no Yamamoto　酒のヤマモト
> 1–17–10 Nishi-funahashi, Hirakata-shi 573–1122
> 枚方市西船橋1–17–10　〒573–1122
> ☎ 0720–57–0082

SAITAMA

Haruyama Shōten Saka Ten　春山商店　酒店
> 24–8 Sasame Minami-chō, Toda-shi 335–0035
> 戸田市笹目南町24–8　〒335–0035
> ☎ 048–421–1885, fax 048–421–7898

Kazusaya Sake Ten　かづさ屋酒店
> 1–35–8 Nishi Kawaguchi, Kawaguchi-shi 332–0021
> 川口市西川口1–35–8　〒332–0021
> ☎ 048–255–1130

Marubun Sake Ten　丸文酒店
> 2–5–11 Matsuyama, Kamifukuoka-shi 356–0027
> 上福岡市松山2–5–11　〒356–0027
> ☎ 0492–61–0240

Matsuzaki　マツザキ
> 1–24–8 Arajukumachi, Kawagoe-shi 350–1124
> 川越市新宿町1–24–8　〒350–1124
> ☎ 0492–43–4022

SHIGA

Tatsuno Sake Ten　タツノ酒店
> 1–15 Oiwake-chō, Ōtsu-shi 520–0064
> 大津市追分町1–15　〒520–0064
> ☎ 077–524–2209

SHIZUOKA

Hagiwara Shōten   萩原商店

228–1 Ugusuhama Kamomura, Kamo-gun 410–3501

加茂郡加茂村宇久須浜228–1　〒410–3501

☎ 0558–55–0009, fax 0558–55–0560

Umenoya Sake Ten   梅野屋酒店

191 Yugano Kawazu-chō, Kamo-gun 413–0507

加茂郡河津町湯ケ野191　〒413–0507

☎ 0558–35–7010

TOCHIGI

Shimamura   しまむら

2909 Ōaza Shizuwa Iwafunemachi, Shimotsuga-gun 329–4304

下都賀郡岩舟町大字静和2909　〒329–4304

☎ 0282–55–4274, fax 0282–55–6814

TOKYO

Koyama Shōten   小山商店

5–15–17 Sekido, Tama-shi, Tokyo 206–0011

多摩市関戸5–15–17　〒206–0011

☎ 0423–75–7026, fax 0423–73–9955

Extensive selection of names; the *kanji* on the many wooden tags advertising the various attractions are all handwritten by the bustling boss, the chuckling Koyama-san himself.

Mikawaya   三河屋

1–3–26, Akatsuki-chō, Hachiōji-shi, Tokyo 192–0043

八王子市暁町1–3–26　〒192–0043

☎ 0426–22–3143, fax 0426–26–3182

Local grocery that also happens to be a dealer in excellent and individual sake. Or is it the other way round?

Sakaya   さかや

1–4–6 Minami Naruse, Machida-shi, Tokyo 194–0045

町田市南成瀬1–4–6　〒194–0045

☎ 0427–27–2655, fax 0427–32–8620

This shop is run by two generations of the Kurihara family and manager Aoki-san, all of whom taste their way round hundreds of sakes every year in their annual tour of the regional and national industry contests for new sake.

Miyata Sake Ten   宮田酒店
   1–18–3 Kamirenjaku, Mitaka-shi, Tokyo 181–0012
   三鷹市上連雀1–18–3   〒181–0012
   ☎ 0422–51–9314, fax 0422–51–9316

YAMAGUCHI

Kajiwara Shōten   かじわら酒店
   12–8 Tanakamachi, Shimonoseki-shi 750–0008
   下関市田中町12–8   〒750–0008
   ☎ 0832–32–3215

Murata   ワインと地酒のムラタ
   75 Kamitake-kōji, Yamaguchi-shi 753–0035
   山口市上堅小路75   〒753–0035
   ☎ 0839–22–3840

YAMANASHI

Ozawa Sake Ten   小沢酒店
   3–9–10 Chūō, Kōfu-shi 400–0032
   甲府市中央3–9–10   〒400–0032
   ☎ 0552–33–5026

10

Selected Restaurants and Bars in the United States

Compiled by Chris Pearce

CALIFORNIA

Asakuma Restaurant
11701 Wilshire Boulevard
Los Angeles
☎ (310) 826–0013

Sake enthusiasts can enjoy two specially imported brews at this popular Los Angeles restaurant and sushi bar: Tatsutaya Oni-goroshi and Azuma-ryū. Both are from Aichi Prefecture, and are shipped to Asakuma through a special arrangement with the breweries. Kubota's Hekijyu label, supplied by a local distributor, rounds out the selection of *reishu*. Haku-tsuru is the *atsu-kan* house sake. A nice assortment of side dishes is available off the appetizer menu.

Hama Restaurant
213 Windward Avenue
Venice
☎ (310) 396–8783

The sake menu here is quite extensive, with around fifty labels imported from Japan. Some, such as Daishichi from Fukushima Prefecture and Sui-gei from Kochi, are well known, but many are from small breweries with no national distribution in Japan. For those looking for unusual sakes, this is the place, but best check with the chef Yokoyama-san for recommendations. The food menu contains a number of "Franco-Japanese" specials, as well as traditional sake side dishes and selections from the sushi bar.

Hamakawa

207–209 S. Central Avenue

Los Angeles

☎ (213) 625–8125

Most sushi bars stock only a few brands of sake. Hamakawa is an exception to the rule, with well over a dozen labels on hand. Two *ginjō* sakes are served, Kurosawa from Nagano Prefecture and Zuichō from Okayama. There is an American Haku-shika *ginjō*, and *ji-zake* imports like Ume Nishiki, Haru-shika and Otoko-yama filling out the list along with a few Nada selections. Ōzeki and Hakusan, two California sakes, are also served.

Hayakawa Restaurant

750 Terrado Plaza #33

Covina

☎ (213) 332–8288

Japanese nouvelle cuisine is the theme here, with items like monkfish pâté with caviar, fresh salmon kelp roll, and mixed seafood ceviche. Sake is an ideal accompaniment for this kind of food, and the restaurant serves Kubota (both Manju and Hyakuju), Otoko-yama, and Shōchikubai. The cozy space seats ten at the sushi counter and forty at tables. A different set *"o-makase"* menu is presented by the chef daily, accompanied by a sake selection.

Matsuhisa

129 N. La Cienaga Boulevard

Beverly Hills

☎ (310) 659–9639

Along with a range of eclectic accompaniments, including items like baby squid with *wasabi* pepper sauce and "new style sashimi," Matsuhisa serves a fine selection of sakes. Hoku-setsu, with both *ginjō* and *junmai* labels, is specially imported from Niigata Prefecture. Hakusan from Napa Valley is sold by the bottle and served chilled. Chef Nobu Matsuhisa sometimes has a few off-the-menu labels on hand—knowledgeable guests should inquire about the "special sake."

Sanuki no Sato

18206 S. Western Avenue

Gardena

☎ (310) 324–9185

With seven tatami rooms and plenty of table seating, this is one of Los Angeles' largest Japanese drinking spots. The sake menu includes such strong contenders as Ume Nishiki, Ichi no Kura, Kubota (both Manju and Hekijyu), Otoko-yama, and Hōō Suishin—all imported by Nishimoto Trading Company. California sakes are also well represented. The extensive appetizer menu lists over a hundred items, including a number of house specialities.

Sushi Ran

107 Caledonia Street

Sausalito

☎ (415) 332–3620

When this fifty-seat restaurant opened three years ago, its minimalist decor and California fusion cuisine quickly put it on the map. About twenty sakes are served, including two premium labels from Otoko-yama and the estimable Bishōnen from Kyūshū. Favorites among the appetizer specials—there are eight or nine different ones each night—include mussels steamed in beer (Sapporo) and tuna carpaccio. Hakusan from nearby Napa Valley is the house sake.

Yuu Restaurant

11043 Santa Monica Boulevard

Los Angeles

☎ (310) 478–7931

For those in search of an authentic Japanese drinking spot in the Los Angeles area, this is the place. Over fifty sakes are on the menu, all supplied by distributors in southern California. Yuu's has both an *izakaya* serving a traditional menu of affordable "*ippin-ryōri*" side dishes, and a sushi bar. In addition to the listed sakes, unusual labels are sometimes brought in by patrons returning from trips to Japan.

COLORADO

Tommy Tsunami's

1432 Market Street

Denver

☎ (303) 534–5050

Haku-shika, brewed in Colorado, is the house sake at Tommy Tsunami's, but the menu also features Shirayuki from Hyōgo Prefecture and several labels from Momokawa, the Aomori brewery that has started up operations in Oregon. Haku-shika makes a *ginjō* at its American brewery, and this is on the list as well. The menu evokes the east-west cuisine of Hawaii, where the restaurant's surfer-turned-millionaire founder spent his youth.

GEORGIA

Sakanaya

6241–A Peachtree Industrial Boulevard
Doraville
☎ (770) 458–0558

The *atsu-kan* house sake here is Shōchikubai, with the *reishu* list featuring Shōchikubai Ginjō (from California), Shōchikubai Nama-zake, Hakusan, and Ki-ippon, all from California.. The restaurant's *robata-yaki* counter serves up grilled fish and vegetables, and at the sushi counter Atlantic sole (*hirame*) from South Carolina and live lobster fresh from the tank are popular choices. Sakanaya is a good late-night noodle stop as well; the spicy *gekikara* ramen is a big favorite with local patrons.

Yakitori Den-Chan

3099 Peachtree Road
Atlanta
☎ (404) 842–0270

The sake menu varies here from month to month, but always includes a half dozen Japanese imports and one or two American sakes. Masumi, an excellent Nagano label, and Tsukasa Botan from Kochi Prefecture were featured on a recent visit. *Yakitori* (skewered chicken) and grilled vegetable or seafood selections, fill out the food menu. Owner Dennis Lange mans the grill with speed and dexterity, giving this spot the authentic feel of a Yurakuchō red-lantern *izakaya*.

HAWAII

Furusato

Hyatt Regency Hotel
2424 Kalakaua Avenue
Honolulu
☎ (808) 922–4991

A frequent caterer of Honolulu sake-tasting events over the last ten years, Furusato has a solid sake list of its own. Kamo Izumi, Otoko-yama, Ume Nishiki, Masumi, Hakusan, Ichi no Kura, and Mine no Hakubai appear on the current menu. Patrons can choose between the sushi bar at street level or the restaurant with tables and tatami seating below. Chef Shuji Abe is a sake enthusiast himself, so his culinary creations go exceptionally well with Japan's national drink.

Hakone Restaurant

5400 Makena Alanui

Makena Resort, Kihei, Maui

☎ (808) 874–1111

Located in the Maui Prince Hotel, this is one of Hawaii's finest Japanese restaurants. Momokawa labels predominate, with the brewery's *daiginjō*, *ginjō*, and *junmai* sakes all listed. Two Tōhoku area sakes, Ichi no Kura and Aramasa, also make an appearance. Sake service here will accompany a meal of sushi, a set dinner or one of the *nabemono* specialities. Chef Katsuhiko Sato also prepares an exquisite *kaiseki* set menu every evening.

Kyo-ya Restaurant

2057 Kalakaua Avenue

Honolulu

☎ (808) 947–3911

Authentic Japanese cuisine impeccably prepared is the hallmark of this Honolulu restaurant. Six sakes appear on the menu, including Momokawa, Otoko-yama, Tama no Hikari, and Kiku-sui. Menu standouts include *katsuo* (bonito) *tataki*, deep-fried sole, and miso butterfish. It's worth a visit just to admire the sumptuous decor and Japanese carpentry.

Senba

2633 S. King Street

Honolulu

☎ (808) 947–1001

This is a lively *izakaya* popular with Honolulu's overseas Japanese community. Most of the dozen or so regional sakes imported by Nishimoto Trading Company are served, but there is no standout; Hakusan represents the American side. Over a hundred appetizers appear on the menu, with nightly specials as well. The atmosphere is warm and friendly and encourages conversation with neighbors or tablemates.

NEW JERSEY

Izakaya Makoto

299 Queen Anne Road

Teaneck

☎ (201) 692–1002

This *izakaya* is located only fifteen miles from New York City, but most of its customers drop in from around the neighborhood. As in the Japanese prototype, there's counter seating for a dozen customers and a scattering of tables. The sakes served here included Ichi no Kura, Haru-shika, Ume Nishi, Wakatake Onigoroshi, and Hakusan. During cold weather, Makoto keeps an *oden* pot simmering and serves up hearty dishes like pork and onions and *maguro carpaccio*.

NEW YORK

Hatsuhana

> 17 East 48th Street
> New York
> ☎ (212) 355–3345

Hatsuhana is one of New York's oldest sushi spots, dating back to the mid-seventies. The premises occupy two stories of a midtown Manhattan building, with a sushi bar on the first that seats thirty people. The sake list includes Otoko-yama, Karatanba, Koshi no Hana, Hatsu-hana, and Ōzeki. In season you'll find Atlantic *saba* (mackerel) and *sawara* on the menu, as well as unusual items (including *maguro* from France) purchased at New York's central fish market.

Nagashima

> 12A–1 Jericho Turnpike
> Jericho
> ☎ (516) 338–0022

Sake aficionados will enjoy a visit to Nagashima, with its extensive sake list and lively menu. The house sake is Hakusan (both mild and premium), and premium brands from Otoko-yama, Namahage, Bishōnen, and Suishin, Sawa no I, and Akita Homare are also on hand. Over thirty items crowd the restaurant's appetizer menu—with standouts like lobster *motoyaki* and clams in garlic sauce—and another hundred or so appear on a separate listing of sake side dishes. The restaurant is located on Long Island, about twenty miles from New York City.

Nobu NYC

> 105 Hudson Street
> New York
> ☎ (212) 219–0500

Nobu's New York venture features the same sake list as its sister restaurant, Matsuhisa, in Los Angeles. The best choice is Hoku-setsu, an exquisite Niigata sake. There are three different labels—a *junmaishu*, a *daiginjō*, and a *junmai daiginjō*—served in traditional *masu* or by the glass. Hakusan represents the California breweries. The menu is so full of delightful surprises that Nobu has been ranked among the best restaurants in New York City.

Sushisay

38 East 51st Street
New York
☎ (212) 755–1780

Sushisay is the American branch of Tsukiji Sushisei, a venerable sushi restaurant located close to Tokyo's fish market. The sake list includes Haku-shika, Otoko-yama, and Yamada Nishiki, an export label from Ōzeki. The restaurant re-creates, in midtown Manhattan, the feel of Tokyo's old *shitamachi* area eatery. The service and selection is strictly traditional, and tatami seating is available.

11

Selected Restaurants, Bars, and Retailers in Europe and Asia

When I started drinking sake in the 1980s, the restaurants and bars I knew to carry a selection of fine sake were rare havens. I had a mental map of Osaka City, like an arid wasteland with fragrant oases of *ginjōshu* spotted sparsely across it.

At that time, I took it for granted that a bar I merely wandered into would probably have nothing more exciting to offer than a cold beer. Now, not quite ten years later, I find that almost any place I come across has its range of sake from far-flung corners of Japan. Ever-more books about sake are published annually, and many express the writers' excitement at the happy state of the industry and the snow-balling interest shown by the public. With so much positive change in its homeland, it is perhaps only a matter of time before fine sake begins to make a stronger impression overseas. After years of despairing of ever finding drinkable sake abroad, there are signs that the heartening developments I have seen in Japan may have their counterparts on a wider stage.

The Meimonshu-kai (Prestige Sake Association) has been exporting for over ten years now, and were kind enough to supply me with the following lists of restaurants and retailers carrying their products. Unfortunately, I have not as yet been able to visit these myself. I would welcome any information from readers which might improve future editions.

■ EUROPEAN RESTAURANTS

FRANCE

Benkay (弁慶)
Hotel Nikko de Paris
61, Quai de Grenelle, 75015 Paris
☎ (01) 40–58–21–26

Isse (伊勢)

56, Rue Saint Anne, 75002 Paris

☎ (01) 42–96–67–76

Kifune (きふね)

44, Rue Saint Ferdinand, 75017 Paris

☎ (01) 45–72–11–19

Kinugawa (衣川)

4, Saint Philippe du Roule, 75008 Paris

☎ (01) 45–63–08–07

Restaurant Suntory Paris

13, Rue Lincoln, 75008 Paris

☎ (01) 53–75–4027

Zen (禅)

18, Rue du Louvre, 75001 Paris

☎ (01) 42–86–9505 (For reservations from Japan, call this Tokyo number: ☎ [03] 5390–1378)

Noon–2:30 P.M., 7:00–11:30 P.M., closed Sunday lunchtime, Mondays

GERMANY

Benkay (弁慶)

Nikko Dusseldorf

Immerman Strasse 41, 40210 Dusseldorf 1

☎ (0211) 834–2600

Deutsche "Nippon-kan" (日本館)

Immerman Strasse 35, 40210 Dusseldorf 1

☎ (0211) 35–31–35

ITALY

Ran (蘭)

Via Bordori 8, 10, 2104 Milan

☎ (02) 669–6997/0177

SPAIN

Yamashita (やました)

Josep, Tarradelles, 145, Barcelona

☎ (03) 419–06–97

UNITED KINGDOM

Donzoko (どんぞこ)
15 Kingley Street, London W1R 5LD
☎ (0171) 734–19–74

Jūjiro (十字路)
18 Frith Street, London W1V 5ST
☎ (0171) 494–38–78

Komasazushi (小まさ寿司)
14 Hanway Street, London W1P 9DD
☎ (0171) 637–77–20

Saga (嵯峨)
43–44 South Molton Street, London
☎ (0171) 408–2236

■ ASIAN AND AUSTRALIAN RESTAU-RANTS

AUSTRALIA

Hanabishi
187 King Street
Melbourne, Victoria
☎ (03) 670-1167

HONG KONG

Fukuki (福喜)
21–25 Wellington Street, Central, Hong Kong
☎ (852) 2877–6668

Gomitori (五味鳥)
Shop LG5, 92 Granville Road
Tsim Sha Tsui East, Kowloon, Hong Kong
☎ (852) 2367–8519

Kaetsu (鹿悦)
Grand Hyatt Hong Kong
1 Harbor Rd., Hong Kong
☎ (852) 2588–1234

Nadaman (なだ万)
Hotel Shangri-la Kowloon
64 Mody Rd.
Tsim Sha Tsui East, Kowloon, Hong Kong
☎ (852) 2721–2111

■ EUROPEAN RETAILERS

FRANCE

Cave Fuji
8, Rue Therese, 75001 Paris
☎ (01) 49–27–04–39

■ ASIAN RETAILERS

HONG KONG

Seibu
1901, Level 19, Two Pacific Place
88 Queensway, Central, Hong Kong
☎ (852) 2971–3382

SINGAPORE

Sogo
250 North Bridge Road
#05 00 Raffles City Tower, Singapore 0617
☎ (65) 330–8195

Sogo Food Hall
290 Orchard Road, #02 35, The Paragon, Singapore 0923
☎ (65) 732–4195

THAILAND

Yaohan
7 Rachadapisek Road,
Dindaeng Sub District, Dindaeng District, Bangkok 10310
☎ (02) 248–4119 (10 lines)

Zen Market Place
4 Rajadamri Road, Pathumwan, Bangkok 10330
☎ (02) 255–9693

12

Sake Producers Worldwide

S
ake has been made outside Japan for a surprisingly long time now. The first overseas sake breweries were responses to two great movements of Japanese people: emigrants and colonialists. The first group founded breweries to serve the needs of the new communities of Japanese living abroad, first in Hawaii and the mainland United States, and, somewhat later, in Brazil. Breweries were also established in the wake of Japan's colonial activities in Southeast Asia, notably in the former Manchurian colony and in Korea.

Extremely varied in their history, capacity, and volume of actual production, all these firms share one huge advantage over Japanese brewers—the low cost of rice. Estimates vary, but American-produced rice, for example, is said to cost about one-sixth to one-tenth of that grown in Japan. The long grained *indica* varieties are not well-suited to sake brewing, but makers in other countries have responded by growing *japonica* strains locally. (One report on American brewing wrote recently of "the short grain rice from Arkansas, *Akita Komachi*"!)

The target market for overseas producers is as diverse as their climates and cultures. Some are enjoying considerable success in their own domestic markets—the extraordinary popularity of the Chiyonha product of Korea's Beka firm being the most striking example—but others have an eye on the Japanese consumer. In 1990, a mere twenty-three kiloliters were imported into Japan; in 1995 and 1996, imports exceeded 3,000 kiloliters. The ball is rolling. At present, Korean sake accounts for 80% of imports, followed by China and Australia. Unless reforms of Japanese agriculture and distribution structure bring about a reduction in the price of rice, Japanese brewers must continue to compete with rivals enjoying a huge head start in production costs—a gap that all the industry's tradition and high standards may find hard to close.

Brewing in the United States

The first American brewery, and the main pillar of brewing in Hawaii, was the Honolulu Sake and Ice Company. Its history reflects many of the events that have influenced production in the United Sates. Brewing was interrupted on three occasions after the firm's foundation in 1908. First, during Prohibition, the brewery survived by making ice cream, an inventive strategy that was made possible by their refrigeration plant, at that stage still unheard-of in Japanese brewing. The second hiatus came with World War II. In the postwar years, the brewing of Takara Masamune, the brand affectionately known to local Japanese Americans as "Hula Girl sake" from the picture on the label, began once more. Then, in 1986, the Honolulu firm was bought out by the large Fushimi concern, Takara Shuzō. A few years later, citing transport costs for raw materials and the finished product, amongst other factors, the new owners discontinued production, bringing Hawaian sake brewing to a close, and shutting the book on the company's quite extraordinary history of perseverance and innovation. Sadly, there are no active sake-brewing facilities remaining in Hawaii. The Takara Masamune brand is still produced, but it is brewed on the mainland.

On the mainland, sake brewing began in the early years of this century, and a succession of more or less short-lived firms have come and gone. At the time of writing, seven breweries are on line, of which five are owned wholly or in part by Japanese producers.

American Pacific Rim

4732 East 26th Street, Vernon, CA 90040

☎ (213) 268–3794

Tasting room: none

Tours: by appointment

Founded in 1977, this is one of the smaller of the American breweries, with an ouput (in 1995/96) of 550 kiloliters. The firm's main product line is the California Ki-Ippon series, which I have spotted once or twice in Japan. The former company President, Taketsugu Numano, has played a considerable role in the recent history of sake in the United States. He began importing Japanese sake in the early 1970s, and was also formerly owner of the concern that became Takara Sake USA when bought out by one of Japan's largest producers.

Gekkeikan Sake USA

1136 Sibley Street, Folsom, CA 95630

☎ (916) 985–3111

Tasting room: 10 A.M.–5 P.M.

Tours: by appointment

Founded in 1989 by Japan's largest sake producer (home base in the famous Fushimi brewing district in Kyoto). Production started in 1991 at 1,000 kiloliters, but has increased. Where most American producers also make *mirin* (sweet "cooking sake"), Gekkeikan has stuck to drinkable sake. For more information on Gekkeikan, see the brewers' listings in the Sake Sampler.

Haku-shika Sake USA

4414 Table Mountain Drive, Golden, CO 80403

☎ (303) 278–0161

Tasting room: available

Tours: hourly, 10 A.M.–noon, 1–4 P.M., Mon–Fri (by reservation)

The White Deer brand is one of Japan's oldest, brewing since 1662 in the preeminent Nada region of western Japan. The American plant was founded in 1991: the site, supplied by local beer giant Coors, was chosen for the quality and the image of Rocky Mountain water. The firm's product range includes a *ginjō* made with California rice. On permanent display in a small gallery are sake-related photography and artwork brought from the museum attached to the mother company in Japan.

Japan American Beverage Company (Momokawa Sake Brewery)

920 Elm Street, Forest Grove, OR 97116

☎ (503) 357–7056

Tasting room: available noon–5 P.M., daily

Tours: call ahead

The newest member of the American sake-brewing fraternity. The parent company is Momokawa, a brewery situated in Aomori Prefecture in the far north of Japan. Brewing of Momokawa Sapphire, their first American effort, began in 1997. It is made from *Akita Komachi* sake rice grown in Arkansas. The company aims to develop a market for high-grade sake, stressing cold sake over the hot stuff that seems to be the rather brutal norm in the United States.

Kohnan (Hakusan)

1 Executive Way, Napa, CA 94558

☎ (707) 258–6160

Tasting room: 9 A.M.–6 P.M.

Tours: 9 A.M.–6 P.M.

The Japanese parent company is not a sake brewer, but the holder of the Japanese Coca-Cola franchise, with links to a conglomerate best known for *shōchū* spirit. The fact that Hakusan ("White Mountain") is an American-only brand name presumably means that they are free of image-related worries in their home market (unlike most of their competitors, who have their domestic image and market share to consider). This firm stocks a well-illustrated book, *The Joy of Sake*, available for $12.

Ozeki Sake USA

249 Hillcrest Road, Hollister, CA 95023

☎ (408) 637–9217

Tasting room: by appointment

Tours: by appointment

This plant was established in 1979, making it the oldest of the breweries currently in service, following the sad termination of the production activities of the Honolulu Sake Company in 1992. The Japanese parent company is one of the Japanese giants. For more information on Ozeki, see the listings in the Sake Sampler.

Takara Sake USA

708 Addison Street, Berkeley, CA 94710

☎ (510) 540–8250

Tasting room: noon–6 P.M.

Tours: none

Founded in 1983, this is the largest sake producer in the United States, with over 2,300 kiloliters brewed in 1996. The parent company, Takara Shuzō, is one of Japan's largest producers of alcoholic beverages, from Shōchikubai sake to *mirin* ("cooking sake") and *shōchū* (a Japanese spirit). The American concern's activities are equally eclectic: apart from a range of sake products, the firm also offers plum wine, *mirin*, and *shōchū*. The brewing water comes from the Sierra Nevada, which gives its name to the low-alcohol sake Sierra (12% by volume). The name Shōchikubai is comprised of the characters for pine, bamboo, and plum. In Japan, these three plants are celebrated for their hardiness—the plum tree in particular blossoming at the chilly peak of the traditional sake-brewing season—and so are a traditional symbol of felicity, used particularly at times of celebration.

Brewing in Asia, Australia, and Brazil

In Southeast Asia, breweries were first set up in the prewar period of Japan's occupation of Korea and parts of China. There are now more breweries operating on a modest scale in China, but Korean sake, though produced by only three firms, has become a booming business. The largest firm, Seoul's Beka, produces on the scale of the big Japanese firms, and has the lion's share of the market. The small firm that hand-brews Chiyohe sake was founded in 1925, and, as far as I know, is the oldest of all overseas breweries still operating.

In Thailand a huge state-of-the-art plant started production in 1995, using specially grown *Japonica* rice (Japanese short-grained varieties). A plant financed by a Japanese producer began construction in Vietnam in 1995. The seventy years of sake brewing in continental Asia can never before have seen such large-scale investment in such a short time.

AUSTRALIA

Sun Masamune

> 29–32 Cassola Place, Penrith, N.S.W. 2750
> ☎ 02–4732–2833
> Tasting room: 9 A.M.–4 P.M. Mon to Fri; 2–4 P.M. Sat, Sun, and holidays
> Tours: arrive by 2/2:30 P.M.

This firm, funded with investment from the giant Itami maker of the Shirayuki brand, Konishi Shuzō, and from Kitajima Shuzō (whose sake, Miyozakae, is listed in the Sake Sampler), began production in 1996. Their product line includes a *junmaishu*, a *junmai ginjōshu*, and a *nama* sake (to be drunk cold). The sake is also being shipped back to Japan for sale (mainly in convenience stores) with the inevitable koala on the label.

BRAZIL

In Brazil, rice grown on a model farm near Sao Paolo was first used to make sake in the 1930s. Nowadays, the firm (making Azuma Kirin— "Eastern Kirin"—sake) produces under the aegis of Japan's biggest beer manufacturer, Kirin. A second firm brews only at an experimental level.

Indústria Agrícola Tozan

> R. Galvão Bueno, 212–5° and CJ, 52 Saõ Paulo, SP 01506–900
> ☎ (11) 278–4299, fax (11) 279–7713

Sakura-Nakaya, Alimentos

> Rua Ordenações N.º 151, São Paulo, SP 03446–030
> ☎ (11) 295–4177, fax (11) 941–0444

13

Sake Exporters and Distributors

EUROPE

Okanaga Europe S.A.R.L. (Mr. Katsutoshi Kamei)
8. Rue Therese, 75001 Paris, France
☎ (331) 4296–1758, fax (331) 4020–9756

UNITED STATES AND CANADA

American Pacific Rim, Inc. (Ms. Yoko Sasaki)
4732 East 26th St., Vernon, CA 90040
☎ (213) 268–3794, fax (213) 268–4956

Nishimoto Trading
410 East Grand Avenue
South San Francisco, CA 94080
☎ (415) 87–2490

Wine of Japan Import, Inc.
235 West Parkway
Pompton Plains, NJ 07444
☎ (201) 835–8585, fax (201) 835–9097

Mr. Kazuhide Yamazaki
100 Vandam St., New York, NY 10013
☎ (212) 924–8189, fax (212) 366–4925

WORLDWIDE

The Sake Export Association
At the time of writing, still a fledgling organization, the Sake Export Association (SEA) aims to export premium sake and educate overseas markets. It boasts a mouthwatering roster of member breweries, as listed below.

Sake Export Association (SEA) Office

407, 5–2–4 Sendagaya, Shibuya-ku, Tokyo 151–0051, Japan

東京都渋谷区千駄ヶ谷5–2–4–407　〒151–0051

☎ (03) 5269–0105, fax (03) 5269–0102

E-mail: sea@ceres.dti.ne.jp.

Web: http://www.ceres.dti.ne.jp/~sea

Azuma Rikishi	Shimazaki Brewery, Tochigi Prefecture
Chiyo no Sono	Chiyo no Sono Brewery, Kumamoto Prefecture
Denshu/Kiku-izumi	Nishida Brewery, Aomori Prefecture
Dewa-zakura	Dewa-zakura Brewery, Yamagata Prefecture
Dewa-zuru/Kariho	Akita Seishu Brewery, Akita Prefecture
Eikō Fuji	Fuji Brewery, Yamagata Prefecture
Fuchū Homare	Fuchū Brewery, Ibaraki Prefecture
Fukuchō	Imada Brewery, Hiroshima Prefecture
Hatsu-mago	Tōhoku Meijo Brewery, Yamagata Prefecture
Kaiun	Doi Brewery, Shizuoka Prefecture
Kiku-yoi	Aoshima Brewery, Shizuoka Prefecture
Kirin	Kaetsu Brewery, Niigata Prefecture
Kokushi Musō	Takasago Brewery, Hokkaido
Maihime	Maihime Brewery, Nagano Prefecture
Masu-izumi	Masuda Brewery, Toyama Prefecture
Nanbu Bijin	Kuji Brewery, Iwate Prefecture
Rihaku	Rihaku Brewery, Shimane Prefecture
Rikyū-bai	Daimon Brewery, Osaka-fu
Sake Hitosuji	Toshimori Brewery, Okayama Prefecture
Shichi-fukujin	Kiku no Tsukasa Brewery, Iwate Prefecture
Shokō	Kumazawa Brewery, Kanagawa Prefecture
Suehiro	Suehiro Brewery, Fukushima Prefecture
Taki Koi	Kimura Brewery, Hyōgo Prefecture
Tama Jiman	Ishikawa Brewery, Tokyo
Tedori-gawa	Yoshida Brewery, Ishikawa Prefecture
Tenju	Tenju Brewery, Akita Prefecture
Tentaka	Tentaka Brewery, Tochigi Prefecture
Tenzan	Tenzan Brewery, Saga Prefecture
Waka no Kotobuki	Wakatakeya Brewery, Fukuoka Prefecture
Yamato-gawa	Yamato-gawa Brewery, Fukushima Prefecture

14

Sake on the Web

A few minutes' mousing about revealed a surprising number of sake-related sites in English. They cover the usual range, from the informative and entertaining to the dull, dubious, and even surreal. The following list includes all the English sites of particular producers I could find, and one or two others that I found interesting. Anyone looking for more English sites related to sake is referred to the lengthy list which is to be found at this address: http://www.gwjapan.org/sakenet/sakelink.html.

Akita Brewer's Union
http://www.media-akita.or.jp/akita-sake-sakeE.html
This offers excellent and extensive technical information, along with an interesting account of the history of brewing in the region. The site is linked to more general, regional information and photos, making it very pleasant to browse through. The prefecture-run information center in Tokyo is also featured.

Echigoya (Retailer)
http://www.echigoya.com/
Kindly informs visitors in English and French that information is given only in Japanese. Hmmm. However, the site includes a lengthy (Japanese!) sake index, with links to the home pages of a considerable number of breweries (the underlined entries), with photographs in many cases.

Hakurei (Producer)
http://www.dancer.or.jp/u/hakurei/english.html
Brief company profile and product notes.

Hakusan (US Producer)
http://www.hakusan.com/index.html
Homepage of the brewery in the wine country of Napa Valley. Includes

directions and a map, and pictures of the facilities, which also has Japanese-style gardens. A printout of the homepage entitles you to a free tasting for up to four people. Goods offered for sale include sake cups and *masu*.

Haku-shika (Japan/US producer)

http://www.sakeweb.com/hakushika/

This site contains a map and directions to the brewery, and a list of "frequently asked questions" with answers.

Harasho (Retailer)

http://www.pjnet.com/harasho/indexl.html

Gives label pictures and information about a few of their top-selling brands.

Hiroshima Sake

http://www.hiware.or.jp/hi2201-e.html

A brief history of brewing in Hiroshima, with links to pages of phone numbers, addresses, and labels of breweries in the prefecture.

Home Brewing

http://www.spagnols.com/handouts/sake.html

Gives home-brewing recipes courtesy of brewing writer Fred Eckhardt.

Izumibashi (Producer)

http://www.sphere.ad.jp/izmibasi/

This charming site introduces the operations of this brewery, with pictures illustrating the various stages of brewing. Though it appears to be offering information in eight languages, I can only find engagingly accented English. They ask for correspondence in English or Esperanto only.

Joy of Sake

http://www.joyofsake.com/IntroPg.html

Basically a reworking of material from the eponymous booklet distributed by the American-based Hakusan brewery (q. v.). Includes pictures illustrating the brewing process, and a few shots of various product labels with vital statistics all under the rather grand heading of "The World's Best Sake."

Kikusui (Producer)

http://www.bic-akita.or.jp/kikusui/new-b.html

The standard product information and photos, but also offering a brewing diary with a number of photographs. The commentary offers drinkers the splendid advice: "You have to find a bridegroom for your sake."

Labels

http://ecbos.tmit.ac.jp/sake/label.html
Simply a collection of sake labels.

Momokawa (Japan/USA producer)

http://www.teleport.com.~momokawa/
Selection of illustrated product introductions, with some information about brewing techniques and policy, including a few photographs of the premises and so on. The site also includes an offer for a free booklet, the "Connoisseur's Guide to Sake."

Otokoyama (Producer)

http://eolassun.eolas.co.jp/hokkaido/otokoyama/otokoyama/otoko03e.html
A variety of pages showing off the firm's varied and, it would seem, lovely facilities. Attractions include a gallery of *ukiyo-e* woodblock prints (under the heading "History of Otokoyama"), and pictures of the brewery's splendid flower gardens in the shadow of the building ("Flower Garden").

Sake World

http://www.sake-world.com/home/.html
Produced by John Gauntner, who publishes the *Sake World* newsletter. The site gives information about the newsletter and a glossary of sake-related terms, and also includes a questionnaire.

Shirayuki (Producer)

http://www.konishico.jp./E/shirayuki/index.html
One of the most enjoyable English sake sites. Lots of information about the firm's venerable history and products, spiced with plenty of cultural and historical detail, making for a diverting read. The section listed under "Shirayuki Presents Special Products" introduces sake for sale in a range of gorgeous containers, including 300 milliliters of sake for a million yen (about $7,500), for those with a taste for luxury. Other features of this varied site include a portfolio of photographs of Mount Fuji taken by the company chairman, and a virtual guestbook to sign.

Suihitsu (Isaka Shōten/Retailer)

http://www.suihitsu.co.jp/eng/lecture/sake/sake.html
The best feature of this site are the illustrations of Edo period (1603–1868) brewing which adorn the text. The hyperbolically named "Sake Dictionary" contains only a very few terms. The section "Isaka's Cellar" gives pictures and details about quite a number of the firm's best-selling brands.

Sun Masamune (Australian Producer)

http://sun-masamune.com.au/

Information on the firm's products, and details (with map) of the visitor's center and local attractions. Also includes a form for online orders.

Tamanohikari (Producer)

http://sake.com/

Pages and pages of information regarding sake in general, and Fushimi's Tamanohikari in particular. It also offers the chance to order the product at US$35 a bottle.

Toshimori Shuzō (Producer)

http://optic.or.jp./companies/tosimoribrewery/tosimoribrewery-e.html

Primarily a request for overseas sales agents.

15

An Extended Directory of Retailers, Bars, and Japanese Restaurants in the United States

ARIZONA

Fujiya Market	1335 West University Dr., Suite 5, Tempe	(602) 968–1890
New Tokyo Market	3435 West Northern Ave., Phoenix	(602) 841–0255

CALIFORNIA

• Anaheim

Hamayu Restaurant	6324 E. Santa Ana Canyon Rd., #A-4, Anaheim	(714) 974–4512
Nippon Foods	2935 W. Ball Rd., Anaheim	(714) 826–5321

• Arcadia

Tokyo Wako	401 E. Huntington Dr., Arcadia	(818) 447–8761

• Arleta

Fuji Restaurant	9071 1/2 Woodman Ave., Arleta	(818) 892–9035

• Berkeley

Musashi Market	2126 Dwight Way, Berkeley	(510) 843–2017
Tokyo Fish Market	1220 San Pablo Ave., Berkeley	(510) 524–7243

• Beverly Hills

Chaco	230 N. Camden Dr., Beverly Hills	(310) 247–1829
Kippan Restaurant	260 N. Beverly Dr., Beverly Hills	(310) 858–0535
Matsuhisa	129 N. La Cienega Blvd., Beverly Hills	(310) 659–9639
Papashon	8635 Wilshire Blvd., Beverly Hills	(310) 360–0807
Sushi Sushi	326 1/2 S. Beverly Dr., Beverly Hills	(310) 277–1165

- **Brea**

Kai Restaurant	518A S. Brea Blvd., Brea	(714) 990–6937

- **Brentwood**

Taiko	11677 San Vicente Blvd., #302, Brentwood	(310) 207–7782

- **Buena Park**

Ginzaya	8682 Stanton Ave., Buena Park	(714) 995–7355

- **Burlingame**

Takemura Market	1360 Broadway, Burlingame	(415) 344–5004

- **Carlsbad**

Sushi Taisho	30 Carlsbad Village Dr., #214, Carlsbad	(619) 729–2437

- **Chatsworth**

Omino	20957–59 Devonshire St., Chatsworth	(818) 709–8822

- **Chula Vista**

Kinokawa	1335 Third Ave., Chula Vista	(619) 426–9592
Koto Restaurant	651 Palomar St., Chula Vista	(619) 691–1418

- **City of Industry**

Kamon Restaurant	17855 Colima Rd., City of Industry	(818) 965–5895
Nijiya Market	17869 Colima Rd., City of Industry	(818) 913–9991

- **Colton**

Sayaka Restaurant	1063 S. Mt. Vernon, Colton	(909) 824–6958

- **Concord**

Jana Market	1099 Reganti Dr., #A, Concord	(510) 682–0422

- **Corona Del Mar**

Genkai Restaurant	3344 E. Coast Hwy., Corona Del Mar	(714) 675–0771
Nagisa Sushi Restaurant	3840 E. Pacific Coast Hwy., Corona Del Mar	(714) 673–3933

- **Costa Mesa**

Sushi Wave	2075 Newport Blvd., #108, Costa Mesa	(714) 722–8736
Yaohan	665 Paularino Ave., Costa Mesa	(714) 557–6699

• Covina

Bishamon Japanese Restaurant	139 N. Citrus Ave., Covina	(818) 967–5900
Hayakawa	750 Terrado Plaza, #33, Covina	(818) 332–8288
Yashima Restaurant	236 E. Rowland St., Covina	(818) 331–4240

• Cypress

Echizen	9111 Valley View Blvd., #113, Cypress	(714) 828–2155
Gyushinte	10953 Meridian Dr., #J-K, Cypress	(714) 995–0691
Harima Restaurant	4009 W. Ball Rd., Cypress	(714) 527–3576
Uzushio Restaurant	10545 Valley View St., Cypress	(714) 236–0678

• Dana Point

Ichibiri	16 Monarch Bay Plaza, Dana Point	(714) 661–1544
Yama Tepan House	24961 Dana Point Harbor Dr., Dana Point	(714) 240–6610

• Diamond Bar

Jubei	20627 Golden Springs Dr., #2K, Diamond Bar	(909) 869–7881

• El Cerrito

Oriental Food Fair	10368 San Pablo Ave., El Cerrito	(510) 526–7444

• Encino

Enshino Japanese Restaurant	17047 1/2 Ventura Blvd., Encino	(818) 783–4621
Hirosuke Sushi	17237 Ventura Blvd., Suite C, Encino	(818) 788–7548
Wakatake	17920 Ventura Blvd., Encino	(818) 996–3164

• Fountain Valley

Ebisu Supermarket	18930–40 Brookhurst St., Fountain Valley	(714) 962–2108
Izakaya Restaurant	16650 Harbor Blvd., #C-5, Fountain Valley	(714) 775–3818
Kappa Horida	18450 Brookhurst St., Fountain Valley	(714) 964–4629
Kasen	9039 Garfield Ave., Fountain Valley	(714) 963–8769

• Gardena

Azuma Japanese Restaurant	16123 S. Western Ave., Gardena	(312) 532–8623
Daisuke	1541 S. Normandie Ave., Gardena	(310) 532–9537
Daruma-Izakaya	15915 S. Western Ave., Gardena	(310) 323–0133

Fukagawa	1630 W. Redondo Beach Blvd., Gardena	(310) 324–4306
Fukuhime	17905 S. Western Ave., Gardena	(310) 324–7077
Furaibo Restaurant	1741 W. Redondo Beach Blvd., Gardena	(310) 329–9441
Genji Restaurant	1425 W. Artesia Blvd., #17, Gardena	(310) 532–4842
Imari	2225 W. Redondo Beach Blvd., Gardena	(310) 532–9520
Isogen	18022 S. Western Ave., Gardena	(310) 327–5159
Kappo Restaurant	15116 S. Western Ave., Gardena	(310) 324–6129
Marukai	1740 W. Artesia Blvd., Gardena	(310) 660–6300
Maruyaki Japanese Style BBQ	1749 W. Redondo Beach Blvd., Gardena	(310) 329–3369
Pacific Super Market	1620 W. Redondo Beach Blvd., Gardena	(310) 323–7696
Sanuki no Sato	18206 S. Western Ave., Gardena	(310) 324–9185
Sennari Sushi	18220 S. Western Ave., Gardena	(310) 324–1970
Shin Sen Gumi	18517 S. Western Ave., Gardena	(310) 715–1588
Spoon House	1601 W. Redondo Beach Blvd., Gardena	(310) 538–0376
Sushi Bei	2021 W. Redondo Beach Blvd., Gardena	(310) 515–5246
Tori-Zen Yakitori Restaurant	16410 S. Western Ave., Gardena	(310) 323–8600
Tsukiji Restaurant	1745 W. Redondo Beach Blvd., Gardena	(310) 323–4077

• Glendale

Zono Sushi	139 N. Maryland Ave., Glendale	(818) 507–4819

• Goleta

Indo China	6831 Hollister Goleta	(805) 968–3353
Kashima	5746 Hollister Ave., Goleta	(805) 683–8724
Nikka	5721 Calle Real, Goleta	(805) 964–7396

• Hermosa Beach

Sushi Sei	50 Pier Ave., Hermosa Beach	(310) 379–6900

• Hollywood

Sushi Dokoro	6065 Hollywood Blvd., #105, Hollywood	(213) 856–9972

• Huntington Beach

Daimon Restaurant	16232 Pacific Coast Hwy., Huntington Beach	(310) 592–4862
Hajime Restaurant	15892 Springdale Ave., Huntington Beach	(714) 891–4848
Matsu Restaurant	18035 Beach Blvd., Huntington Beach	(714) 848–4404

• Irvine

Eiko Market	14805 Jefferey Rd., #E, Irvine	(714) 551–3200
Goro	3931 Alton Parkway, #C, Irvine	(714) 252–1872
Sushi Riki	4790 Irvine Blvd., #103, Northwood, Town Center, Irvine	(714) 731–1543
Taiko Restaurant	14775 Jeffrey Rd., Irvine	(714) 559–7190
Uo Ki Sushi	15435 Jeffrey Rd., #119, Irvine	(714) 786–3420

• La Mesa

Shizuoka Japanese Restaurant	9118 Fletcher Pkwy., La Mesa	(619) 461–1151

• La Palma

Sushitatsu	5511 Orangethorpe Ave., La Palma	(714) 522–3792

• Laguna Niguel

Mijouri Sushi Bune	30251 Street of The Golden Lantern, Laguna Niguel	(714) 363–8840

• Lake Forest

Uoko Restaurant	23600 Rockfield Blvd., #2–1, Lake Forest	(714) 837–7231

• Lomita

Club Stallion	2230 Pacific Coast Hwy., Lomita	(310) 325–7577
Eboshi Noodle Bar	2383 Lomita Blvd., #116, Lomita	(310) 325–6674
Kotobuki Sushi Restaurant	1817 Pacific Coast Hwy., Lomita	(310) 530–7615
Tora Tora	1814 W. Lomita Blvd., Lomita	(310) 539–6607

• Long Beach

Kinokawa	1611 E. Wardlow Rd., Long Beach	(310) 427–8737

• Los Angeles

Aloha Grocery	4315 Centinola Ave., Los Angeles	(310) 822–2288
Asakuma Restaurant	11701 Wilshire Blvd., Los Angeles	(310) 826–0013

Asuka Restaurant	11941 Westwood Blvd., Los Angeles	(310) 474–7412
Café Sushi	8459 Beverly Blvd., Los Angeles	(213) 651–4020
Enbun Market	124 Japanese Village Plaza, Los Angeles	(213) 680–3280
Furaibo Restaurant	368 E. 2nd St., Los Angeles	(213) 613–1854
Granada Market	1820 Sawtelle Blvd., Los Angeles	(310) 479–0931
Hamakawa	209 Central Ave., Los Angeles	(213) 625–8125
Hassho	239 S. Vermont Ave., Los Angeles	(213) 387–1233
Hirozen	8385 Beverly Blvd., Los Angeles	(213) 653–0470
Hokkaido	1257 W. Temple St., Los Angeles	(213) 250–7502
Horikawa Restaurant	111 S. San Pedro St., Los Angeles	(213) 680–9355
In and Out Liquor	2130 Sawtelle Blvd., Los Angeles	(310) 312–5729
Isshin	10861 Lindbrook Dr., Los Angeles	(310) 208–5224
Itacho	6779 Santa Monica Blvd., #3, Los Angeles	(213) 871–0236
Kagaya	418 E. 2nd Street, Los Angeles	(213) 617–1016
Katsu Restaurant	1972 N. Hillhurst Ave., Los Angeles	(213) 665–1891
Katsu Restaurant	8636 W. 3rd St., Los Angeles	(310) 273–3605
Kokekokko	203 S. Central Ave., Los Angeles	(213) 687–0690
Komasa Restaurant	351 E. 2nd St., Los Angeles	(213) 680–1792
Kuishinbo	4001 Wilshire Blvd., #E, Los Angeles	(213) 380–5049
Kushinobo	123 S. Onizuka St., #305, Los Angeles	(213) 621–9210
Mako Sushi	123 S. Onizuka St., #307, Los Angeles	(213) 613–0083
Mame No Ki	2068 Sawtelle Blvd., Los Angeles	(310) 444–1432
Michi	11301 Olympic Blvd., #203, Los Angeles	(310) 473–5657
Mishima 2	8474 W. 3rd St., #108, Los Angeles	(213) 782–0181
Nagisa Sushi Restaurant	11330 Santa Monica Blvd., Los Angeles	(310) 478–1591
Nanbantei of Tokyo	123 S. Onizuka St., #203, Los Angeles	(213) 620–8744
Nanohana	319 E. 2nd St., #205, Los Angeles	(213) 687–7087
New Otani Hotel	120 S. Los Angeles, Los Angeles	(213) 629–1200
Noshi Sushi	4430 Beverly Blvd., Los Angeles	(213) 469–3458
Oiwake	122 Japanese Village Plaza, Los Angeles	(213) 628–2678
Oomasa Restaurant	100 Japanese Village Plaza, Los Angeles	(213) 623–9048
Sakura House	13362 Washington Blvd., Los Angeles	(310) 306–7010
Sobadokoro Taiko	11677 San Vicente Blvd., #302, Los Angeles	(310) 207–7782

Sushi Aki	11513 Santa Monica Blvd., Los Angeles	(310) 479–8406
Sushi Gen	422 W. 2nd., Los Angeles	(213) 617–0552
Sushi Kappo	456 E. 2nd., Los Angeles	(213) 617–1008
Tasuki Restaurant	416 Boyd St., Los Angeles	(213) 613–0141
Ten Sushi	4339 W. Sunset Blvd., Los Angeles	(213) 663–8890
Tokyo House	6333 W. 3rd St., Los Angeles	(213) 931–1928
Tokyo Kaikan	225 S. San Pedro St., Los Angeles	(213) 489–1333
Toricho	319 W. 2nd St., Los Angeles	(213) 485–0800
Usui Restaurant	343 E. 1st St., Los Angeles	(213) 680–1989
Yabu Restaurant	11820 W. Pico Blvd., Los Angeles	(310) 473–9757
Yagura Ichiban	101 Japanese Village Plaza, Los Angeles	(213) 623–4141
Yaohan	333 S. Alameda St., Los Angeles	(213) 687–6699
Yaohan	3760 Continela Ave., Los Angeles	(310) 398–2113
Yutaka	456 E. 2nd St., Honda Plaza, Los Angeles	(213) 617–1008
Yuu	11043 Santa Monica Blvd., Los Angeles	(310) 478–7931

• Malibu

Something's Fishy	18753 Pacific Coast Hwy., Malibu	(310) 456–0027
Zooma Sushi	29350 Pacific Coast Hwy., Malibu	(310) 457–4131

• Manhattan Beach

Octopus	1133 Highland Ave., Manhattan Beach	(310) 545–2826

• Marina Del Rey

Kifune	405 Washington Blvd., Marina Del Rey	(310) 822–1595

• Menlo Park

Naks Oriental Market	1151 Chestnut St., Menlo Park	(415) 325–2046

• Mission Viejo

Shin Sushi	26002 Marguerite Pkwy., Mission Viejo	(714) 582–1011

• Monterey Park

Kayo Restaurant	816 S. Atlantic Blvd., Monterey Park	(626) 282–7525
Shinano	1106 S. Atlantic Blvd., Monterey Park	(626) 300–0130
Taihei Restaurant	2195 S. Garfield Ave., Monterey Park	(213) 726–1787
Yoshino Market	111 N. Lincoln Ave., Monterey Park	(626) 573–0662

• Moreno Valley

Matsuri Restaurant   25100 Alessandro, #E, Moreno Valley   (909) 247–0767

• National City

Hanaoka Restaurant   1528 Sweetwater Rd., National City   (619) 477–5173

• Newport Beach

Kitayama Restaurant   101 Bay View Pl., Newport Beach   (714) 725–0777
Koto Restaurant   4300 Von Karman Ave.,   (714) 752–7151
Newport Beach

• North Hollywood

Nippon Restaurant   10155 Riverside Dr., North Hollywood   (818) 506–6167

• Northridge

Hatano Japanese   19401–9 Parthenia St., Northridge   (818) 885–6175
Restaurant
Kabuki Sushi   9701 Reseda Blvd., Northridge   (818) 886–8266

• Orange

Koisan Japanese   1132 E. Katella Ave., Orange   (714) 639–2330

• Oxnard

Kampai Restaurant   2367 N. Oxnard Blvd., Oxnard   (805) 988–0252

• Pasadena

Sushi Polo   927 E. Colorado Blvd., Pasadena   (818) 356–0099

• Rancho Cucamonga

Satsuma Sushi   9950 Foothill Blvd., #G,   (909) 941–7415
Rancho Cucamonga

• Redlands

Ichiban   1630 W. Redlands Blvd., Redlands   (909) 792–7177

• Reseda

Ramen Nippon   6900 Reseda Blvd., #D, Reseda   (818) 345–5946

• Riverside

Akina Sushi-Teppan   195 E. Alessandro Blvd., #8A, Riverside   (909) 789–2691
New Tokyo   5180 Arlington Ave., Riverside   (909) 689–8054
Restaurant
Teriyaki House   10170 Indiana Ave., Riverside   (909) 352–0675

• Sacramento

Ot's Japan Food   5770 Freeport Blvd., #49, Sacramento   (916) 424–2398

• Salinas

Tokyo Oriental Food   24 San Miguel Ave., Salinas   (408) 424–1175

• San Clemente

Ichibiri   1814 N. El Camino Real, San Clemente   (714) 361–0137

• San Diego

Chopstix	4633 Convoy St., #101, San Diego	(619) 569–9171
Fusako	4212 Convoy St., San Diego	(619) 277–7722
Hayama	911 Camino Del Rio South, San Diego	(619) 692–1152
Katzra	4229 Convoy St., San Diego	(619) 279–3430
Kobe Sushi	3944 W. Point Loma Blvd., San Diego	(619) 223–7624
Sushi a la Kaz	3870 Valley Center Dr., #302, San Diego	(619) 792–5509
Sushi Bar Nippon	532 4th Ave., San Diego	(619) 544–9779
Sushi Ota	4529 Mission Bay Dr., San Diego	(619) 270–5670
Tajima	4681 Convoy St., #1, San Diego	(619) 576–7244
Yaohan	4240 Kearny Mesa Rd., #119, San Diego	(619) 569–6699

• San Dimas

Little Tokyo   150 E. Bonita Ave., San Dimas   (909) 599–0666

• San Francisco

Maruwa Foods   1737 Post St., San Francisco   (415) 563–1901

• San Gabriel

39 Sushi	8151 Arroyo Dr., S., San Gabriel	(818) 573–5308
Natori	140 W. Valley Blvd., #118A, San Gabriel	(818) 307–8802
Tozai Food Market	1326 Potrero Grande Dr., S., San Gabriel	(818) 288–5124
Yaohan	515 W. Las Tunas Dr., San Gabriel	(818) 457–2899

• San Jose

Dobashi Mart	240 E. Jackson St., San Jose	(408) 295–7794
Santo Market	245 E. Taylor St., San Jose	(408) 295–5406
Yaohan	675 Saratoga Ave., San Jose	(408) 255–6690

• San Mateo

Draeger's Market	222 E. Fourth Ave.	(650) 685–3725
Supermarket Spark	175 W. 25th Ave., San Mateo	(415) 571–8620
Suruki Super Market	71 E. 4th Ave., San Mateo	(415) 347–5288
Takahashi Market	221 S. Claremont St., San Mateo	(415) 343–0394

• Santa Ana

Sankai	3940 S. Bristol St., #112, Santa Ana	(714) 241–7115

• Santa Barbara

Arigato Sushi	11 W. Victoria St., #16, Santa Barbara	(805) 965–6074
Edo Masa	202 Santa Catalina, Santa Barbara	(805) 963–3041
Edo Masa	271 De la Vina St., Santa Barbara	(805) 687–0210
Ichiban	1990 Cliff Dr., Santa Barbara	(805) 564–7653
Ichiban	650 Russell Way, Santa Barbara	(805) 687–1235
Kashima	179–F Camino De Vida, Santa Barbara	(805) 683–4987
Piranha	714 State St., Santa Barbara	(805) 965–2980

• Santa Monica

Hakata Restaurant	2830 Wilshire Blvd., Santa Monica	(310) 828–8404
Light House Buffet	201 Arizona Ave., Santa Monica	(310) 451–2076
Taka Sushi	1345 2nd St., Santa Monica	(310) 394–6540
Zipangu	802 Broadway, Santa Monica	(310) 395–3082

• Sherman Oaks

Kuishinbo	14622 Ventura Blvd., Sherman Oaks	(818) 386–0255
Mako Sushi	13905 Ventura Blvd., Sherman Oaks	(818) 789–1385

• Simi Valley

Fuji Restaurant	2845 Cochran St., Simi Valley	(805) 581–1225
Ken of Japan	4340 E. Cochran St., Simi Valley	(805) 527–6490

• Solana Beach

Samurai of Japan	979 Lomas Santa Fe Dr., Suite A, Solana Beach	(619) 481–0032

• South Pasadena

Ai Restaurant	1013 Fair Oaks Ave., South Pasadena	(818) 799–0534

• Stanton

Daimaru Market	11360 Beach Blvd., Stanton	(714) 891–0877
Mitsuyoshi	12033 Beach Blvd., Stanton	(714) 898–2156

• Studio City

Teru Sushi	11940 Ventura Blvd., Studio City	(818) 763–6201

• Tarzana

Kushi Yu	18713 Ventura Blvd., Tarzana	(818) 609–9050
Mon Restaurant	19463 Ventura Blvd., Tarzana	(818) 342–0307
Sushi Spot Restaurant	19658 Ventura Blvd., Tarzana	(818) 345–8651
Ueru-Ka-Mu	19596 Ventura Blvd., Tarzana	(818) 609–0993

• Thousand Oaks

Kashima	412 W. Hill Crest Dr., Thousand Oaks	(805) 496–7377

• Torrance

Bayside	2212 W. Artesia Blvd., Torrance	(310) 769–5548
Benihana of Tokyo	21327 Hawthorne Blvd., Torrance	(310) 316–7777
Cocono Sushi	1541 Crenshaw Blvd., #L, Torrance	(310) 534–5600
Daisuke	2814 W. Sepulveda Blvd., #G, Torrance	(310) 539–9020
Dojima-An	23737 Hawthorne Blvd., Torrance	(310) 373–0566
Eikoh Sukiyaki Garden	800 W. Carson St., Torrance	(310) 320–9012
Fukamoto	2621 Pacific Coast Hwy., Torrance	(310) 534–5445
Honda, Japanese Restaurant	3629 Pacific Coast Hwy., Torrance	(310) 373–8272
Housenka	1880 W. Carson St., #A, Torrance	(310) 618–8357
Iccho	25310 Crenshaw Blvd., Rolling Hills Plaza, Torrance	(310) 325–7273
Jarinko	1607 W. Sepulveda Blvd., Torrance	(310) 325–7034
Kantaro-Sushi	1542 W. Carson St., Torrance	(310) 320–0200
Kazan	1757 W. Carson St., #1, Torrance	(310) 320–5511
Kikusui	24584 Hawthorne Blvd., Torrance	(310) 373–5271
Koraku	2531 Pacific Coast Hwy., Torrance	(310) 517–0064
Kozan Yakiniku House	1510 Cabrillo Ave., Torrance	(310) 328–4140
Matsushima	1644 W. Carson St., #B, Torrance	(310) 787–8088
Mishima	21605 S. Western Ave., #G, Torrance	(310) 320–2089
Musha	1725 W. Carson St., #B, Torrance	(310) 784–7344
Nijiya Market	2121 W. 182nd St., Torrance	(310) 366–7600
Nijiya Market	2533–B Pacific Coast Hwy., Torrance	(310) 534–3000
Seafood Club	1757 W. Carson St., #S, Torrance	(310) 782–0530
Shuchan Restaurant	2143 W. 182nd St., Torrance	(310) 719–7102
Sushi Cocono	24631 Crenshaw Blvd., #L, Torrance	(310) 534–0600

Tsukuba Restaurant	2210 W. Artesia Blvd., Torrance	(310) 538–4828
Yaohan	21515 Western Ave., Torrance	(310) 782–0335

• Tustin

Osaka Kappo	13681 Newport Ave., #9, Tustin	(714) 730–7051
Suginoko	14215 Red Hill Ave., Tustin	(714) 832–3323
Taka Sushi	13112 Newport Ave., #D, Tustin	(714) 573–1571

• Van Nuys

Koyo Fish & Sushi	7032 1/2 Van Nuys	(818) 786–8093
Kyushu Ramen	15355 Sherman Way, Van Nuys	(818) 786–6005

• Venice

Hama Restaurant	213 Windward Ave., Venice	(310) 396–8783

• Walnut Creek

Diablo Oriental Food	2590 N. Main St., Walnut Creek	(510) 933–2590

• West Covina

Sakura of Tokyo	533 S. Glendora, West Covina	(818) 960–7155
Shizu	116 N. Grand Ave., West Covina	(818) 966–5279

• West Hollywood

Sushi on Sunset	8264 Sunset Blvd., West Hollywood	(213) 656–3242
Take Sushi	8866 Sunset Blvd., West Hollywood	(310) 659–6580

• West Los Angeles

Hana Sushi	11831 Wilshire Blvd., West Los Angeles	(310) 473–6828
Mishima	11301 Olympic Blvd., #210, West Los Angeles	(310) 473–5297
Nijiya Market	2130 Sawtelle Blvd., #105, West Los Angeles	(310) 575–3300
Safe & Save Market	2030 Sawtelle Blvd., West Los Angeles	(310) 479–3810
Sushi Sasabune	11300 Nebraska, West Los Angeles	(310) 268–8380
U-Zen	11951 Santa Monica Blvd., West Los Angeles	(310) 477–1390

• Westminster

Gesshin	16492 Beach Blvd., #J–14, Westminster	(714) 842–5581

• Woodland Hills

Something's Fishy	21812 Ventura Blvd., Woodland Hills	(818) 884–3880

FLORIDA

Japanese Market	1412 79th St., Causeway, North Bay Village	(305) 861–0143
Sushi Chef	3100 Coral Way, Miami	(305) 444–9286

GEORGIA

Food Mart Inoue	6253 Peachtree Ind., Blvd., Doraville	(404) 454–9234
Nippan Daido	2399 Chamblee Tucker Rd., Chamblee	(404) 455–3846
Oriental Farmers Food market	5345 Jimmy Carter Blvd., Norcross	(404) 368–8888
Tomato Japanese Groceries	2086–B Cobb Parkway, Smyrna	(404) 933–8808

HAWAII

Daiei Kaheka Store	801 Kaheka St., Honolulu	(808) 973–4800
Daiei Kailua Store	345 Hahani St., Kailua	(808) 261–8526
Daiei Waipahu Store	94–144 Farrington Hwy., Waipahu	(808) 678–6800
Marukai Wholesale Mart	2310 Kamehameha Hwy., Honolulu	(808) 845–5051
Shirokiya Ala Moana	Ala Moana Shopping Center, Honolulu	(808) 973–9111
Shirokiya Pearlridge	Pearlridge Shopping Center, Aiea	(808) 483–7711
Taniguchi Store	2065 S. Beretania St., Honolulu	(808) 949–1489

ILLINOIS

• Arlington Heights

Kitakata	20 E. Golf Rd., Arlington Heights	(847) 364–7544
Yaohan	100 E. Algonquin Rd., Arlington Heights	(847) 956–6699
Yaohan (Market)	100 E. Algonquin Rd., Arlington Heights	(847) 956–6699
Yuraku Tei	234 E. Golf Rd., Arlington Heights	(847) 437–2323

• Barlington

Sagano Restaurant	110 N. Hough Ave., Barlington	(847) 382–8980

• Buffalo Grove

Kamon Japanese Restaurant	129 Arlington Heights Rd., Buffalo Grove	(847) 537–7550

• Chicago

Ginza Restaurant	19 E. Ohio St., Chicago	(312) 222–0600
Hatsuhana Restaurant	160 E. Ontario St., Chicago	(312) 280–8808
Itto Sushi	2616 N. Halsted St., Chicago	(312) 871–1800
Kamehachi of Tokyo	1400 N. Wells St., Chicago	(312) 664–3663
Restaurant Suntory Chicago	11–15 Huron St., Chicago	(312) 664–3344
Star Market	3349 N. Clark St., Chicago	(312) 472–0599
Tsunami	1160 N. Dearborn, Chicago	(312) 642–9911

• Deerfield

Wakaba	20504 N. Milwaukee, Deerfield	(847) 541–7777

• Elk Grove Village

Wako Japanese Restaurant	1112 W. Devon Ave., Elk Grove Village	(847) 529–8822

• Evanston

Kuni's Japanese Restaurant	511 Main St., Evanston	(847) 328–2004

• Highland Park

Happi Sushi	600 Central Ave., Highland Park	(847) 432–1516

• Hoffman Estates

Kinokawa Japanese Restaurant	1578 W. Algonquin Rd., Hoffman Estates	(847) 705–9200
Sun San Corporation	1625 Arrowick Dr., Hoffman Estates	(847) 881–3800

• Horwood Heights

Fuji-ya	7201 W. Wilson Ave., Horwood Heights	(847) 887–3000

• Itasca

Hirano Restaurant	500 Park Blvd., Itasca	(847) 250–9010

• Lake Forest

Sushi Kushi Toyo	825 S. Waukegan Rd., Lake Forest	(847) 234–9950

• Lincolnwood

Renga-Tei Restaurant	3956 W. Touhy, Lincolnwood	(847) 675–5177

• Mt. Prospect

Torishin	1584–6, Busse Rd., Mt. Prospect	(847) 437–4590
Yasuke Inc.	1827 W. Algonquin Rd., Mt. Prospect	(847) 952–0450

• Northbrook

Fujiyama Japanese Restaurant	3057 Dundee Rd., Northbrook	(847) 714–1319
Kegon Japanese Restaurant	569 Waukegan Rd., Northbrook	(847) 498–1109

• Rolling Meadow

Sakura Restaurant	4011 Arbor Dr., Rolling Meadow	(847) 397–2166

• Vernon Hills

Tsukasa	700 N. Milwaukee, Vernon Hills	(847) 816–8770

• Westmont

Sushi House, Ltd.	830 Ogden Ave., Westmont	(847) 920–8948

• Wilmette

Akaihana	3223 W. Lake Ave., Wilmette	(847) 251–0384
Akaihana Japanese Restaurant	3217–23 W. Lake Ave., Wilmette	(847) 251–0384
Kappo Kamakura	1116 Central Ave., Wilmette	(847) 256–6783

NEVADA

Japan Food Express	1155 E. Sahara Ave., Suite 8, Las Vegas	(702) 737–0881

NEW JERSEY

• Cliffside Park

Izakaya Fukuchan	671 Palisades Ave., Cliffside Park	(201) 941–6665
Komachi Restaurant	458 Palisades Ave., Cliffside Park	(201) 941–5777

• Edgewater

Yaohan USA Corp.	595 River Rd., Edgewater	(201) 941–9113

• Fort Lee

Fort-Lee Hilton (SUGI)	2117 Route 4 East, Fort Lee	(201) 461–9000

| Tamaya | 2347 Hudson Terrace, Fort Lee | (201) 585–7009 |
| Yamaguchi (NJ) | 2165 Route 4, Fort Lee | (201) 947–3456 |

• Hackensack

| Tomi of Tokyo | 388 Route 40, Hakensack | (201) 641–3260 |

• Teaneck

| Izakaya Makoto | 252 Degraw Ave., Teaneck | (201) 907–0888 |

NEW YORK

• Ardsley

| Sushi Man | 724 Sawmill River Rd., Ardsley | (914) 693–8800 |

• Carle Place

| Marumi Restaurant | 540 Westbury Ave., Carle Place | (516) 333–3434 |

• Commack

| Kurofune Restaurant | 77 Commack Rd., Commack | (516) 499–1075 |

• Elmsford

| Hanaki Restaurant | 83 E. Main St., Elmsford | (914) 592–0004 |
| Ichiriki No. 2 | 1 E. Main St., Elmsford | (914) 592–2220 |

• Fort Lee

| Nippan Daido | 1385 16th St., Fort Lee | (201) 944–0020 |

• Harrison

| Momiji Restaurant | 261 Halstead Ave., Harrison | (914) 631–6842 |

• Hartsdale

| Akaihana | 17 E. Hartsdale Ave., Hartsdale | (914) 328–2199 |
| Tsuru | 259 N. Central Ave., Hartsdale | (914) 761–0057 |

• High Park

| Culinary Institute of America | 433 Albany Post, High Park | (914) 451–1545 |

• Huntington Station

| Kohaku | 2089 New York Ave., Huntington Station | (516) 351–9888 |
| Musashino Restaurant | 107 E. Jericho Tpke., Huntington Station | (516) 549–2784 |

• Jericho

Nagashima Japanese Restaurant	21A 1 Jericho Tpke., Jericho	(516) 338–0022

• Levittown

Sushi Ko	170A Gardeners Ave., Levittown	(516) 731–8232

• Mamaroneck

Top Sail Wines & Spirits	623 E. Boston Post Rd., Mamaroneck	(914) 698–6930

• Nanuet

Ume Sushi	237 W. Rt. 59, Nanuet	(914) 623–3110

• New Rochelle

Karuta Restaurant	77 Quaker Ridge Rd., New Rochelle	(914) 693–6688

• New York City

Akaihana-En	2164 Broadway, New York	(212) 724–8666
Ariyoshi	226 E. 53rd St., New York	(212) 319–3940
Astor Wine & Spirits	12 Astor Pl., New York	(212) 674–7500
Azusa of Japan	3E. 44th St., New York	(212) 681–0001
Beckman Liquors	500 Lexington Ave., New York	(212) 759–5857
Blue Ribbon	119 Sullivan St., New York	(212) 343–0404
BTM Liquors	1347 3rd Ave., New York	(212) 373–0790
Caviar Russe	538 Madison Ave., 2nd Fl., New York	(212) 980–5908
Chanterelle	2 Harrison St., New York	(212) 966–6065
Chikubu Restaurant	12 E. 44th St., New York	(212) 818–0715
Cotan Japanese Restaurant	121 W. 3rd St., New York	(212) 677–2370
East 55 Restaurant	251 W. 55th St., New York	(212) 581–2240
East Restaurant	210 E. 44th St., New York	(212) 687–5075
Eisay Restaurant	27 Thames St., New York	(212) 608–2992
Esashi Restaurant	32 Avenue A, New York	(212) 505–8726
Hamaya	152 E. 46 St., New York	(212) 867–6198
Hanami Restaurant	213 E. 45th St., New York	(212) 687–0127
Hasaki Restaurant	210 E. 9th St., New York	(212) 473–3327
Hatsuhana Restaurant	17 E. 48th St., 3rd Fl., New York	(212) 355–3345
Hatsuhana Restaurant	237 Park Ave., New York	(212) 661–3400
Hi-Life Restaurant	1340 1st Ave., New York	(212) 249–3600

Hizen	203 E. 45th St., New York	(212) 557–0299
Honmura An	170 Mercer St., New York	(212) 334–5253
Ikeno Hana Restaurant	1016 Lexington Ave., New York	(212) 737–6639
Iroha Restaurant	152 W. 49th St., New York	(212) 308–9049
Izakaya Decibel	229 E. 9th St., New York	(212) 228–3030
Izakaya Riki	141 E. 45th St., New York	(212) 986–5604
Japas	137 E. 47th St., New York	(212) 980–7909
Katsu Hama	11 E. 47th St., New York	(212) 758–5909
Kelley and Ping	127 Greene St., New York	(212) 228–1212
Kiraku	127 E. 56th St., New York	(212) 751–1088
Kitchen Club	30 Prince St., New York	(212) 274–0025
Kodama Restaurant	301 W. 45th St., New York	(212) 582–8065
Kurumazushi	7 E. 47th St., 2nd Fl., New York	(212) 317–2802
Little Tokyo Restaurant	252 W. 47th St., New York	(212) 719–9055
March Restaurant	405 E. 58th St., New York	(212) 754–6272
Maruchan Restaurant	160 W. 54th St., New York	(212) 246–0955
Match Restaurant	160 Mercer St., New York	(212) 343–0020
Menchanko-Tei 45	131 E. 45th St., New York	(212) 986–6805
Mikaku Restaurant	67 Liberty St., New York	(212) 349–0060
Mirezi	59 5th Ave., New York	(212) 242–9709
Nakagawa Restaurant	7 W. 44th St., New York	(212) 869–8077
Naniwa Restaurant of Japan	4 E. 46th St., New York	(212) 370–4045
Nippon Club	145 W. 57th St., New York	(212) 581–2223
Nobu Restaurant	105 Hudson St., New York	(212) 219–0500
Oikawa Restaurant	805 3rd Ave., New York	(212) 980–1400
O-Ishi Restaurant	430 3rd Ave., New York	(212) 481–8060
Onigashima Restaurant	43–45 W. 55th St., New York	(212) 247–1585
Park Ave., Liquor Shop	292 Madison Ave., New York	(212) 685–2442
Red Eye Grill	890 7th Ave., New York	(212) 541–9000
Restaurant Tokyo	342 Lexington Ave., New York	(212) 697–8330
Rikyu Restaurant	210 Columbus Ave., New York	(212) 799–7847
Ryoyu Foods Enterprise	10 E. 52nd St., New York	(212) 759–8484
Sakagura	211 E. 43rd St., B-1, New York	(212) 953–7253
Season Food Corp.	235 E. 4th St., New York	(212) 674–1727

Sekku Japanese Restaurant	343 Lexington Ave., New York	(212) 697–9020
Sesume Restaurant	1649 2nd Ave., New York	(212) 879–1024
Sharaku Restaurant	14 Stuyvesant St., New York	(212) 598–0403
Sherry-Lehmann	679 Madison Ave., New York	(212) 838–7500
Shinbashi An	141 E. 48th St., New York	(212) 752–0505
Shinbashi Restaurant	280 Park Ave., New York	(212) 661–3915
Sushi Jun	9 Barrow St., New York	(212) 929–3353
Sushi Masa	141 E. 47th, New York	(212) 715–0837
Sushi-Hatsu	1143 1st Ave., New York	(212) 371–0238
Take Sushi	71 Vanderbilt Ave., New York	(212) 867–5120
Takino	1026 2nd Ave., 4th Fl., New York	(212) 750–2108
Tamura Restaurant	106 Liberty St., New York	(212) 964–2247
Tango Restaurant	43 W. 54th St., New York	(212) 765–4683
Tanokyu	7 W. 46th St., New York	(212) 921–9365
Tatany 52	250 E. 52nd St., New York	(212) 593–0203
Temple Bar	332 Lafayette St., New York	(212) 925–4242
Tenkai	20 W. 56th St., New York	(212) 956–0127
Thomas & Inagiku International	111 E. 49th St., New York	(212) 355–0440
Thompson Wine & Spirits	222 Thompson St., New York	(212) 353–3566
Tobato Restaurant	356 E. 51st St., New York	(212) 826–4319
Toraya	300 1/2 E. 52nd St., New York	(212) 838–4351
Tsukiji Sushisay	38 E. 51st St., New York	(212) 755–1780
Tsukushi	346 1/2 E. 49th St., New York	(212) 758–8920
Village Yokocho	8 Stuyvesant St., New York	(212) 598–3041
Wave Japanese Restaurant	21 South End Ave., New York	(212) 240–9100
Windows on the World	One World Trade Center, 106th Fl., New York	(212) 524–7079
Yakitori Taisyo	5 St. Marks Place, New York	(212) 228–5086
Yakko Restaurant	114 E. 40th St., New York	(212) 986–2205
Yamaguchi 212	212 E. 52nd St., New York	(212) 754–4840
Yamaguchi Restaurant	35 W. 45th St., New York	(212) 840–8185
Yodo Restaurant	13 E. 47th St., New York	(212) 751–8775
Zen	31st St., Marks Place, New York	(212) 533–6855
Zutto Restaurant	77 Hudson St., New York	(212) 233–3287

- **Peral River**

Yuki House	11–21 E. Washington Ave., Peral River	(914) 735–8885

- **Port Washington**

Tsuruno Mai Restaurant	166–168 Main St., Port Washington	(516) 944–7490

- **Scarsdale**

Zachys Wine & Liquor Store	16 E. Parkway, Scarsdale	(914) 472–6390

- **Spring Valley**

Akira Sushi & Steak	49–38 Spring Valley Mkt., Spring Valley	(914) 426–5472

- **Suffern**

Koto Restaurant	83 Lafayette Ave., Suffern	(914) 357–8877

- **Thornwood**

Yama Japanese Restaurant	677 Commerce St., Thornwood	(914) 747–0377

- **White Plains**

Ajiyoshi	291 Central Ave., White Plains	(914) 948–6651

TEXAS

- **Addison**

Siegel's #5	15003 Inwood Rd., Addison	(214) 387–9873

- **Dallas**

Danny's Liquor	2001 W. Northwest Hwy., #120, Dallas	(214) 556–0148
Lakeside Liquor	2806 W. Northwest Hwy., Dallas	(214) 352–6991
Lucky Discount Liquor	2835 N. Henderson, Dallas	(214) 824–8456
Monticello Liquor	4855 N. Central, Dallas	(214) 520–6618

- **Houston**

Kazy's Gourmet	11346 Westheimer, Houston	(713) 293–9612
Nippan Daido	11138 Westheimer, Houston	(713) 785–0815

WASHINGTON

• Ballinger

Thrittway	20036 Ballinger Rd., Ballinger	(206) 368–7221

• Bellevue

K's Beverage	1100 Bellevue Way N.E., Bellevue	(425) 455–4301
Larry's Market	699 120th Ave. N.E., Bellevue	(206) 453–0600
Pete Wine	134 105th St. N.E., Bellevue	(425) 454–1100
Q.F.C. #826	15600 N.E. 8th St., Bellevue	(425) 865–0282
Uwajimaya	15555 N.E. 24th St., Bellevue	(425) 747–9012

• Bothel

Q.F.C. #850	22833 Bothel Everett Hwy., Bothel	(425) 485–1991

• Edmonds

Ho Do Ri Market	23830 Hwy. 99, #105, Edmonds	(425) 672–9611
Top Food	21900 Hwy. 99, Edmonds	(425) 672–4545

• Federal Way

Saerona Oriental Market	31260 Pacific Hwy. S., #112, Federal Way	(253) 839–6255
Top Food	31515 20th St., Federal Way	(253) 839–9299

• Issaquah

Fine Wine & Cigars	710 N.W. Gilman St., #112, Issaquah	(425) 392–6242

• Kirkland

Larry's Market	12321 120th Place N.E., Kirkland	(425) 820–2300

• Lynnwood

Food Emporium	13619 Muklteo Speedway, Lynnwood	(425) 745–8545
Pal Do World Market	17420 Hwy. 99, Lynnwood	(425) 742–2237

• North Seattle

Larry's Market	100 Aurora Ave., North Seattle	(206) 527–5333

• Redmond

Fine Wine & Cigars	16535 N.E. 76th St., #D1, Redmond	(425) 869–0869
Q.F.C. #371	8867 161st Ave. N.E., Redmond	(425) 869–8006

• Seattle

Ballerd Market	1400 N.W. 56th St., Seattle	(206) 783–7922

Big Star Grocery	1117–1119 N. Northgate Way, Seattle	(206) 729–0797
Larry's Market	100 Mercer St., Seattle	(206) 213–0782
Maruta Shoten	1024 S. Bailey St., Seattle	(206) 767–5002
McCarthy & Schering	2209 Queen Anne Ave. N., Seattle	(206) 282–8500
McCarthy & Schering	6500 Ravena Ave., S., Seattle	(206) 524–9500
Mutual Fish	2335 Rainier Ave. S.	(206) 322–4368
Pioneer Ship Supply Inc.	5505 1st Ave., S., Seattle	(206) 762–5999
Q.F.C. #807	2746 N.E. 45th., Seattle	(425) 523–5160
Q.F.C. #847	1401 Broadway, Seattle	(206) 860–3818
Seattle Cellars	2502 2nd Ave., Seattle	(206) 256–0850
Thrittway	1908 Queen Anne Ave. N., Seattle	(206) 284–2530
Uwajimaya	519 6th Ave. S., Seattle	(206) 624–6248

• Tacoma

Boohan Oriental Market	9122 S. Tacoma Way, Tacoma	(206) 588–7300
Pal Do World Market	8730 S. Tacoma Way, Tacoma	(253) 581–7800

Glossary

akai sake あかい酒—"red sake." Made by a method patented in Niigata Prefecture, using a variety of *kōji* (*beni-kōji*) that gives a red color. In contrast, *aka-zake* (赤酒) refers to a rare type of sake particular to Kumamoto Prefecture, which takes its color from a type of ash added to the fermenting mash. Still other pink products receive their coloring from bio-engineered yeast varieties.

amai 甘い—sweet.

amakuchi 甘口—literally "sweet mouth." Used as an adjective to describe sweet sake.

ama-zake 甘酒—"sweet sake." Not a sake at all, but a sweet drink made from saccharified rice.

arabashiri あらばしり—the first run-off when a batch is pressed. Sometimes sold separately, carrying this name.

aru-ten アル添—"alcohol-added," the abbreviated form of

arukōru tenka アルコール添加—the addition of brewer's alcohol.

atsu-kan 熱燗—*see "kan-zake."*

awamori 泡盛り—type (or rather archetype) of *shōchū* (q.v.), distilled in Okinawa, the most southerly islands in the archipelago. Noted for highly distinctive methods of production and maturation.

brewer's alcohol—rectified alcohol, which may be used to fortify some kinds of sake, according to specific guidelines. *See "honjōzō* (shu)," "triple sake," and "*futsūshu*."

choko (o-choko) 豬口、ちょこ—the tiny china cups used for drinking sake. *See also "guinomi."*

chū-ginjō (chū-gin) 中吟醸—*see "ginjō(shu)."*

"cloudy sake"—*see "nigori-zake."*

daiginjō 大吟醸—*see "ginjō."*

futsūshu 普通酒—misleadingly named "ordinary sake." Made by a style of brewing in which much more alcohol may be added than for Special Designation Sakes—but less than for "triple sake" (q.v.). Additions of sugars are not permitted.

genmaishu 玄米酒—"brown-rice sake." Obviously, sake brewed from unpolished rice. Rare.

genshu 原酒—undiluted sake. May have more than 20% alcohol. Most sake is diluted (commonly to 15% or so) before sale, but a little is sold in this form.

ginjō(shu) 吟醸(酒)—Special Designation Sake, in Japanese originally signifying selected or special brew sake. The highest grade of sake. Further divided into middle and great *ginjō* (*chu-ginjō, daiginjō*, 中吟醸, 大吟醸).

ginjō-ka 吟醸香—the characteristic aroma of a *ginjō* sake.

gōseiseishu 合成清酒—"synthetic refined sake." Not sake in the true sense at all, it is synthesized from a variety of ingredients by a range of methods. The original method fermented sugars, with amino acids added to adjust the flavor. It was the product of research into the production of "sake" without using rice, at a time when shortages of the staple food were severe enough to provoke riots. Production has declined to a fraction of its 1960 peak, but this extremely economical beverage infuriates purists by refusing to die out.

guinomi ぐい呑み—a sake cup, but larger than the tiny *sakazuki* or *choko* (q.v.).

hi-ire 火入れ—literally the "putting in of fire"; pasteurization.

hine-ka 老香—literally "aged smell." It refers (not always flatteringly) to the characteristic aromas that arise when sake matures. Some prefer to distinguish between the (*hine-ka*) aromas of sake aging downhill, and *jukusei-ka* (熟成香), the rounded aromas of maturing sake.

hire-zake ひれざけ—"fin sake." Sake with the grilled fin of a blowfish in it, with distinctive flavor as a result. Frowned on by purist connoisseurs, as the real flavor of the sake tends to be smothered.

hiya-oroshi ひやおろし—autumn sake, with a rounded flavor, several months after pasteurization in spring.

hiya-zake 冷酒—"cool sake." May refer to chilled sake, or that served at room temperature. Sometimes just "*hiya*," though "*o-hiya*" is also ordinary water in drinker's parlance. Also called *reishu*.

honjōzō(shu) 本醸造(酒)—Special Designation Sake in which up to a quarter of the total alcohol is brewer's alcohol added to the fermenting mix before pressing. (Strictly speaking, the brewer may add 116 liters of pure alcohol per ton of white rice.)

izakaya 居酒屋—variously translated, the word refers to a generally quite homey breed of eating and drinking establishment.

ji-zake 地酒—"local sake." An overused and underdefined expression. *See* the sidebar for "J" for details.

jukusei-ka—*see* "*hine-ka*."

junmai(shu) 純米(酒)—"pure rice sake."

kanpai 乾杯—vital word in drinker's conversation: cheers!

kan-zake 燗酒—hot or warm sake. Sake should not be fiercely heated and, in places that care, "*atsu-kan*" (piping hot sake) is actually less common than "*nuru-kan*" (the warm variety). Often referred to honorifically as *o-kan*. Don't let anyone tell you heating sake is wrong. *Over*heating is a sin: *warming* has been the commonest way to serve sake for hundreds of years.

kan-zukuri 寒造り—the winter-only pattern of brewing which became the rule during the Edo Period (1603–1868). Though some larger firms now brew almost year round in refrigerated factories, most *kura* still adhere to this traditional pattern.

karai 辛い—dry (though it also means "hot," in the sense of hot, spicey food).

karakuchi 辛口—from characters for "dry" and "mouth"; an

adjective used to describe dry sake. *See also "tanrei karakuchi."*

"keg sake"—*see "taru-zake."*

kijōshu 貴醸酒—written with characters meaning "precious brewed sake." A portion of the water used in brewing is replaced with sake in a method with similarities to the making of port. The resulting sake is very sweet and heavy, rather liqueurlike. Generally matured for several years before sale.

kikishu きき酒—this is the term for "sake tasting."

kimoto 生酛—"raw" or "live" *moto* (q.v.). Yeast starter made by an old, laborious, and time-consuming method, giving a sake with a complex aroma. A revised version, *yamahai* (q.v.), is now the most common form of the *kimoto* school.

kinshōshu 金賞酒—literally, "gold prize sake." Refers to sake which has received the highest honor in the annual trade contest for new sake, held every spring. Sometimes sold as a premium item at deluxe prices. Sake being the tricky business it is, the contents may not always show the same charisma that impressed the judges in the spring, by the time it reaches the customer weeks or months later. Don't be misled by labels which read, not *kinshōshu*, but *kinshōgura* (金賞蔵), "gold prize *kura*." This merely indicates that a sake made by the brewery took the gold medal—not necessarily the one in the bottle.

kōbo 酵母—yeast.

kōji 麹—properly, any of a number of molds used in the making of sake, soy sauce, *shōchū* spirit, or *miso*, and in brewing in some Southeast Asian countries. Sake brewing uses "yellow *kōji*" (*Aspergillus oryzae*) propagated on steamed rice. The word is also commonly used colloquially to refer to this "rice *kōji*."

koshu 古酒—"old sake," aged or matured sake.

kura 蔵—a sake brewery, also called a *sakagura*. (The character 倉, also pronounced *kura*, simply refers to a warehouse, though originally both characters were used interchangeably.)

kura-bito 蔵人—brewery worker. *See also* the sidebar for "K."

masu 枡—a square, wooden box, sometimes used to drink sake from (most commonly at weddings and festivals). The flavor of the wood tends to overpower that of the sake, so higher-grade sakes are not usually drunk from *masu*.

Miyamizu 宮水—superb brewing water discovered in Nishinomiya in the Nada region of present-day Hyōgo Prefecture in the nineteenth century.

moromi 醪—the main mash; fermenting sake before pressing.

moto 酛—yeast starter. Also known as *shubo* (酒母, literally "sake mother"), this early stage in the brewing process is a dense preparation of pure sake yeast. The standard method is the *sokujō* (速醸), or quick-fermentation method. The older *kimoto* (raw, live *moto*) styles are now much less common.

nama-zake (*namashu*) 生酒—"live sake." It has not been pasteurized, which means that yeast bacteria, enzymes, and so on are still active. This also means that the taste is very prone to change. *Nama* sakes must be refrigerated, and are best drunk quickly once opened.

nigai 苦い—bitter.

nigori-zake にごりざけ—"cloudy sake." At the pressing stage, passed only through a wide mesh, and consequently contains quite large rice particles in suspension.

nihonshudo—*see* "sake meter value."

nomiya 飲屋—colloquial expression for a "drinking shop."

nuru-kan ぬるかん—*see* "*kan-zake.*"

o-choko—*see* "*choko.*"

o-kan—*see* "*kan-zake.*"

ori-zake 滓酒 おりざけ—"lees sake." Like *nigori-zake*, it contains a sediment made of rice particles. "*Ori*" means "lees," and signifies a finer sediment than that found in *nigori*.

ōte 大手—"big hand." Refers to the giant sake breweries.

"plum sake"/"plum wine"—*see* "*umeshu.*"

"pure rice sake"—*see* "*junmaishu.*"

"red sake"—*see* "*akai sake.*"

reishu 冷酒—"chilled sake"; *see also "hiya-zake."*

rice polishing ratio 精米歩合—*Seimai buai* in Japanese. A figure denoting the grade of white rice. Given as the percentage of the grain remaining. A ratio of 70% means 30% of the grain has been removed.

sakagura 酒蔵—*see "kura."*

sakaya 酒屋—literally a "sake shop." This can be a confusing term, since it is used to refer to both retailers and producers. The matter is sometimes clarified by referring more exactly to a brewery as a *"tsukuri-zakaya."*

sakazuki 盃—*see "guinomi."*

sake meter value 日本酒度—a figure used as an index of sweet and dry. The sake meter itself is a device like a hydrometer for measuring residual sugar. A plus reading indicates a dry sake, a minus figure shows a sweeter brew. The larger the figure the sweeter or dryer the sake in question should be.

sanmi 酸味—sourness. The expression *sanmi ga tsuyoi* (the sourness is strong) is rather more commonly used than the apparently more straightforward *suppai* (sour).

sanzōshu 三増酒—"triple sake." Low-grade sake, named for the method of production. Raw alcohol, sugars, monosodium glutamate, and so on are added to the mix before pressing, tripling the yield.

seimai 精米—rice "polishing."

seimai buai—*see* "rice polishing ratio."

seishu 清酒—"clear," or "refined" sake. All (legal) modern sakes fall into this category. To qualify, the sake must be passed through a mesh or net of some kind. Since all sake must be strained in some way according to sake-related legislation, *"seishu"* is simply the generic name for sake. As a result, just about every bottle of sake carries this designation.

shiboritate しぼりたて—"just pressed." Sometimes used as a generic brand name.

shibui 渋い—"astringent."

shinshu 新酒—"new sake."

shizuku 雫—literally "droplets." This is sake that has not been pressed in the conventional manner. Instead, the *moromi* is poured into sake bags which are then hung up, and the liquid that drips out under its own weight is collected. Time-consuming, laborious, and inefficient, this method (known in the trade by the gruesome epithet *kubi-tsuri,* "hanging by the neck") results in sake of great softness and refinement of flavor.

shōchū 焼酎—spirit, distilled in a number of regions from a variety of ingredients (wheat is most common). Distinguished from Western spirits by use of *kōji* at stage of initial fermentation. Main area of production is southern island of Kyūshu.

shubo 酒母—*see "moto."*

Special Designation Sake (*Tokutei Meishōshu*) 特定名 称酒—group of high-grade sakes, falling into three broad categories: *junmai, honjōzō,* and *ginjō* (q.v.).

sugi-dama 杉玉—also *sakabayashi;* a globe of the needles of the cryptomeria (sometimes rendered as "Japanese cedar"); the symbol of a sake brewery. The *sugi* is a holy tree, associated with the sake deity of the Miwa Shrine in Nara Prefecture, where *sugi-dama* are made. A sake festival, held at the shrine every autumn, is attended by brewery owners and *tōji* (q.v.) to pray for a successful season. The globes received at that time are still green. In days past, it is said that when the color of the globe hanging from the eaves changed to brown in the spring, this served as a sign to the locals that the new sake was ready for sale.

tachi-nomiya 立飲み屋—a shop where the customers stand and drink at the counter. Often attached to a retailer.

tamago-zake 卵酒—"egg sake." A hideous cold remedy, made of raw eggs and hot sake. Only for the desperate.

tanrei karakuchi 淡麗辛口—"*tanrei*" means, approximately, light and crisp; "*karakuchi*" is dry. In combination, they refer to the crisp, dry, light style of sake that has become increasingly popular in recent years.

taru-zake 樽酒 たるざけ—"keg sake." Sake that has been aged in Japanese kegs, taking on their flavor. Rather uncommon.

te-zukuri 手造り—making by hand; handmade.

tōji 杜氏—a master brewer. *See also* the sidebar for "T."

tōketsushu 凍結酒—"frozen sake." The sake is frozen, and some kinds are drunk while still half frozen, in a slushlike state of a frozen cocktail.

tokkuri 徳利, とっくり—the small decanters used to hold and pour sake.

"triple sake"—*see "sanzōshu."*

umai/umami うまい/旨み—generally used to mean delicious/deliciousness, these words also carry an untranslatable extra meaning, referring to a rounded fullness of flavor.

umeshu 梅酒—"plum sake," frequently called plum wine. Not wine, not sake! It's made from green plums, pickled in *shōchū* (q.v.), or white spirit.

yake-zake やけざけ—not a kind of sake, but a way of drinking: the despairing sort indulged in by the unlucky in love or the recently-fired, when drowning their sorrows. Not recommended. "Drowning yourself in drink."

yamahai 山廃—sake for which the *moto* (q.v.) was made by the traditional, time-consuming, *yamahai* method. Though it is not an inalienable law, most people associate this style with full flavors and high levels of acidity. *See also "kimoto."*

Sake Listed by *Kanji*

Recommended Reading

Japanese

For those who can read Japanese, there is an abundance of literature available. From such a wide field, just a few recommendations.

Akiyama Yūichi. *Nihonshu* (Sake). Tokyo: Iwanami Shoten, 1994.

An excellent general introduction, containing historical and technical information; written for the general public by one of the sake world's most eminent researchers.

Matsuzaki Haruo. *Nihonshu Gaidobukku* (Sake Gaidobukku) *Guidebook.* Tokyo: Shibata Shoten, 1995.

Uncannily apt tasting notes on no less than 1,212 brands of sake: information on over 400 breweries, regional characteristics, and so on.

Oze Akira. *Natsuko no Sake* (Natsuko's Sake). Tokyo: Kodansha, 1988.

Comic-book series packed with thoroughly-researched detail.

Other

Antoni, Klaus. *Miwa: Der Heilige Trank* (Miwa: The Holy Drink). Stuttgart: Franz Steiner Verlag Wiesbaden GMBH, 1988.

Somewhat abstruse German text focused on the religious significance of sake from prehistoric times onward.

Gauntner, John. *Sake World.* Newsletter, published bimonthly.

A columnist for the *Japan Times*, Gauntner also publishes his own newsletter on the brew, available at a yearly subscription rate of $35 or

¥3,500. Each issue contains his reviews of *izakaya* and sake brands. Contacts: John Gauntner, Setagaya Mishuku Mansion 502, 2–27–14 Mishuku, Setagaya-ku, Tokyo, Japan 154–0005 (fax 81–3–3413–3039, e-mail: zowie@twics.com); Kate Kamakahi, Sensei Incorporated, 304 S.E. 3rd St., St. Stephen, MN 56375 USA (toll free ☎ 1–888–273–6734, fax 320–203–8578, e-mail: gosensei@aol.com).

Kodama K., and Yoshizawa K. "Sake." In *Alcoholic Beverages.* London and New York: Academic Press, 1977.

Professional's description of contemporary sake brewing.

Kondo Hiroshi. *Sake: A Drinker's Guide.* Tokyo, New York, London: Kodansha International Ltd., 1984.

As the first English book on sake, it surely needs no introduction.

Nunokawa Yatarō. "Sake." In *Rice Chemistry and Technology.* American Association of Cereal Chemists, Inc., 1972.

A description of contemporary sake brewing.

Index

Acknowledgments

This book is the fruit of the kindness and generosity of many, many people, first and foremost of my colleagues and employers at Ume no Yado. Despite the length of this list, I feel sure I will have forgotten some benefactors who deserve better, and hope they will forgive my oversight and take my wholehearted thanks as given.

My thanks are due to the host of brewers, retailers, wholesalers, bartenders and miscellaneous sake lovers whose time, information, sake, and most of all, enthusiasm, made researching such a pleasure.

A large number of breweries, their staff and owners, have helped me in various ways, from moral support to guided tours and much information and inspiration. The following firms have been particularly generous with time, tours, information and support: Aihara Shuzō (Ugo no Tsuki), Fuchū Shuzō (Fuchū Homare, Wataribune), Ikemoto Shuzō (Biwa no Chōju), Miyoshino Shōten (Hana Tomoe), Nishiyama Shuzō (Kotsuzumi), Saijō Gōshi Gaisha (Ama no zake). In addition, my heartfelt thanks to the following individual members of the industry for their cooperation, friendship, support, and for the daunting examples of commitment they set: Junichirō Aihara, Shūji Fujimoto, Akira Sunda, Akira Tanaka, Takaaki Yamauchi, Toshiaki Yokomichi (as well as Chimachan), and Yasuo Yokosaka.

My gratitude also to the following firms for showing me around their premises: Asabiraki, Doi Shuzōjō (Kaiun), Fushimi Meishu Kyōdōkumiai, Imanishi Seibei Shōten (Harushika), Kariba Shuzō (Shūgetsu), Kinshi Masamune, Kizakura (Tanba plant), Nakamoto Shuzō (Yamazuru), Nishioka Shuzō (Tsukimaru), Ōzeki (Tanba plant), Saitō Shuzō (Eikun), Tsuki no Wa Shuzōten.

Particular thanks also to Kobori Michio of Kawai Shuzō, Matsukawa Hiroshi of Konishi Shuzō, and Matsumoto Takashi of Wakazuru Shuzō, for gratefully received materials and encouragement.

🍶 ◦● ◦●

Many more retailers than can be listed here have offered me much support and the opportunity to learn a great deal, both professionally and as regards research for this book. Shimada Shōten and Isodaya (both in Osaka) have been particularly rich sources for me. My thanks are also due to my closest sake suppliers: Wine Plaza Matsumura, Momotarō, Abetaya, and Nobori Sake Shop (all in Nara). In Osaka: Hayashi Shōten, Shimizuichi Shōten, Hyōtanya, and Yamanaka Sake no Mise. In Tokyo: Kōshuya, Sakaya, and Honma Shōten; and, elsewhere, to Shimaya (Chiba-shi); Hiraoka Sake Shop (Kobe), Hagiwara Atsushi of Hagiwara Shōten, Shizuoka, Masuyoshi (Chiba), Hamada Tetsuya of Hamadaya, (Tottori), Sakashō Yamada (Hiroshima), and Sake no Maeda (Fukuyama-shi).

Bars and restaurants and their staff and clients have been one of my most valuable sources. My thanks to the Suchi family of Tōmorokoshi; Minoru; Mugitarō; and the Yamamoto family who own Tanbaya (all in Osaka). In Tokyo: Akaoni; Ikesu; and Sakuragi-san of Ichinochaya. In my own area, I must thank Matsuribayashi and Ajisai, which have provided opportunities for research locally.

The staff and management of Ōboshi Okamura kindly introduced me to some of their valued clients. The Prestige Sake Association's Iida Eisuke was enormously generous with his valuable time and information.

Groups that have given me access to either a large audience, a large selection of fine sake, or both, include Hachiōji Meishukai, Honmonono Nihonshu o Ajiwau Kai, the International Business Association, Amnesty International (Osaka), Rakusuikai, Kobe International Community Center, and the Brewing Society of Japan.

Yoshiaki Chatani was one of the many individuals who gave me valuable advice; the late Tadahiko Hozumi kindly supplied information about brewing overseas. My appreciation also goes out to Toshio Yoshida for sharing his boundless enthusiasm and some of his fund of information with me. John Gauntner provided a spur to get some of my thoughts on paper in his newsletter, *Sake no Koto* (now *Sake World*). Nobuo Ishida of the Chūgoku Shinbunsha helped me with useful information, both in person and in the form of his excellent book on the subject of breweries outside Japan.

Many thanks to the head of the National Brewing Research Institute,

Yūichi Akiyama, for the generous loan of his copy of Atkinson's 1888 treatise on the chemistry of sake brewing, and much kind encouragement. With general instruction and support, the following teachers have been most kind: Masaharu Nagatani, Naomichi Nishiya of the Central Brewer's Union, and Kiyoshi Yoshizawa of Tokyo Agricultural University. In addition to the gratefully received professional guidance of the members of the Osaka Tax Office, I am indebted to them for some of the data in this book which they kindly provided.

I must also thank the Dobson family for helping and putting up with me during research activities in Tokyo, and for general friendship and encouragement during the writing of this book. The Kyōgoku family of Shinjuku also offered me their inimitable brand of hospitality. Roddy ("Edward") Llewellyn gave helpful criticism of the manuscript early on. Andrew Hare helped spread the load on my liver, and kindly made perceptive and extremely necessary suggestions for improvements in the final stages.

Haruo Matsuzaki gave me important help and advice early on in this manuscript's life, for which I extend my heartfelt thanks. His peerless practical writing for sake lovers is a source of wonder and inspiration.

▄● ●● ●▄

While writing this book, I have spent the winters in the close company, first, of the great brewer Tetsuo Ishihara and his veteran team, and, later, *Nanbu tōji* Mikio Takahashi and his staff. It has been an honor to live and work with them. Their dedication, conscientiousness, modesty and good humor have shown me new standards that I can admire, but never hope to equal. The stories of their long careers have taught me much and given me precious first-hand glimpses of pre-modern brewing—for such it was when they first left home to work the winter season. My wholehearted thanks to them for camaraderie and support through the long winter seasons, and for the opportunity to see the traditions of centuries they embody.